Cuttings from My Garden Notebooks

The gardener is the trustee of a world of fair living things.
William Robinson, *The English Flower Garden*

BY THE SAME AUTHOR

The Rose Book
Perennial Garden Plants
Plants for Ground-Cover
Trees in the Landscape
The Art of Planting
Colour in the Winter Garden
Three Gardens
The Complete Flower Paintings and Drawings of Graham Stuart Thomas
The Rock Garden and its Plants
Ornamental Shrubs, Climbers and Bamboos

Cuttings from My Garden Notebooks

GRAHAM STUART THOMAS
OBE, VMH, DHM, VMM
Garden Consultant to the National Trust

Introduction by
DAVID WHEELER
Foreword by
ALLEN LACY

A Ngaere Macray Book
SAGAPRESS, INC.
Sagaponack, New York

Arthur Tysilio Johnson and his Garden in Wales, The Tea-Noisette Roses and The Portland Roses are reprinted by kind permission of the Editor of *Hortus.*

Lady Moore is reprinted by kind permission of the Editor of *Moorea,* the journal of the Irish Garden Society.

George Rowland Jackman is reprinted by kind permission of the Editor of *The Garden,* the journal of The Royal Horticultural Society.

Floral and end paper illustrations by Graham Stuart Thomas. Line drawings on pages 25, 46, 101, 113, 114, 157, 158, 190, 209, 211, 214, 218, 219, 230, 235, 254, 257, 287, 300, 301, 303, 304 and 305 by Simon Dorrell.

Copyright 1997 Sagapress, Inc., Sagaponack, NY
All rights reserved

Edited by Liz Robinson
Design and composition by Greg Endries
Jacket design by Sydney Butchkes
Plant zones provided by John Elsley
Production coordinated by Carol Lewis

Printed in the United States of America

Distributed by Timber Press, Portland, Oregon

Library of Congress Cataloging-in-Publication Data

Thomas, Graham Stuart.
    Cuttings From My Garden Notebooks / Graham Stuart Thomas
        p.   cm.
    "A Ngaere Macray book."
    Includes index.
    ISBN 0-89831-032-6 (hard)
    1. Landscape gardening. 2. Thomas, Graham Stuart. I. Title.
  SB473. T52   1996
  635.9—dc20   96-21433
                                         CIP

DEDICATION

Sixty-three garden essays
commemorating the holders of the Victoria Medal of Honour
instituted in 1900 to commemorate Queen Victoria's reign by
The Royal Horticultural Society, and to the memory of my father
who drew, in terra cotta crayon, the Grecian head below.
I have never discovered whom the drawing represents.

CONTENTS

A pencil sketch by the author of a farm scene in Surrey, with an old Cambridge field roller in the foreground.

INTRODUCTION

By David Wheeler

From the opening page of this book Graham Thomas takes the novice's hand, 'with the idea of helping those who are setting out on the garden path'. But these essays comprise much more than a starter manual for hopeful horticulturists. A text of Promethean range spans almost everything, from diminutive alpine plants to hefty forest trees, but never in that fearful tone of voice reminiscent of classroom or lecture hall. Here is a friend, a kindly 'uncle' keen, simultaneously, to educate and to amuse: in short, the perfect companion to lead you (literally) down the garden path.

My own encounter with his 'helping hand' began in the 1960s when I was seventeen or eighteen and I bought my first Graham Stuart Thomas book. Second-hand, priced at only a few pennies in a jumble sale, devoted to what my few gardening friends at that time called 'posh' flowers, it was *Old Shrub Roses* (1956). I knew nothing of the author, and certainly nothing about old roses; as a teenager in that wobbly decade of sham brightness, I was growing some pretty awful varieties — among them, I confess, 'Super Star', whose day-glo pink has stained my retina for all time.

Old Shrub Roses, illustrated with a few photographs, and with a foreword by V. Sackville-West (of whom at that time I also knew nothing), was my somewhat unlikely bedtime reading for several weeks. I gardened then on the south coast of England in a built-up plot around a new house with prim back and front spaces. My father had recently died, and in some mysterious way I had inherited his passion for gardening, at an age when my contemporaries were more keen on motor bikes, bad haircuts and late-night coffee bars.

Ours was a unique front garden in that quiet road: instead of the ubiquitous lawn with a specimen tree surrounded by narrow borders planted out with annuals in summer, my father had made a formal design in concrete of two paths criss-crossing a central bed in the shape of a heart (yes, he was a romantic). In the in-between beds he grew whatever came his way, for though he was a keen and energetic gardener, he did not have that acquisitive streak which today would label him a plantsman. The one or two roses in our front garden were Hybrid Teas, bought for a few shillings at Woolworths, and when I took over the garden, more HTs went in as I earned the necessary money to buy them. They gave me great pleasure; they were weeded, sprayed, manured, and pruned at the right time, and I doubt if I ever waited for the blooms to fade fully before dead-heading them in an eager attempt to maintain a tidy suburban appearance. How we move on!

Looking back, *Old Shrub Roses* must have been a sharp contrast to my usual diet of gardening literature — the offerings of the weekly gardening press, bought as much for the back pages crammed with classified advertisements offering every conceivable gadget, seed and plant that appealed to my magpie mind, as for the instructive text. Gradually, as my taste in garden reading widened (dare I say improved?), I saw Graham Thomas's name more often, and I liked the articles he wrote. As I tracked down other books by him, he became increasingly an idol, a man to read both for pleasure and for information. And I quickly realised, too, that he was enamoured of all garden plants, not just roses.

Twenty years later I started my own gardening periodical, *Hortus,* and by what still seems to me a privileged turn of events, I became one of that (presumably) proud and happy band of men who could add G.S.T.'s name to his list of authors. Then, as a result of a commission to interview Mr Thomas for *Horticulture* magazine (of Boston, Massachusetts), I finally met my hero, at his home near Woking in Surrey.

Curiously, I was more daunted by the prospect of meeting him at that time than if I had come across him in my more horticulturally innocent years. A little knowledge, they say, is a dangerous thing, and even though I had by then been gardening steadily for thirty years, I knew I was no match for this walking encyclopedia. Would I say the right things? Would I be asked to identify some rarish plant in his patch and reveal myself as a fool for not being able to discriminate between an uncommon snowdrop and a little-known snowflake? I need not have worried. G.S.T. is the least intimidating ardent gardener I have ever met. In truth, I think he was a little nervous of meeting me, not at all because of whatever reputation may be mine, but because in his modest and private way he perhaps feared a battery of personal inquiries from a stranger working in a business not always known for its sensitive line of questioning.

I had, of course, gathered a few facts: Graham has written his own gardening autobiography (*Three Gardens*, 1983), making the particulars of his career known to us all. In that book we glimpse his childhood, then follow him through his student days at the Cambridge Botanic Garden to the making of his own two Surrey gardens (at Oak Cottage near Chobham and, later, Briar Cottage where he still lives), and his partnership with James Russell at Sunningdale (the most beautiful nursery in the country). To a wider public Graham Thomas subsequently became well known as Gardens Advisor to The National Trust. As I write, in the summer of 1995, G.S.T. is in his eighty-seventh year but his brain is far from redundant, and like a wise old horticultural eagle he acts still as a Consultant to the Trust, whose custodianship of English gardens now numbers more than 115 properties. Although he has given us sixteen books, the printed word is not his only tool. He is an illustrator, too, having down the years made countless pencil drawings and watercolour paintings of cherished flowers (see *The Complete Flower Paintings and Drawings of Graham Stuart Thomas*, Sagapress, 1987). He is also a musician with an especial love of the piano and the human voice (a madrigal group he formed more than forty years ago still sings on), and I think it is this other aspect of him which gives harmony to his whole life, to his writing, to his gardens, and to his treatment of individual plants. Single-issue fanatics, after all, rarely get it right.

And now we have *Cuttings from My Garden Notebooks*, a collection of sixty-three elegant, mostly new garden essays which display the ripeness and fecundity of his years. But why, in this age of casual rounding-up, sixty-three essays? The significance lies in the book's dedication, to the sixty-three men and women (one to mark each year of Queen Victoria's reign) who at any one time may hold the Victoria Medal of Honour, the Royal Horticultural Society's highest award.

And what booty there is in these Cuttings: scented rhododendrons, fragile dog's-tooth violets, lustrous blue poppies, perfumed jasmines, roses (of course), all manner of herbaceous perennial plants, showy climbers, exotic shrubs, domestic apple trees and stately pines. We also meet some of his old friends, in recollections of Lady Moore (at Rathfarnham in Ireland); Rowland Jackman (another Surrey nurseryman, whose name is remembered in *Clematis* × *jackmanii* and *Ruta graveolens* 'Jackman's Blue'); Arthur Tysilio Johnson, who in North Wales made a garden around an old mill that was widely admired in his day, and Nancy Lindsay (daughter of the dauntingly fashionable Norah), who in the 1930s collected plants in the Caspian province of Persia, north of the Elburz Mountains.

"Cuttings" is, therefore, an apt title. It reminds us of a favourite way of increasing our stock of plants, while at the same time suggesting a scrapbook, a scrapbook full of happy moments, true friends, hard work well rewarded, beautiful flowers, leaves, bark and berries, and glad days spent in glorious gardens. Every late-twentieth-century gardener owes a debt to Graham Thomas, and this book puts each of us further in the red.

DAVID WHEELER
Bryan's Ground, Stapleton, Herefordshire

FOREWORD

If the word *plantsman* did not exist, it would have to be invented to describe Graham Stuart Thomas. Indeed, in a sense the word does not exist: in my dictionary there is a conspicuous lacuna where it ought to be, between *plant louse* and *planula.* But everyone in the world of gardening knows what a plantsman — and of course the word must cover women as well as men — is. A plantsman is someone whose whole attention is absorbed by green and growing things in all their variety, provided that they satisfy the eye, the mind, and the spirit. Botanists are interested in plants as plants, without discrimination. A germinating lima bean or alfalfa sprout suffices to attract their interest: the mere fact of photosynthesis is enough to get them going. Landscape architects and garden designers are more discriminating about plants, but for them plants are one element in an overall aesthetic scheme. Plantsmen are different creatures altogether, for in them two things coincide: encyclopedic knowledge and deep passion. They know their plants down to the last jot and tittle, and they are hopelessly smitten with their favourites (and their favourites make a long list indeed).

The rest of us are singularly fortunate when a master plantsman who is also a writer comes along, someone who knows the differences among two dozen cultivars of *Crocosmia* and is able to set them down on paper. I cannot imagine having to get by without Mr Thomas's authoritative books of reference, such as *Ornamental Shrubs, Climbers and Bamboos, Perennial*

Garden Plants, and *Plants for Ground-Cover.* I consult them constantly, even if often somewhat wistfully, like an impoverished child gazing into a candy store: a considerable number of the plants they describe are not available — or not available yet — to North American gardeners. They are the stuff of dreams (or envy). These reference works, however, are not impersonal, for they are generously larded with quotations from other writers and other plantsmen Mr Thomas obviously admires. With them, he carries on a conversation that continues, even though they no longer walk this earth. We are privileged to eavesdrop, and we eventually learn, for example, that A.T.J. stands for another writer of encyclopedic knowledge and deep passion, Arthur Tysilio Johnson. Of him, Thomas wrote in his book on shrubs and climbers: A.T.J. and his wife Nora gardened in North Wales and he wrote about their gardening life together in characteristic prose, packed with words and well-turned phrases, revealing his close association with plants.

Although plantsman may accurately describe Mr Thomas, it does not define him; neither does plantsman-writer. He is that rare kind of person who is as talented with pen-and-ink and paintbrush as with the written word. He not only writes books, but also can illustrate them, when the chance comes along, as in *The Complete Flower Paintings and Drawings of Graham Stuart Thomas,* one of the most handsome garden books of the late twentieth century. Furthermore, although he has lived his life in the world of plants, he also lives in a broader world whose dimensions are not restricted to horticulture. He is passionate for classical music and for English poetry, from Chaucer's time onward to our own.

In *Cuttings from My Garden Notebooks,* we find the complete Graham Stuart Thomas. Among its sixty-three pieces there is great variety. We find him sorting out the rhododendrons and the roses and the jasmines. He tells us about the uses of pergolas, water, and troughs made of tufa for alpine plants. He reminisces about the nurserymen and the other gardeners whose paths have crossed his own. We follow him when as a very young man he bicycled one June day through Guildford and Godalming to

Munstead, where he strolled through Gertrude Jekyll's garden, and then had tea with her. He still recalls the wafts of scent from *Lilium auratum* that day in her garden, and he notes that when she died the following year, William Robinson, another extremely influential garden writer, attended her funeral. Thomas's conclusion to his piece on Jekyll is worth pointing out. Of both Robinson and Jekyll, he writes: 'We all have profited almost unbelievably from their examples and written words; most of what we do in our gardens today stems from their ideas.' Here we catch a characteristic glimpse of Thomas's generosity of spirit. He knows how to appreciate other people, and holds back nothing. He gives credit where credit is due — no small virtue in a world where writers often allow their egos to play the petty games they should have abandoned in their playpens.

But Thomas also has a fine sense of humor and an uncanny, almost wicked eye for the excess and high pretension that sometimes turn up among devoted gardeners. I strongly recommend that readers turn immediately to the cutting of Nancy Lindsay and her rose catalog (a masterpiece of embroidery and exaggeration coupled with spelling mistakes and a more unbridled use of adjective and adverbs than it has ever been my fortune to find excelled). This piece alone would make this book worthwhile — but it is only one of its many treasures.

George Waters once called Graham Stuart Thomas an amiable wizard. I can add only — and a gentle man.

ALLEN LACY
Linwood, New Jersey

The bridge at Ardgour, western Scotland, from a pencil sketch by the author

PREFACE

Cuttings from My Garden Notebooks

This book has been written with the idea of helping those who are setting out on the garden path, of perhaps saving them from pitfalls, and of encouraging them to think things out before setting spade to the soil. Having been gardening for more decades than can be counted on the fingers of one hand, I have had plenty of time to think about the matter, from digging and hoeing to pruning and taking cuttings. The taking of a cutting is the removal of a portion of the parent plant, encouraging it to take root and prosper in its own separate life — and so I should like you to look on your reading of this book: as the taking of my thoughts and turning them to your profit and advantage, so that in your fresh soil they may not only take root but will help you to overcome some of the difficult decisions that we all have to make in the art and craft of gardening.

I have gardened in a sticky limy soil, a very light sandy acid soil, and another less light, also acid, which when I started with it I fondly thought was the answer to the gardener's prayer — a medium loam. Strangely, though it was at one time part of a large kitchen garden, it has proved less fertile than the other two. In the rather heavy limy plot I could grow *Lilium candidum*, *Helleborus niger*, *Daphne mezereum* and aubrietas; these were indicative of that particular soil, and I have not been able to grow them satisfactorily on the acid soils. Conversely, in my early craving for the (almost) impossible, by means of bracken peat (moss peat was unheard of in those days) I managed on the limy soil to flower the then new

Meconopsis betonicifolia, Lilium nobilissimum and *L. speciosum* — by means of lining a hole with clay, I made bog plants such as *Rodgersia podophylla, Darmera (Peltiphyllum)* and *Cypripedium reginae* thrive on the untoward soil. Looking back on it now, I realise these were wasted efforts in the art of gardening, however much they may have given satisfaction in the craft. Later in my lime-free sand and loam such difficulties did not appear; while certain plants will not thrive on limy soils there are few that will not thrive on neutral or acid soils.

Have I leapt in at the deep end, as it were? Is this fundamental difference between lime and acid soils widely understood? If not, be patient and all shall be revealed.

It is quite obvious that I went in for gardening at an early age because of a love of plants or the beauty of flowers, not for any other reason. This is the usual approach of people with any such desire — or, I might add, the need. To many, the need for "doing the garden" does not come until it is part of the home, but fortunate is the child who has had a small patch of the parental garden set aside for his or her personal enjoyment. To what high fancies does it lead, and what gems does it sow! Thus do we learn early the difference between root and shoot, seed and flower, growth and death, and the seasons.

Another very common desire in a garden is to have a source of flowers for the house. This touches on the art side of the matter, whereas the growing of vegetables is more allied to the craft. Apart from the innate love for and awareness of the beauty of flowers and their exquisite frailty, this craft is where gardening started. It has blossomed and grown in the great walled gardens of the last two hundred years or so, until today when it has come to be looked upon as an art as much as a craft. It is a very worthy endeavour, to make your garden produce both flowers and vegetables, to say nothing of their companions, the fruit trees and bushes, and for many people I believe this is what is looked upon as gardening.

On the other hand, a garden may be no more than a place where the dog can enjoy itself, or an area for football or cricket for the children.

In spite of the fact that hedges have to be clipped and lawns cut, it cannot then be considered as art, scarcely as craft. There is seldom a garden, though, that makes no demands on either qualification, even if it is just a place to sit in or walk around.

There will usually be a principal window out of which can be seen a lawn or paved patio, plants, shrubs and trees. This is where the art begins — for there is no doubt that gardening is an art, though few are the colleges where it and its history are taught. The subject does not seem to appear in the curriculum of lectures on art in general, despite the long history of formal garden design in (particularly) Italy and France, and of the informal approach in England. I like to think that an awareness of garden art has come about as a result of the great enthusiasm for visiting noted gardens during the last forty years or so. A little of the history of garden design must seep into our minds when we think of the fact that no two gardens are the same, nor even alike. The taste, the means and the conditions have been different in every great endeavour.

Today there is certainly a tendency to think along historic lines in creating a garden from scratch. It may be that the owners want a reminder of what might have been, to set off an old house of a given period; or, beside a new house, a hark-back to forgotten ways. There is the possibility of creating something new, but except in special circumstances and with the use of original materials, it is seldom that anything entirely unique is achieved, apart from planting. Most garden design is a re-hash of ideas that have been used before. It is necessary to refresh our minds after browsing through the many finely illustrated books of the last hundred years in order to realise this, and to profit from it with deep thinking.

❧

There are however certain things with which I cannot help you, over which in truth I have no jurisdiction. I will list them briefly because they are what we all have to cope with on our own.

First and foremost are the soil and the climate. A failure to take both into deep consideration from the start will only lead to disaster and distress. I have already mentioned lime, which has a great bearing upon what will thrive or what will refuse to grow. Generally, a glance round neighbouring gardens will indicate whether it is absent: rhododendrons and azaleas and Hortensis hydrangeas, summer-flowering heaths and heathers all thrive in lime-free soils, but will not live on those containing limestone. In between is a series of soils which are described as neutral. If in doubt, have your soil analysed; it is a good plan to do this anyway, because a thorough analysis often reveals the absence of important trace elements which can have a profound effect on the growth of plants.

I remember being asked to recommend a lavish planting of rhododendrons and azaleas in a newly purchased semi-woodland site: unfortunately, it was in a limestone area, and the owner had to put up with species of rose, lilacs, forsythias and *Philadelphus* hybrids instead.

As to climate, it varies considerably over the British Isles, although these differences are nothing compared with the variation in the United States and other parts of the world. Rainfall and average winter temperatures are very important, but there are no generalisations to be made: in the United States, the only solution is to refer to the USDA map for a guide to its seasonal temperatures.

Next in importance for consideration I would list the local conditions: the colour and style of the house, its aspect and exposure, any surrounding trees, and the presence or absence of shade. I had a friend who preferred pinks and reds on the blue side of the spectrum — the crimsons, purples and mauves — and also whites. Unfortunately, she moved to a house built of a rather insistent orange-brown brick, with red roof tiles. In spite of my advice to eschew mauve-pinks near the house, she persisted in her choice, with the consequence that house and flowers "swore" at one another in no uncertain way. I have written of colour and its importance in *The Art of Planting;* suffice it to say here that the most important rule in colour work is to keep the reds and pinks with yellow in them (the flames, oranges and salmons) away from reds and pinks with blue in them (mauves, purples and crimsons).

It makes the garden seem bigger if neighbouring trees are considered to be part of the scene, and both these and what may already be growing on your area have a profound effect in planning a garden. When I last moved I inherited a yellow variegated *Elaeagnus*. I should not have chosen it, but it was large, blocked out the fence and much of the neighbour's car-port, and next to it was a large *Philadelphus* 'Monster'. Together they made a considerable screen, and dictated the colours for that side of the garden, taking whites, yellows, blues and a touch of orange to the accompaniment of some coppery foliage. The old roses and their tints were kept firmly to another area.

❧

There come two thoughts about colours, apart from what I have already written. One is that every colour has beauty, but depends for our appreciation of it on its neighbours. The other is that, in spite of this, there is no doubt that certain people prefer certain colours. Furthermore, in a small garden it doesn't do to be too venturesome in colour; the cooler, softer, paler shades will create a more soothing and satisfying garden than bright orange, flame and scarlet. At the same time, some very dark tones of purple or murrey are needed, to provide the bass notes of the orchestra, as old Bobbie James used to say (see Cutting 60, "The Dark Colours").

Another fundamental to be considered is the style of the garden. Is it to be formal or informal? Sometimes it is possible to have both, but not usually in small plots. Even so, whatever the design it is desirable to disguise the hard lines of the boundaries with growing plants — unless, indeed, the fence or hedge can be considered as part of the design. I have enlarged upon this aspect of things in Cutting 53, "Hedges".

For those who want a garden of fragrant plants, it is as well to know at what time of day each plant most readily sheds its scent. Many pale flowers not only show up most at dusk, but are most fragrant then. Examples are Night-scented Stock, white Tobacco plants and most honeysuckles. These are specially prized in gardens belonging to commuters.

Some gardeners may wish to specialise in a single genus, or the plants from a single country, or plants which were in cultivation before a given date. And, of course, we all have favorite plants, but may find that it is not possible to accommodate them all in a single garden, for one or more of the reasons already noted.

I do not intend this to be a treatise on garden design, merely a note of some of the difficulties which beset us all. Maybe your garden has been designed by previous owners. Before accepting it *nem. con.*, out-of-hand, it is as well to consider whether the principal ingredients of a good design are there — access to and from gates and doors, to and from garden shed and greenhouse, and whether the compost and rubbish area is suitably screened. On clay or sticky soil, dry access is imperative and drainage paramount. It is as well to watch the garden for a year before doing any planting. This is to get to know the soil's capabilities, to find out what weeds are prevalent and whether they are of annual duration or troublesome perennials. If the latter, no planting should be done until total eradication by weedkiller or manual labour is secured.

&

Let us imagine that we have stepped from the furnished house into the unfurnished garden. Planting a garden should be looked at in the same way as furnishing a home, each room according to its size and surroundings. In a room few people would be content to have tubular steel furniture mixed with mahogany or oak; hooked rug next to Persian; velvets or satins mixed with cheap calico. The garden should be given just as much consideration, but in these days of instant establishment from nurseries or plant centres, very often a hotch-potch results. I have in mind one garden plot which has received just such thoughtless attention. Into the borders have been placed — all about a yard apart — a Pampas Grass, a Blue

CUTTINGS FROM MY GARDEN NOTEBOOKS

Cedar, a golden Cypress, gooseberries, a Delphinium, golden Privet, Lavender, marigolds, hollyhocks and many more — all disparate things, though each with a special word to say in garden design if it is allowed. The only way that such a collection might be united into a reasonable whole is by the inclusion of areas of ground-cover plants linking some of them together.

On a limy soil the choice is rather more limited than on acid soils, but there are plenty of good and well-tried old garden favourites which will make a blend of old-time charm. Take apples, for instance, which blend as well with flowers as with kitchen gardens; snowdrops and daffodils, Old Roses, peonies, delphiniums, anchusas, lilacs, arches and pergolas and topiary. But refuse slim conifers if you are in a country area of arable farming; choose instead a slim holly. If it is to be a purely flower garden, choose dahlias, gladioluses, sweet peas and tulips; Floribunda and Hybrid Tea roses. If the soil is acid the pointers are fairly clear: rhododendrons, azaleas, hydrangeas of the *H. macrophylla* species, ericas, species roses, ornamental grasses, prostrate or erect conifers. Such a selection, with a birch or two if there is room, would provide a heathland style of planting.

These are merely three selections, at random, from an almost limitless range of plants and shrubs, each grouping having as it were a flavour of its own. It is very difficult to think out a complete planting scheme; apart from the question of whether the separate plants may thrive, there are the flower colours and seasons to consider; foliage; height, spread and speed of growth . . . all adding up to one of the most challenging of all arts. And then seeing, in a beautiful garden open to the public, what seems to be the perfect *fait accompli,* one is oblivious of how many years of thought, rearrangement, cultivation and pruning have gone into what appears to be effortless. It is this sort of reassessment we need to make every year, with a notebook, in order to achieve our own goal.

Time was when one's purchases in the way of plants would be packed in straw bales and sent by rail. The package might arrive on a murky or frosty December day when planting was impossible or inconvenient.

At least one had thought out what one wanted and knew where it was to go. How blessed we are today when, on a nice planting day, we can go along to the plant centre or nursery, get what we need and plant it. Having been a nurseryman for most of my life I can see what a wonderful change has taken place, when legitimately higher prices enable the nurserymen to provide good working conditions, and containerisation means that plants are suitable for handling in all but the worst weathers; to add to this we have the almost universal car, which saves both sellers and buyers endless trouble.

The biggest danger is from temptation: a firm resolution should be made to purchase only a plant for a place, and never to come home wondering where to place a plant.

As in our rooms, blending and fitting together should be the order of the day, not just the formation of a collection of plants. Almost as soon as we step into a garden we realise whether the owner is a collector of plants, or a selector and arranger. This little book is much concerned with the selection of plants for specific purposes. Most of us, for example, do not give enough space to each shrub; they nearly all exceed the size which is in our mind's eye. We need help in arranging plants, remembering not only their ultimate size, but their style of foliage and flower and season of bloom. It is almost too much to expect from anyone who has not had years of experience, and is one reason why professional garden designers tend to think along stereotyped lines, choosing the same plants again and again because they can rely upon them to give the required touch. We hear a lot about "texture" and "plant associations" these days: they are the essentials of garden design, and prove that thinking is proceeding along the right lines. They will help to create that sense of harmony and contentment that should be the aim, consciously or unconsciously, of every gardener — the opposite, in fact, of the jumbled and thoughtless planting which I remarked upon earlier. There are many courses advertised today for training in garden design (just how the eventual graduates are to secure work for themselves is another matter). So it is with learning about plants — without which there would be no gardens: in addition to the few terms with a drawing board it is necessary to spend hours, weeks and years getting to know the potentialities of plants. There is no better key to this knowledge than visiting gardens of every kind in every season.

Most of what we do today in gardens has its origin in the thoughts of Gertrude Jekyll. She was so right when she wrote the following (published in *The World*, August 15, 1905), entitled "A definite Purpose in Gardening":

> Just as an unassorted assemblage of mere words, though they may be the best words in our language, will express no thought, or as the purest colours on an artist's palette — so long as they remain on the palette — do not form a picture, so our garden plants, placed without due consideration or definite intention, cannot show what they can best do for us.

These are her thoughts on colour. The same thoughts should cover all the other attributes of plants.

So, if you have the hormone rooting powder ready and your knife is sharp, the sand and compost are prepared and the frame at the right temperature, come with me and select what cuttings you may want from my garden of experience. All will grow and transplant safely into yours.

ع

Here and there in the following pages will be found short quotations which I have added to illustrate a point or to bring a fresh experience forward. A few are tied to their sources; the remainder are all from *Flowers — a garden note book* by Sir Herbert Maxwell, Bt, who gardened so ably in the earlier part of this century. The book was published in 1923, and is not only a thoughtful and instructive commentary on gardening on the west coast of Scotland, but was written with such knowledge, expertise and enthusiasm that it is surprising it was never given a second edition, especially as it was illustrated with twelve full-page paintings in water colours, of the author's own work. He had earlier published a book on *Scottish Gardens* (1911), and *Trees, a Woodland note book* (1914); all reveal to us a gardener of rare perception, ability and learning who travelled widely and met all the great names in gardening of his day. Moreover, he was able to communicate his personal findings and experiences in easy prose. I hope these few words of mine may result in libraries and second-hand bookshops being besieged with requests for at least the two last volumes. They will never become out-of-date and must rank among the best books of this century about plants.

A pencil sketch of La Morna by the author.

PRELUDE

Crown winter with green,
And give him good drink
To physic his spleen
Or ever he think.

Robert Bridges, *Shorter Poems*

The Year's Awakening

After a night of storm towards the end of November, sometimes it happens that one awakes to a garden transformed. The best tinted leaves have fallen and all have been driven into corners off the paths and lawns, revealing the fresh green of the grass and the contrast of paving and gravel. The leaves are off the trees, giving more light to the garden, and the spectral shadows of bare branches steal across the lawn. The old year has gone, all its glory, its successes and failures, and we are abruptly brought to face winter, with berries and leaves almost alone as colour-givers. The holly berries are ready for Christmas and Candlemas if the birds leave them alone; they seldom touch those of the brilliant skimmias and certain cotoneasters — *C. simonsii, C. horizontalis* and *C. conspicuus* are among them.

Then the eye alights on the evergreens, in thankfulness to all those dauntless travellers who gathered them from other countries to grace our gardens. Three hundred years ago we in Britain only had our few natives to furnish our gardens — the Scots Pine, Holly, Yew, Box and Ivy. "Above all the natural *Greens* which enrich our *home-born* store, there is none certainly to be compar'd to the *Aquifolium* in our holly." Thus saith John Evelyn in *A Discourse on Forest Trees,* 1679. Now we have "greens" of every sort, dull or glittering, pale or dark, on shrubs large or small, coupled with a variety of perennials and ferns. The garden now, in late autumn, has a new dimension and shape. To me it is the beginning of the garden year. And see — snowdrops and crocuses are with us already in sunny corners; the first Snowdrop of autumn, *Galanthus reginae-olgae*, may be nearly over, but *G. caucasicus 'Hiemalis'* will soon be flowering, and the scent of a few flowers plucked from *Crocus laevigatus* will fill a room with fragrance from pale lilac stars with central orange stigmata and purple stripes without; I find they increase freely in well-drained soils. And at any moment we may have the first flowers on the Algerian Iris, *I. unguicularis.*

As a rule, no sooner have the leaves fallen from the Autumn Cherry and Fragrant Guelder than they put forth their first flowers. The former is *Prunus subhirtella* 'Autumnalis' in white, and pale pink in 'Rosea', whose blossoms will soon be thronging the little trees; and an old-established bush of the latter (*Viburnum farreri*) will be covered in heads of small blush flowers for many weeks, flooding the garden with fragrance. In cool temperate climates these two valuable plants will normally be producing flowers throughout winter in mild spells, and on into early spring.

Those who are lucky enough to live where winters are not long or cold may place near to a sunny wall (on lime-free soil with humus) the Japanese *Camellia sasanqua*, in its several varieties from white through blush to crimson. They all flower in autumn, and except for 'Crimson King' they are all fragrant. These camellias are hardy over most of England and in Zones 7 to 9 in the United States, but do not flower freely except in warmer

Galanthus 'S. Arnott'

regions, though a cool greenhouse may work wonders. By the way, the word "greenhouse" grew up because the early glass shelters which supplanted the opaque-roofed orangeries were used to house the many newly discovered "greens" as they were called — so few were the evergreen shrubs previously known, and so uncertain was the hardiness of the new-comers considered.

There is no doubt that these few notes would have been written with less enthusiasm thirty or so years ago, before the great boon among November—December flowering evergreen shrubs of the new hybrid mahonias. These are called *Mahonia* ✕ *media* and are hybrids between *M. lomariifolia*, which is truly autumn-flowering and a tall, gaunt, upright shrub, and the long-known *M. japonica*, whose sweetly-scented creamy yellow bells do not really appear much before Christmas. *Mahonia lomariifolia* has similar flowers, less scented, and of bright yellow in dense upright spikes. Both have magnificent pinnate leaves. Some of the crosses, like the original 'Charity', are also of gaunt upright habit, but can be chopped back after flowering with impunity and will flower just as well the following year. And who would not be prepared to do just this to the earliest (usually) to flower, 'Lionel Fortescue', with long stiff spikes of brilliant yellow, lightening the dark days? My own choice, however, is 'Underway', flowering rather later, in cool citron yellow; it has a more bushy habit. There is no doubt that this group of fine evergreen shrubs has brought new life into our autumn gardens. In unusual colour contrast is *Mahonia* 'Moseri', whose leaves are tinted with bright coral-red from autumn until the flowers appear in spring.

In general the winter-flowering shrubs do not flower until after Christmas, during mild spells. I wish I could find again the special autumn-flowering form of *Daphne mezereum* (*D. m.* 'Autumnalis'), but I have not seen it since before the Second World War.

However, we do not expect to find many hardy flowers open in the November garden, and for beauty and variety must select plants with good leaves. It so happens that two good perennial plants put up their new leaves in autumn, a refreshing and unusual sight. The most important is *Arum italicum* var. *italicum* ('Pictum' of gardens) whose handsome arrowhead leaves are of rich shining green marbled with grey and white. They stand aloft, obscuring the pale green arum-flowers in spring, which are themselves succeeded by handsome spikes of scarlet berries in summer. The second is *Geranium malviflorum*, whose leaves are of lacy outline and last in good condition until May, when lovely violet flowers are produced.

I should not like to be without *Campanula latiloba* 'Alba', whose rosettes of fresh light green are welcome in winter. In complete contrast are the black-green fingered leaves of the native British hellebore, *Helleborus foetidus.* This is a very noble plant producing sheaves of pale green bells early in the year. It appreciates shade, and seemingly will thrive in any soil short of a bog.

For the fronts of borders, where they look so well in contrast to paving or gravel, are the bergenias. Gardeners seem to be in two minds about them; they are either admired, or totally eschewed. There are two whose leaves turn to a rich plum colour at the approach of cold weather: *B. purpurascens* and *B.* 'Sunningdale' (the leaves revert to green in the spring). Another wonderful plant in this class of colouring is the purplish-leafed form of *Phormium tenax*, the New Zealand Flax, whose great sword-shaped leaves stand aloft to 5 feet or thereabouts where the climate suits them; there are handsome variegated forms available too, for large gardens.

One can easily make a very satisfying picture for late winter by using small shrubs such as the Rue, *Ruta graveolens* 'Jackman's Blue', whose filigree of glaucous grey leaves looks so well with bergenias; or the feathery tumps of silvery-grey santolinas, variegated *Arabis*, glaucous *Hebe albicans* and *H. pinguifolia* 'Pagei', all of receding tone. For a sunshine effect in winter we must resort to some yellow variegation. *Euonymus fortunei* 'Emerald 'n' Gold' comes to mind, and the graceful arching rush *Carex morrowii* 'Variegata'.

I have left out of this little assembly two very notable plants. One is the statuesque *Euphorbia characias* subspecies *wulfenii,* whose tall stems are clothed like bottle-brushes in grey-green leaves which bear at their apices heads of yellow-green flowers in spring. The other is that strangely-tinted low shrub whose leaves are a mixture of grey and yellow, giving an effect of bluish khaki, *Phlomis chrysophylla*. It is only beaten into second place by the new 'Sundance' variety of *Choisya ternata* whose leaves take on a permanent bright yellow when exposed to the light. There is nothing so insistently bright throughout the winter, but until it is thoroughly proved in hardiness, I recommend a sheltered position; indeed, all these plants are best where winters are mild.

The female *Skimmia japonica* has the brightest of all scarlet berries of the winter, while its male relative 'Rubella' earns a place for its red-brown flower buds, which are revealed in autumn and last in colour the winter through until its scented flowers open in April. This 'Rubella' is a shrub to treasure for shady places — if it is starved or gets too much sun, its leaves become a sickly yellowish tint.

The hollies are prolific in their forms. The females alone carry berries, of course, but some of the males are so good in their leaf colours that they cannot be left out of these notes. Their leaf-shape and shining texture give the glitter to all hollies, whereas the mahonias and skimmias are of a more sober green. Funnily enough, one of the most brilliant of the so-called "golden" hollies is named 'Golden Queen', though it is a male, whereas 'Golden King' is a female — and a big, substantial shrub it is, too. On the whole I prefer the white- or cream-variegated kinds: their names are many, 'Silver Sentinel', 'Silver Queen', 'Handsworth New Silver', the graceful 'Argentea Marginata', and others; these are all female. An excellent plain green variant of the common holly is 'J. C. van Tol', a good berrying female.

I did not really intend to write about variegated evergreens; there are so many, and variegation can easily be overdone in gardens, where a wide variety of *greens* is the first essential. Take for instance the bright and cheerful light green of *Hebe rakaiensis*, which used to be known as *H. subalpina*; even the fresh green of the lawn does not surpass its insistent hummocks. On the other hand, the dullest of dark greens is found in the good old Laurustinus, or *Viburnum tinus.* The most attractive form to grow is 'Gwenllian' with blue berries, pink buds and white flowers all at the same autumnal and winter moments. No shrub can beat it — but keep it away from doors and windows: in some temperatures and some weather conditions it gives off an unpleasant smell, as do many other viburnums. Forewarned is forearmed.

Cutting Two —

A Christmas Bunch

After a cold snap or two during November, December had been mild. I thought it worth while to walk round the garden in search of a few flowers, leaves and berries to fill a bowl. My garden is in Surrey on lime-free soil in a reasonably sheltered and built-up area, though I have noticed my plants are always a week or so later than those in a friend's garden which lies in an area more sheltered by trees and not so open to cold winds.

Of course I went straight to *Rhododendron* 'Yellow Hammer', which always blesses us with a late autumn crop of creamy yellow tubular flowers amongst its tiny dark leaves. It is a neat upright grower, quite different from the normal Hardy Hybrid type of rhododendrons, but among which is that invaluable R. Nobleanum 'Venustum'. This is the most reliable of winter-flowering varieties, making a large bush and opening its flowers — good generous trusses of deep pink, fading paler — at any time in mild weather from November to March. Of course if frost comes the flowers will be spoilt, but fresh buds are always there, ready for the next mild spell.

Some dark colour was provided by the form of *R. ponticum*, 'Foliis Purpureis', with coppery purple leaves, illustrated in my book *Colour in the Winter Garden*. It is a relatively compact plant with small leaves of remarkable richness, echoed by the warm-coloured buds of *Skimmia* × *reevesiana* 'Rubella'. With them were plucked a few plum-red leaves of *Bergenia purpurascens,* carefully placed so that their red undersides would not be lost. The leaves of *B. crassifolia* were also making a good reddish, burnished show and these, coupled with the almost black of the ivy *Hedera helix* 'Atropurpurea', made me feel that a few such richly tinted things would add a depth and background to the little assembly that was growing. As a complete contrast I found a large leaf or two of *Hedera colchica* 'Dentata Variegata' of pure primrose yellow.

Viburnum farreri (*V. fragrans*) had dropped all its flowers, but not so *V. foetens*, whose descriptive name applies to the smell of the bruised leaves and twigs, not to the sweet-scented substantial creamy white flowers. Light-coloured leaves were found in trails of *Hedera helix* 'Adam' and 'Danny' and *Euonymus fortunei* 'Emerald Gaiety'. All of these are white-variegated, the last with an added pink flush after hard weather. I always find it particularly cheering that autumn brings us fresh leaves, rising up from the bare ground, on *Arum italicum*, which is specially appealing in the form 'Pictum'; it has dark green spear-shaped leaves marbled with grey and white. And it is only a few weeks since it cheered us with scarlet berries — truly a plant of great worth.

There were one or two roses which went in to the bunch — pink 'Nathalie Nypels' and the creamy flesh of 'Mme de Sombreuil', a climbing Tea Rose of intense fragrance. But I wasn't really looking for out-of-season flowers, rather for legitimate winter blooms, such as *Prunus subhirtella* 'Autumnalis Rosea' , which was just ready for picking, in the pink-bud stage. It is a non-stop flowerer from late autumn until spring. And of course the wonderful Winter Jasmine — *Jasminum nudiflorum* — was ready in long sprays well set with clear yellow blooms — in fact, I could have filled the entire bowl with it. Its only failing is a complete lack of scent, but we can surely forgive this when we consider its willingness to grow almost anywhere, in almost any soil, and to flower freely every year during mild spells in winter.

I always wish the holly which was here when I came had proved to be a red-berried form instead of the yellow-berried *Ilex aquifolium* 'Fructu Luteo'. It would have made a better contrast to *Clematis cirrhosa* var. *balearica*, which has swarmed up to its topmost shoot and threatens to engulf it.

But there is something rather nice about the yellow-berried holly — I am reminded that it tones well on the Christmas pudding with the rum-and-butter sauce! Nor was yellow wanting from other plants. A sprig or two of *Elaeagnus* × *ebbingii* 'Gilt Edge', broadly variegated, is always a good standby in winter, but I find it fouls the water very quickly. As for *Mahonia* × *media*, the cultivar 'Underway' was still just presentable, though it would only last for a day or two before dropping its sticky petals. *Mahonia* 'Moseri' added its coral-red leaves, and scented flowers were just opening on *M. japonica*.

More pink came from the winter-flowering heather *Erica* × *darleyensis*, of which 'Arthur Johnson' is the best for cutting because of its longer spikes. With it a few sprigs of 'Jackman's Blue' Rue made a lovely contrast.

The bunch needed a touch of bright scarlet. This was found in *Cotoneaster* 'Gnom' and, brightest of all, a berrying female *Skimmia japonica*. The birds often take the Cotoneaster after Christmas, but the Skimmia they usually leave alone. Another good piece of red is *Pyracantha atalantioides*, usually neglected by the birds.

Looking at the little bunch — by now more than a handful — one felt all colours were fairly represented except lilac and blue. Blue could have been provided by *Symplocos paniculata*, but alas I had not protected the berries from the birds. On the other hand, a few berries were left on *Callicarpa bodinieri* 'Profusion', a good rich lilac. But the finishing touch was given by some buds of the Algerian Iris, *I. unguicularis*, which tomorrow would open with quivering delicacy and fragrance.

It would have been a nice touch to add a few fronds of evergreen ferns, but I have not discovered how to make them last in water. Just think what could have been done with *Polystichum squarrosum* and *P. munitum* in shining dark green, or the crisped form of Hart's Tongue, *Asplenium scolopendrium* 'Crispum'. But they must be left, to be enjoyed in the garden.

The bowl of beauty from the garden needed two more items which were readily available — a twig or two of scarlet-barked Dogwood to support the Clematis and ivy trails (*Cornus alba* 'Sibirica'), and the silvery grey filigree of Santolina.

These many plants plucked from the open air a day before Christmas lighted my room with a great variety of shapes and colours, and saved me going to a florist for one of those ravishing cyclamens which I always speedily kill. But stay — there were three more little things, which had to have a tiny vase on their own: the last blooms of the late autumn snow-drop *Galanthus caucasicus* 'Hiemalis' and the amazingly fragrant *Crocus laevigatus* 'Fontenayi', whose small rich lilac flowers are striped externally with fawn and violet. These had for companions a few marbled grey leaves of *Cyclamen hederifolium* (*C. neapolitanum*) and a bud of *Narcissus* 'Cedric Morris', always the first of them all and a foretaste of spring.

Narcissus from Christmas until mid May: 'Jana' (top left), 'Folly' (top right), 'Cedric Morris' (bottom left), and *poeticus* var. *recurvus* (bottom right)

THE
VERNAL
MIRACLE

Wanton with long delay the gay spring leaping cometh;
The blackthorn starreth now his bough on the eve of May:
All day in the sweet box-tree the bee for pleasure hummeth:
The cuckoo sends afloat his note on the air all day.

Robert Bridges, *Shorter Poems*

Cutting Three —

Desert Island Flowers

In idle moments I have sometimes considered what are the fewest genera I could be content with on a desert island — presuming they could be made to thrive there. Again and again I have come to the same conclusion: *Narcissus, Iris, Rosa.* These few could span the year with flowers. And then the thought comes, how could I possibly omit lilies, Japanese anemones, lilacs and *Aster* × *frikartii* 'Mönch'? The more one thinks, the more difficult the choice becomes.

In various forms *Rosa* can be in flower from early June until October, to say nothing of the long-lasting heps of some. Irises will be in flower from winter until July, with berries in autumn from *I. foetidissima.* And daffodils, the true flowers of spring, may be had in flower from the end of December until mid May. That is, I think, a fair assessment of these three genera and makes them strong candidates for my choice.

The daffodil season usually starts a few days before Christmas in my garden, the flowering of 'Cedric Morris' being faithful to these dark days. How lucky we are with this little plant, only 6 to 8 inches high with very small trumpet-blooms of light yellow, lasting through to February or even March. How fortunate indeed that that great artist and gardener, its namesake, brought home from the Costa Verde, Portugal — where it had been found by Basil Leng about 1950 — the stock of this plant, nursed it and increased it and passed it to Beth Chatto for further propagation and distribution. It is now in many gardens where such little joys are cherished. Before it is over several others may be in flower, among them a real miniature, *N. asturiensis* (*N. minimus*), only 3 to 4 inches high with tiny flowers of bright yellow, whose trumpet narrows before it opens into the mouth. This is a character also found in 'Cedric Morris', thus indicating the likely parentage of the foundling.

Apart from some rather delicate little plants, such as *N. bulbocodium* 'Romieuxii' and *N. watieri*, which are most suited to frame- or alpine-house culture, these small treasures are followed by ordinary bold trumpet-daffodils in bright yellow, such as 'Rijnveld's Early Sensation', which in spite of its foreign name was raised in Sussex. In Cornwall this is picked from the open fields in early January. I have had it in flower in mid January in Surrey; it has nothing to recommend it especially apart from its earliness and steadily increasing habit, whereas my next favourite owes everything to its exquisite shape, apart from its earliness. It was named 'Jana' — for Januarius (January) — by the raiser, Alec Gray, and it has a strangely large bulb which is not given to prolific increase. However, I know of no trumpet-daffodil of the whole season with more refinement and elegance.

True to its name, 'February Gold' is a prolific and bold charmer which combines its earliness with some of the pretty, swept-back segments of *N. cyclamineus*, which species, rather like the shape of a Christmas cracker, is now upon us in moist places, together with *N. bulbocodium*. This is naturalised all over the alpine meadows at The Royal Horticultural Society's Garden at Wisley in Surrey, in bright yellow, while its 'Citrinum' variety is distributed with even greater abandon in marshy turf in the Savill Gardens at Windsor. These little Hoop-Petticoat narcissi have a pert charm all of their own. With them are the native Welsh Leek, *N. obvallaris*, in bright uniform yellow with bluish foliage, and our native English Lent Lily, *N. pseudonarcissus*, in two tones of delicate yellow. The latter seeds itself abundantly but the Welshman does not; it does, however, increase freely by the bulb.

I am always ready for a little leavening of the bright yellows and at this time find it in Alec Gray's little 'Rockery White' (the perianth is white, the trumpet lemon-yellow), and *N. pallidus* 'Praecox', a Spanish counterpart of our Lent Lily in pale lemon-yellow throughout. Even paler, in creamy ivory, are *N. moschatus* and its rare double form (*N. cernuus* 'Plenus'), the best flowers of which are not untidily double, but have their trumpets neatly filled with small petaloids.

By this time, which is the end of March or early April, the main mass of hybrid daffodils and narcissi is upon us. They are, today, of every combination of colour, yellow and white with even pink or red cups or trumpets, enough to satisfy the greediest among us. White hybrids increase in number as the season advances, owing mainly to the influence of breeding with the Angel's Tear Daffodil (*N. triandrus*), with its short round cup and swept-back petals, and with the Pheasant-Eye Narcissus, *N. poeticus;* 'Thalia' and the later 'Silver Chimes' lean towards the former and 'Actaea' and 'Cantabile' towards the latter. There are many white-flowered trumpet-daffodils for midseason, before 'Cantabile' flowers. Two popular varieties for which one does not need a bottomless pocket are the favourite 'Beersheba', and 'Cantatrice'. The jonquils have given us many good late varieties, but I will only mention Alec Gray's exquisite light yellow 'Tittle Tattle' and the late doubles, 'Cheerfulness' and 'White Cheerfulness'.

This little selection leads us to the final joy of *N. poeticus recurvus*, the late Pheasant-Eye, which is frequently in flower in early May, a pure white flower with a tiny "eye" in place of a trumpet and a pronounced sweet fragrance. The last to flower is its double form, which does well in the western counties of Britain where the air is soft and mild, but seldom opens in dry Surrey.

The story of the irises is even longer, usually starting in autumn when the first few buds appear on the Algerian irises, *I. unguicularis* (*I. stylosa*). These flower best when planted hard against a south wall in full sun and left undisturbed. Throughout the winter, during mild spells, the flowers of quivering delicacy and soft perfume continue to appear on short stalks, the usual lavender-blue being augmented by palest lilac 'Walter Butt', purple

Iris missouriensis

'Mary Barnard', and the white often attributed to E. A. Bowles. In the early year *I. histrioides* 'Major' is most desirable, with stiff little flowers of violet blue. It is classified under *I. reticulata*, which heads the section. This species is variable in colour, sweetly violet-scented and may be of royal purple, red purple, or light blue; some are probably hybrids of *I. histrioides*. All are about 8 inches high and cheer us as soon as the weather turns towards spring; *I. histrioides* 'Major' will even poke up through a covering of snow and does not usually suffer.

Whereas all daffodils are two-dimensional with their trumpet and perianth, the irises have six segments of which three (the standards) usually stand aloft and three below them (the falls) are usually drooping. Besides these are the curved styles, all contributing to a flower of great beauty.

The Juno Section is strange, in that the standards are reduced to a mere nothing, hanging down below the falls. Even so, the flowers could not be mistaken for anything else and are uniquely poised between the leaves, which themselves are arranged opposite each other up the stem. Two of the most reliable are *I. bucharica*, white with yellow blotch, and *I. orchioides*, usually yellow but sometimes lilac. They both like warm sunny positions.

It is difficult not to find an iris in flower in the early year. The main mass of bearded irises starts with the dwarf relatives, *I. pumila* and *I. chamaeiris*, from whites and pale yellows through to lavender blues, purples and maroon. They are not bulbous, as are the above-mentioned species, but rhizomatous, as is the Algerian Iris, and like their woody roots to be *on* the ground to absorb the warmth of the sun. Some charmers are 'Green Spot', 'Austrian Sky' and 'Langport Carnival'.

A little taller and a little later are the varieties of the Intermediate Section with as big a range of colouring; all are fragrant. They lead us into the Tall Bearded Section, which has absorbed almost all the energies of the iris breeders on both sides of the Atlantic. There is a wonderful array of colours available to blend with or accentuate any scheme. In their efforts to produce something different the breeders have allowed themselves to become obsessed with flowers so goffered, flounced and frilled that the true shape of the iris is gone. But is this any more than what they have done with the daffodil, by breeding those with the trumpets slit into six segments and folded back on to the outer petals? Surely this is the biggest insult ever perpetrated on a uniquely shaped flower. If we compare the goffered irises with the simple original shape of the blossom, it will be seen how far we have gone in the prostitution of a flower of inimitable charm. A good iris of the Bearded Section should show the outline of the R, back to back. Groups of these beauties fill the garden with lovely colours, but only those of light tints enter fully into garden scheming. The lavender-blues and light yellows compete beautifully with the whites. They may be described as the last great flowers of spring: their crystalline texture would wilt under hot summer sun.

Quickly following them is the Sibirica group: grassy tall leaves and elegant flowers on tall wiry stems in white, lavender-blue and purple. Somewhere about midseason for irises comes *I. missouriensis*, forming a dense clump of grey grassy foliage topped with bright lavender-blue flowers, thin and shapely. I give it top marks. The annual display nearly finishes with *I. spuria* and *I. orientalis*, *I. aurea* and their hybrids. These are very tall, often achieving 4 feet but needing no staking, and their greyish leaves and extra elegant flowers in lavender-blues, whites and yellows contribute something very special to the garden, just when the old French roses are at their best. But we have missed some moisture lovers — the Japanese *I. ensata* (formerly known as *I. kaempferi*) in rich purples and whites, large and flat and magnificent. With these come *I. laevigata* in lavender-blue, or white, which will grow in shallow water, and its hybrid 'Rose Queen'.

Even into July we may enjoy the strange brown-red flowers of *I. fulva* and its plum-purple hybrid *I.* ✕ *fulvala*. And it seems that even then the iris season may be elongated, or repeated, by some of the new, twice-flowering, Tall Bearded varieties which give their second crop in late September.

Meanwhile the roses, my third choice for my desert island, are in full swing. I need not write again about the long succession of beauty to be found among them, from early *R. × anemonoides* and 'Frühlingsgold' till the last flowers are gone from *R. rugosa,* and we are left the autumn and winter season to enjoy the scarlet heps. Their full glory has been covered in my books. Let us end on a note of joy and thanksgiving, that the hybridisers in their production of innumerable single, semi-double and fully double varieties have not succeeeded in spoiling the shape of the rose, though they have produced some strident colours. Most are fragrant, a point they share with *Narcissus* and *Iris.*

Cutting Four —

Blue with the Yellow of Spring

'Green's forsaken and yellow's forsworn,
But blue's the prettiest colour that's worn.'

So runs the old distich, and one parts with a blue flowering herb
more reluctantly than with those of other hues.

Apart from the Witch Hazel and Winter Sweet, which really belong to
winter, the first glimmer of spring yellow comes from the male catkins of
the hedgerow hazels and willows. Thereafter the earliest forsythias greet us
in the garden, followed by the several species of *Corylopsis* and *Mahonia*.
Keeping pace with them are the daffodils in infinite variety, early and late,
tall or short, yellow, white and particoloured. They bring us the first great
glory of the garden's year. It is yet too early to produce those studied grada-
tions which we call colour schemes; they belong to later in the year, when
the first gasp at spring's bounty is over and we long to drag art into our
garden pictures. It may be said that it is never too early to resort to art, but
too careful a study of it can sometimes ruin the spontaneous enjoyment of
a garden. In the early year I tend to omit certain dominant tints from a
portion of a garden so that those that are left greet us with their full
impact. We do need some colour other than yellow in our spring gardens.
We have the choice of reds and pinks or blue and purple. Reds and pinks
are unsatisfactory, being too dominant. White, blue and purple, to my
eyes, are the right colours to use at daffodil time. Fortunately the daffodils
and narcissi themselves provide the white; blue and purple are at hand in

quantity if only we look for them, and no other colours enhance so well the sudden almost overpowering yellow of daffodils.

We can begin with purple crocuses and the pure blue of *Scilla bifolia*, especially the variety praecox. "*S. bifolia* leads the procession, sometimes flowering before the end of January." Its hybrid × *Chionoscilla allenii* creates an even more decisive patch of cobalt blue. The chionodoxas themselves follow on directly after these are over. The richest blue is *C. sardensis*, from Sardinia; it has a small white eye, and is a free-seeder, making a veritable carpet of colour if left to itself. The better known *C. forbesii*, which used to be *C. lucilleae*, is a little taller, equally free to seed and spread but of a less definite blue and with a rather larger white eye. In all of them two leaves enfold the flower stalk, each of which displays several starry flowers. They coincide with *Narcissus* 'February Gold' and other earlies.

Following almost immediately are the nodding *Scilla sibirica*, a bright clear blue, and the larger and more pro-lific *S.s.* 'Spring Beauty', of richest Prussian blue; these have a long flowering season, partly because each strong bulb produces more than one flower stem. Like the chi-onodoxas they spread by seed as well as by increasing at the bulb. While these are in flower the main mass of daffodil hybrids is upon us, benefiting greatly from the lowly stature of these little blues. *Scilla messeniaca* is another small bulb for naturalising anywhere, in-creasing freely by seed and sending up countless small spikes of clear, pale lilac-blue.

Mahonia japonica

Blue of quite another kind can be found in the ordinary hyacinths used so freely for forcing for indoor bloom. There are dark and light blues available, any of which give a touch of opulence to the garden and flood it with fragrance as well. When forced for the house the spikes are apt to be rather clumsy and stodgy, but when established in the garden they become less full and more elegant. Nothing gives such a depth of blue as do the darker shades, except *Scilla sibirica* 'Spring Beauty'. White hyacinths are unsurpassed for quality and size of bloom, to say nothing of scent. Further, I find hyacinths static; they renew their spikes every year, although they are slow of increase.

One of the best blue flowers of spring is *Anemone apennina*, a gregarious small plant which increases readily by seed and by its spreading roots, especially on limy soils. In my acid soil they are not so prolific, nor is the near relative, rather smaller, *A. blanda.* Both have white varieties, and the latter varies to dazzling cerise.

By the time that scillas and hyacinths are over, so is the bulk of the yellow daffodils, though there are yet a few, such as 'Tittle Tattle'; the white hybrids of *N. triandrus* and *N. poeticus* carry us on for a few weeks. Fortunately, more excellent blues are to be found in grape hyacinths (*Muscari*), which have very sweetly scented dense little spikes of tiny bell flowers. Their leaves appear in autumn and last through till late spring. The rich blue of the ordinary *M. armeniacum*, or its selected form 'Heavenly Blue', is one of the best for general garden use; it is followed by 'Blue Spike', which has looser spikes of a feathery nature and often reverts to an ordinary type. Its lateness is a great boon. As the grape hyacinths go over we have *Ipheion uniflorum*, a relative of the onions and free of increase. The pale green, narrow leaves are offset by the pale flowers, which are nearly white in some forms although there are several good selections of light blue, such as 'Wisley Blue'. These little bulbs have a long flowering period and will thrive in the driest of positions.

Clumps of bulbs can be a nuisance to the cultivator in autumn and winter unless their positions are clearly and permanently marked. By the end of June most spring-flowering bulbs will have died down, having spent some weeks detracting from the appearance of the border with their dying foliage. It is therefore a good plan to plant them around clumps of other plants whose foliage does not start growing until May, such as hostas and agapanthuses. Rather earlier in leafing are peonies. All produce good spreading leaves which will cover up those of the bulbs. Fortunately these other plants also thrive on a diet of bonemeal and humus; both should be applied in early spring with a view to providing nourishment by the autumn, and to discourage weeds during the growing season.

Cutting Five —

Coppicing

My title is one which would be readily understood by a woodsman or forester but less easily by a gardener. Yet there is one sort of pruning which we gardeners might well call coppicing, which consists of cutting down shrubs so that the resultant growth makes an effect by its uniformity. It is mainly practised with willows and dogwoods in late winter so that a thicket of young shoots may spring up, making a dense mass of bark-colour the following winter. Particularly does it apply to those species with bright red, orange or yellow bark, or sometimes bright green, and the willows (*Salix*) and dog- woods (*Cornus*) excel in these tints. It is the bark on the youngest (one-year) twigs and branches that is the bright- est, hence the cutting-down.

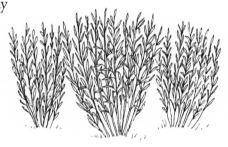

The most rewarding among species of *Salix* are variants of *S. alba*, of which the best known is *S. a.* 'Britzensis' whose twigs are orange-red. There are other similarly coloured variants but 'Britzensis' has the advan- tage of being a male clone and consequently has good spring catkins, covered with yellow stamens. If grown as a tree it will make a narrow specimen (which has been likened to the shape of a round paint-brush) and the leaves are of a strange khaki-grey, less silvery than those of *Salix alba*, which is a tree with a wide head. 'Britzensis' or similar variants are widespread in limestone or chalky valleys in Britain, and enliven the landscape on clear winter days. The variant with the brightest yellow bark is *S. a.* var. *vitellina.* Lit by the winter sun, it is as if a tin of rich yellow paint had been emptied over the bushes.

For darker colour, approaching crimson, there are forms of *Cornus alba,* itself a large bushy shrub for all but the driest of positions, like the willows. In the typical form, giving good autumn colour and bunches of grey-white berries, the bark is a rich dark plum-crimson. A much brighter but not quite so vigorous form is known as *C. a.* var. *sibirica.* Little is known about this plant; it has become designated the Westonbirt Dogwood, despite the fact that in that celebrated arboretum in Gloucestershire it does not thrive as does *C. alba* itself. Whether rabbits abound in Siberia I do not know, but they have certainly curtailed its growth at Westonbirt. Those with gardens invaded by these pests, take note! Though not conspicuous on a winter's day except in certain lights, the form *C. a.* 'Kesselringii' has bark so dark as to be almost black.

There is another species of *Cornus* for use on our palette, and that is *C. sericea,* of which the form *stolonifera* 'Flaviramea' has bark of a bright, greenish yellow, which can be very effective when grouped with the other colours.

All these plants, both the willows and dogwoods, are vigorous growers, and when established and regularly cut down will make large bushes up to 6 feet high and wide, or even more. The most compact is the Westonbirt Dogwood. It is usually recommended to cut down — to coppice — the bushes almost to ground level every spring. This ensures the brightest mass of stems for effect the following winter, but also means that until late summer there is no shrub to look at. This is all very well in large gardens and parks, but in small gardens where there is perhaps only one bush it is unfortunate that the shrub concerned shall be, as it were, "absent" just when the garden as a whole is at its best and needing the support of every bush in its furnishing. My solution to this is to cut down the two year old wood only; in other words, to leave each stem to grow for two years so that there will be something to look at during the summer months. With the willows in particular this may result in growth over one's head, but nobody would plant these willows and the dogwoods if space was at a premium. With this specialised treatment, our term "coppicing" is not applicable, since it describes, in woodsmanship, the complete pruning down of Hazel, Sweet Chestnut or Ash trees to what are known as "stools", every two or three years, for the production of walking sticks and larger poles.

There are several shrubs and shrubby plants which will repay annual cutting to ground level in order to encourage some winter beauty, and also in some species, maximum flowering potential. One is that unusual shrub *Leycesteria formosa,* with nodding heads of white flowers enclosed in mulberry-black bracts, borne on tall arching stems of rich Hooker's Green, of bamboo-like quality. In winter, after you have enjoyed the flowers in late summer and autumn and their black berries — if such things appeal to you — the green stems have much beauty. Alongside, if you have a large garden, you might plant one of the so-called white-washed brambles, species of *Rubus* to which the blackberries belong. If there were space enough I should choose *R. biflorus* which has gleaming cream-white stems, but it is a prickly monster to cope with. *Rubus cockburnianus* is not quite so large and its purple stems are also covered in a white "bloom", giving it grey-white effect. Much smaller is *R. thibetanus,* with ferny leaves, but it has a more invasive root. As an utter contrast you might plant *R. subornatus* var. *melanadenus* which has glossy, maroon stems. None of these has great beauty of flower or fruit, so that an annual cutting down does not rob us greatly.

There is an important point to observe in placing these shrubs for winter colour: to get the most of the bark colour they must be positioned so that the weak sunshine lights upon them, otherwise they will look like silhouettes.

For small gardens there is a good shrub or sub-shrub with grey-white stems, *Perovskia* 'Blue Spire', which is a hybrid of *P. atriplicifolia,* the Russian Sage. This brings us to the first plant in these notes whose flowers actually benefit from the encouragement of the growth of strong, fresh shoots annually from the base. The greyish leaves have a pungent sage-like fragrance and the small flowers, in lavender-blue, are in good branching spikes up to 4 feet. And through the winter you can enjoy the grey-white stems.

Most fuchsias die down in winter, at least in cold districts, but in mild maritime gardens where they do not succumb to frost it is best to cut them down — to coppice them — otherwise they tend to develop an untidy mass of weak stems. This specially applies to the small-flowered species and hybrids.

There are several good shrubs which flower better and give a longer display from an annual cut-down, though they are not noted for winter bark colour. Allied to the *Perovskia* is *Elsholtzia*, this time with mint-like leaves and fragrance. The spikes of lilac-pink flowers do not appear until very late summer, which makes it valuable in the garden. And although the scarlet tubular flowers are freely produced on a full grown shrub, I think it is best to treat *Phygelius capensis* and its new hybrids as herbaceous plants, to get a more manageable display.

It may seem strange to single out one of the less hardy hypericums, considering there are many first rate hardy ones, but *H.* × *moserianum*, if cut down in spring, gives an uninterrupted succession of flowers from mid-summer till autumn; and they are sumptuous flowers, too, with orange anthers. *Indigofera heterantha* (*I. gerardiana*) will make lovely large feathery shrubs in mild districts with lilac-pink pea-flowers in bunch after bunch from midsummer onwards. If cut down in early spring the display will be more concentrated over as long a period, about 4 feet high. Before finishing this little dissertation with some worthy spiraeas, I feel that *Lespedeza thunbergii*, which used to be called *Desmodium penduliflorum*, deserves notice. In a good sunny autumn no shrub can surpass in beauty its waving masses of crimson-purple pea-flowers, borne on arching stems growing up from ground level. If you can plant it on a bank so that it sweeps down over some grey-leafed shrub you will be able to realise one of the great sights of the year. But you must arrange for a fine, warm October.

And so to my last, the spiraeas, which I want to include. Everybody knows *Spiraea japonica* 'Anthony Waterer' and some of its relatives, but it is not every gardener who understands that to get the largest heads of flowers and the longest flowering period the plants need to be "coppiced". This applies to all the strongest-growing variants, 'Anthony Waterer' itself and the form 'Walluf' with larger heads of richer crimson flowers and without the odd variegated leaves; the tall 'Fastigiata' with immense flat heads of creamy white; and the small pink-flowered 'Macrophylla', which when annually pruned down is one of the most richly coloured shrubs for autumn leaves.

The plants I have mentioned in the last few paragraphs will of course make shrubs rather larger if left to themselves than they will if annually cut down, but the crop of flowers will thereby be better and of longer duration. And is not this what we all want from our shrub garden when the summer is waning?

Cutting Six —

After the Daffodils

March and April are resplendent with daffodils but the garden is suddenly bereft of their glory as May approaches. Those of us who have a garden of formal design, or at least one with formal areas, can resort to tulips, but I cannot feel they lend themselves to the mixed informal borders of shrubs and plants where the daffodils so happily bloomed. For these areas we have to look elsewhere for bloom at April's end.

But hold hard: we can have daffodils and narcissi from Christmas Eve until the middle of May if we plan well (see Cutting 3, "Desert Island Flowers"). And for early May we have *Narcissus poeticus* and its hybrids, such as 'Cantabile', that delicate Pheasant-Eye, and for yellow there is the extremely sweetly scented 'Tittle Tattle', one of Alec Gray's best. Even so, to my mind we have to wait for *N. poeticus* var. *recurvus* for the supreme last moment — those snow-white small flowers with their bird's eye and unforgettable scent. And those who garden in cooler, damper climates can glory in the double Pheasant-Eye, whose buds seldom open properly in dry areas. With these varieties the daffodil season is truly over. What will cheer the garden best at this time?

At the back of the border, under the shrubs, the Munstead Honesty, rich claret purple — or the white if you prefer it — will vie with the yellow of *Doronicum* 'Miss Mason'. If Honesty is too much of a nuisance in its biennial life and unlimited seedlings, try the perennial *Lunaria rediviva* in palest lilac. It has similar (but longer) pods to the biennial *L. annua*, and produces seedlings freely when left to itself, but if you gather the pods and dry the seeds in a packet, nary a one will germinate. This pale, bland lilac tones well with the equally bland pale orange of the single *Kerria japonica* — the finest is 'Guinea Gold'; I also have a soft spot for the dainty variegated *Kerria*, but usually eschew the gawky double variety.

The most obvious successor to daffodils in the less formal parts of the garden is the Spanish Bluebell which now, after many changes of name, seems settled under the title of *Hyacinthoides hispanica*. It is slightly paler than the British native Bluebell, *H. non-scripta*, and, if anything, is even more prolific and more amenable to any soil than the native, which is a little later in flowering. I specially like the white varieties, and tolerate the pink ones. They are, however, all inveterate spreaders by root and seed and must be controlled by removing the seed pods in all cases, and digging up unwanted bulbs. An old friend of mine used to say that they actually choked out the daffodils and narcissi from the rough grass in his orchard, so prolific were they.

In early May the very first of the hardy geraniums will be in flower — *Geranium malviflorum*, whose fingered leaves appeared in autumn. The flowers are borne above them, of rich violet blue, beautifully veined. It is strong enough in colour to assort with that earliest of peonies, *Paeonia* 'Early Bird', a hybrid of *P. tenuifolia*, with similarly lacy foliage and single flowers of vivid crimson, lit by the yellow stamens. It is very soon followed by that old double red *P. officinalis* which overwhelms all the colours in the garden.

There are many shrubs to comfort us in this period bereft of yellow, though the vivid orange of the *Berberis darwinii* clan may stare us out of countenance. One of my favourites is *Viburnum* 'Chesapeake', one of Donald Egolf's most successful hybrids, between *V.* × *carlcephalum* and *V. utile*. It is dense-growing and is usually covered with bloom, rounded heads of cream flowers opening from pink-tinted buds. It is a stolid, solid shrub of excellence, the very opposite to the arching shoots of *Rubus deliciosus* with wide-awake wild rose blooms of snowy whiteness.

Along the border front, when the Pasque flowers have turned into fluffy seed, the little *Tulipa batalinii* in creamy yellow and its hybrids of orange-amber are, I find, amenable and free-flowering. Their tones are delicate enough to mingle with the white and pale lavender of the dwarf alpine phloxes. Some of the strong pink varieties of these need careful placing, but 'Benito' — a rampageous ground-cover — is good value in full sun. For a shady site, a combination of the dainty little butter-yellow *Narcissus* 'Hawera' and a carpet of true blue from *Omphalodes cappadocica* is hard to beat. On wall or fence those charming species of *Clematis, C. alpina* and *C. macropetala,* have no competitors in their softest lavender-blues, pinks and whites. The former is a no-nonsense four-petalled single, the latter a ballet dancer with many petticoats.

Dicentra formosa is another spreader, with ferny foliage and an abundance of mauve lockets on upright stems; a charmer indeed but nothing when compared with the elegant *D. spectabilis,* whose rosy pink dangling lockets eclipse in beauty all its seasonal companions. Also nodding are the white bells of *Leucojum aestivum* 'Gravetye Giant', a bulbous plant of elegance and vigour.

The most brilliant yellow comes from the tall *Euphorbia wulfenii* and its even more brilliant but shorter relative, *E. polychroma.* They both benefit from the contrasting blue of forget-me-nots and *Brunnera macrophylla. Euphorbia polychroma* lasts in beauty of flower or foliage until the autumn, while *E. wulfenii* carries on through the winter as well.

Leucojum vernum

One of the most treasured shrubs for early May is *Exochorda* 'The Bride'. It is of pendulous, vigorous habit and smothers all its growths with particularly cold white flowers. As companions I can think of nothing better than a good clear pink form of *Rhododendron (Azalea) vaseyi*, an American species noted for its vivid autumn colour; this could be joined by those bluest of small-leafed rhododendrons, the tall 'Blue Diamond' and short *R. scintillans*. At the back could be added the extra good form of *R. campanulatum* which has been named after me. Its flowers are large and well shaped, emerging from buds of dark lilac to a lovely lighter shade, best described perhaps as clear amethyst-lilac, and paler in the throat, which is marked by delicate spotting. To accentuate its blue tone try it with the palest yellow of *R.* 'Ightham Yellow' or slightly darker 'Damaris Logan'. I wish there were a small-flowered, light yellow *Rhododendron* to flower with it, for it is my belief that contrast of size of bloom is almost as important as contrast of colour.

Meanwhile, a plant for a sunny border-front is that scintillating white daisy with silvery, lacy foliage, *Anthemis cupaniana*. It is dazzling with the *Geranium* and *Paeonia* and requires a well-drained soil. It tends to get leggy with age, but rooted pieces pulled off soon make new clumps.

Camassias are useful and beautiful bulbous plants steadily increasing at the root, and will seed themselves if naturalised. They make grassy tufts and produce slender spires of blue, white or cream in the best species, *C. leichtlinii*. They mostly flower at the junction of April and May with me, though the elegant double creamy form *C. l.* 'Plena' is later. 'Electra' is a stalwart light blue but the best blue form — a rich violet blue — is 'Eve Price' which originated at Wakehurst in Sussex. In good soil they may ascend to four feet.

By mid May one expects to see the splendid old columbines which seed about very freely but are not long-lived. We all know the podgy little Granny's Bonnets of old gardens in purple, crimson and pink. These are not what I am recommending; they are rather dull and dowdy. Years ago in a Scottish garden *Aquilegia alpina* developed into a blue strain which is called 'Hensol Harebell'. Over the years A. T. Johnson and Norman Hadden let them seed in their gardens, crossing with the old Granny's Bonnets and gradually eliminating the latter. The results were generously shaped columbines embracing not only the original blue and the white, but numerous shades of soft pink and purple, "selfs" and "bicolors". They are just what is required as the daffodils go, seeding themselves with abandon but easy to eliminate, and it is a simple matter to cut off the flower stems before the pods ripen, if they become too numerous. While Granny's Bonnets are self-explanatory from the close-gathered pleatings of the nodding blooms, columbine is not so easily understood. It likens the shape of the flowers to a cluster of doves, their necks and heads erect and their wings half-spread (*columba* being a dove, just as *aquila* is an eagle and thus *Aquilegia*).

Cutting Seven —

Spring Greens

For those of us who live in districts where overgrown hedges and bosky woodlands abound — where there is some shelter from the coldest winds — there often comes a day in early March, in Britain, or even in late February, when it suddenly steals upon our senses that Spring is on the way. The thickets have a film of green over them from the tiny, early buds of brilliant green of the May or Hawthorn. Its vivid colour invades old hedges as well and is not excelled in brilliance of true green by any other green of spring.

But cast your eye aloft, too; it may be that a tall tree is also sporting a film of green, of pronounced yellow tint this time. One of the first trees to delight us in this way is the Italian Maple, *Acer opalus*, whose tassels of yellowish flowers usually precede those of the Norwegian Maple, *Acer platanoides*. These are both large trees best enjoyed outside our small gardens, and excel not only in this early flowering but also in their yellow colouring at the end of the growing season.

The coming of the green of spring is what we all yearn for at the end of winter, when the evergreens which have kept us interested in the garden for weeks begin to pall and look tawdry. We have been comforted by the vivid orange and red of certain heathers, mostly *Calluna vulgaris* varieties, the invaluable *Mahonia* 'Moseri' and the yellow and orange-tinted conifers. They add brilliance to a winters's day, but are at best only a hectic flush directed at Old Man Winter's declining days. What we need most is the fresh green of new leaves, and our gardens with their multitudes of

Geranium maculatum

foreign plants help us as much as the broad greenery of the Lords and Ladies (*Arum maculatum*) and filigree of Cow Parsley (*Anthriscus sylvestris*), both early performers nestling at the foot of hedgerows.

In the garden I can think of no early greenery of any size and solidity to compete with the broad shining blades of colchicums, often called autumn crocuses, though they belong botanically to the Lily family. (Have you noticed how the leaves squeak when pulled together? Remembering E. A. Bowles's epithet for *Bergenia* leaves as "pig-squeak", it seems to me that *Colchicum* might be known as "mouse-squeak".) Some gardeners cannot bear the size and overweening aspidistra-like proportions of colchicums' leaves, but when they have reached 8 to 10 inches there is no clump of greenery in the garden to compete with their rich foliage. They outshine in both quality and colour other earlies, like daffodils, and the comforting, precocious *Geranium macrorrhizum*.

But perhaps I am going too fast. The Weeping Willow holds I think the prize for the tree most responsive to the call of Spring. Sometimes as early as late January in Britain its hanging twigs, meeting the ground vertically, in sheltered places will be tinted with brilliant green from the emerging leaf-buds. This is a tree that the botanists have played games with in regard to nomenclature over the years: it now seems fairly settled as *Salix* 'Chrysocoma', though nobody is certain of its origin. It is the best known Weeping Willow and excels in the yellow tint of its pendulous, lengthy twigs.

Now that our gardens are thronged with evergreens of varied hues it is perhaps the yellowish spring leaves that give us the greatest delight. They augment the yellow of the daffodils and make us believe the sun is shining even when it is obscured by dull clouds. No fresh yellow-green can compete with that of *Philadelphus coronarius* 'Aureus', the Mock Orange, whose young foliage lasts in almost true yellow from the opening buds in March until the sun gains strength in May to bleach and burn them. It is true that we have had plenty of this tint from the bright yellow conifer varieties and *Choisya ternata* 'Sundance', but these evergreens begin to fade after a time

Cornus mas

and become tarnished. Another early starter in yellow is *Physocarpus opulifolius* 'Luteus' — or, even brighter, 'Dart's Gold' — while the genus *Cornus* offers us several competitors: witness *Cornus alba* 'Aurea', less known than the variegated clones, but a brilliant and uniform spectacle until the autumn, augmented by the reddish plum-coloured young twigs. This is not as vigorous as the variegated forms 'Spaethii' and 'Elegantissima' and is a wonderful complement to the blues of various ceanothuses from spring until late summer.

But we are straying from our point, which is spring greenery. Things move so fast in spring that the garden, in spite of inclement weather, does not stand still. Every plant is doing its best and after being held up by the receding efforts of winter is putting forth a variety of greens that defy description. Some are not greens or even yellow-greens; there are blue-greens and purplish tints from Seakale, quite apart from the dark greens of colchicums, already mentioned. Some of the loveliest of spring greens are found in the warm-hued leaves of certain epimediums such as *E. rubrum* and *E. perralderianum*. In these, while the veins are of pale fresh green, the intervening spaces are a warm rosy brown; truly a miracle of beauty, especially when accompanied by the dainty flowers in pink, cream or yellow. And they are everybody's plants, thriving heartily in widely differing conditions and soils, though on the whole appreciating some shade.

One border in my garden inherited a plant of the yellow-flushed *Philadelphus coronarius* 'Aureus'. I planted nearby some of the hybrid photinias. Several evergreens among them have a habit of making very early young growth of brilliant coppery red. The most desirable seems to be *P.* × *fraseri* 'Red Robin', with close runners-up in 'Birmingham' (of Alabama) and *P. glabra* 'Rubens'. 'Birmingham' is a tall open shrub, but the other two are more compact and brilliant. The reddish colouring of the young leaves is touched with coppery brown, and has not the clear scarlet of certain *Pieris* forms, but on the other hand they are not harmed by frost and do not fail to thrive on limy soils. All in all these photinias have, I think, come to stay, and will contribute much to our gardens in the future. Not only their rich colouring will hold the eye, but as with all foliage their effect will outlast the display of daffodils and tulips, irises and peonies and thus be ready for conjuring up the warm effects of summer. Truly may it be said that with the passing of each floral spectacle it is leaves that create the lasting display. We have finished with tints scarcely green but they are worthy contributors to our garden schemes; it is the yellowish and reddish tones which are most in tune with spring, leaving the blue-greens and greys to the summer and early autumn borders when the season has spent itself before its final fling of glory.

It so happened that my predecessors had planted in this same border the double-flowered *Kerria japonica*, an invasive, tall and gawky shrub, but with an early spring display of rosette-flowers of soft light orange. The flowers are long-lasting both in the garden and when gracing our rooms;

they augment the copper of the photinias and the yellow *Philadelphus,* making a most brilliant spectacle, driving away winter's cold and rivalling any summer display.

Geranium malviflorum, meanwhile, has cheered us monthly throughout the winter, for though its rich violet-blue flowers do not appear until late spring, the new foliage arises in autumn.

One of the most cheering sights at the turn of the year is from *Helleborus foetidus.* Above an imposing pedestal of deeply cut leaves of darkest, almost black-green the pyramid of palest greens grows up with every lengthening day to produce those small bells of delicate green rimmed with red-brown. But these are to be the flowers, and we are looking for leaves.

Two other herbaceous plants respond early to the new year. The aconitums are first among the few and *Aconitum angelicum* the first and brightest green of all; the erect stems are clad in filigree leaves. In contrast, *Euphorbia myrsinites* has trailing stems set with small, glaucous green, sharply pointed leaves from summer onwards, to bear at their tips the clustered heads of flowers in April. Their tint is one of the most conspicuous yellow-greens, and the clusters may be likened to curds on the whey of the old glaucous trails. This *Euphorbia* is one of the most elegant of frontal plants, a true perennial in a sunny well-drained spot, and lasts a long time in beauty. As if this were not enough, its seeding heads, of parchment tone, later often become tinged with pink; and after all that, the stems should be cut away to make room for the next lot.

> Soon o'er their heads blithe April airs shall sing,
> A thousand wild flowers round them shall unfold,
> The green buds glisten in the dews of spring
> And all be vernal rapture as of old.

Cutting Eight —

Scented Rhododendrons

The flooding of the garden with the fragrance of azaleas is well known, and is given due note in Cutting 14, "The Pinxterbloom and Its Relatives". It is not generally realised that rhododendrons — as opposed to what we have long called azaleas — give us two very distinct assets in fragrance. Apart from flower fragrance there is also that priceless quality of aromatic foliage which delights us when working with them, layering or making cuttings, or bruising in any way. The rich odour from a propagating frame full of cuttings is only equalled by that from a frame of *Cistus* cuttings. On some warm and humid days the aroma hangs in the air; it mostly emanates from small-leafed species and hybrids such as those of the Saluenense and Hippophaeoides Series. In winter the aroma is strong when picking buds from *R. dauricum,* and on some mild and humid days *R. augustinii* and its relatives deliver a delicate whiff of heliotrope.

A visit to Cornish gardens in April and May will reveal an astonishing fragrance in the air. At Trengwainton, for instance, there are many species and hybrids of a tender sort, mostly with flowers white or faintly flushed or striped with pink, in every part of the garden. There are *R. edgeworthii* (*R. bullatum*), *R. johnstoneanum, R. lindleyi,* and such hybrids as 'Princess Alice', 'Countess of Haddington', 'White Wings' and the well-known 'Fragrantissimum'. One has to conjure up all the best far-eastern lilies, like *Lilium speciosum,* to get a scent to approach that of the rhododendrons. The above are all small to medium size in growth and lend themselves to pot or tub culture, by which means they can be given winter protection in

Rhodendron Cilpinense (top), *R.* 'Ptarmigan' (left)
and *R.* Praecox

colder districts. They are worth almost any trouble to gain for us the exotic delicacy of their blossoms to grace our rooms at flowering time, or "may be successfully cultivated under the shelter of a north wall, even where winter is sometimes severe".

Among hardier and larger-growing species are *R. fortunei*, which has flowers of delicate creamy pink or mauve and excellent foliage. Later in the season are its subspecies *discolor*, and *R. decorum*, mainly white but sometimes tinted with pink; the lovely foliage sets off the shapely crinkled flowers.

It must be tantalising to many when I keep writing about tender rhododendrons, but there is no doubt that they embrace some of the most gracious species. Remember that what we might call the epicentre of the genus is in those folded hills of western China and the Himalaya where the monsoon is not far away. Very few species, comparatively speaking, are found in the drier parts of the northern hemisphere. So most of us must yearn for the extreme beauty of bark, foliage, poise of flower and scent of the tender *R. griffithianum* from East Nepal, Assam and Bhutan; the flowers are in varying tones of pink, of the size and shape of a superb Lily. In fact, most of these large, scented rhododendrons have more in common with the flower of a trumpet lily than anything else. *Rhododendron griffithianum* has proved a splendid parent, not only in producing the ubiquitous 'Pink Pearl' but, united with *R. fortunei*, gave us *R. × loderi*.

In Great Britain we need only go to the Sussex gardens, in one of which — Leonardslee — the cross was made, to experience the delight of the very fragrant *R. × loderi* in May. The great lily-like flowers are white or pale pink, poised in loose open trusses at the extremes of every branch. They are very fine and large. A number of special forms have been named, such as 'King George', almost white, and 'Pink Diamond'. In spite of their size of bloom the plants are mostly large and fairly open, and thus made Mrs A. T. Johnson in North Wales claim that "they are never so smothered with blooms as to appear vulgar". They are fit to grace the largest of gardens where semi-woodland conditions obtain.

By choosing to cross the superb *R. griffithianum* with *R. discolor* a similar race of hybrids was raised at Exbury in Hampshire, named 'Angelo'. In fact, Lionel de Rothschild did a wonderful job in the many hybrids he made resulting in June- and July-flowering plants. Several distinct seedlings have been named, their corollas white or pink with dark or light centres, flowering early or late in the season. To walk through a glade strung along with plant after plant is a remarkable experience. I also take special delight in *R. discolor*, not only because of its scent but because of its lovely shape and later blooms coupled with neat grey-green leaves.

Not many of the Hardy Hybrids which have for so long held the stage in more exposed gardens show the influence of these fragrant species, but where *R. fortunei*, *R. griffithianum*, *R. discolor* and *R. decorum* have been used as parents, fragrance is often an added delight. I can think of no better example than the fine white 'Mrs A. T. de la Mare'. I should be willing to rearrange any shrub planting to accommodate this so-shapely beauty, white with a green eye, gracefully poised.

It is a long season, that of rhododendrons. As I write, in December, *R. dauricum* is in bloom, and for the next six or seven months we may expect various species and hybrids to come into flower, culminating in the brilliant months of May and June, but even after that showing what can be done with the later woodland hybrids.

The genus has another surprise in store. It is usually August before that supreme species *R. auriculatum* blooms, bearing trusses of great white lily-flowers with a rich lily-scent; a further attraction is the scarlet bracts which start unfolding at flowering time. It is remarkable also for its sturdy, almost tabular growth and great leaves, which by the way resist the call of spring and wait until after the flowers drop to produce their new crop. In many ways this may be called the king of rhododendrons. I was surprised to find it so tolerant of my rather dry soil — perhaps because of its reluctance to give its seasonal beauty until the longer nights and dews of August have effect. It is a species all on its own.

Taking a close relative of *R. decorum* as a parent, J. B. Stevenson at Ascot in Berkshire selected *R. diaprepes* (which is now classed as a subspecies of *R. decorum*) to cross with *R. auriculatum*. Both are sweetly scented and white; while *R. auriculatum* is comparatively low, widely branched and sturdy the other is a tall plant, usually tree-like. The result of the cross is the well-known 'Polar Bear', frequently to be seen 20 or 30 feet high, often with a single trunk. It is a great moment in August when this imposing plant breaks into flower, bringing the rhodo season to a close except for *R. serotinum* and the usual autumn crop on little 'Yellow Hammer': but these are not scented.

Some gardeners may bemoan the fact that so many of the scented rhododendrons are white or blush. A thought comes then that in the most hybridised or selected races of garden plants it is usually true that the white or pale forms have the most quality. Besides this, I might add that I find white and pale colours the most acceptable in the garden, and certainly of an evening when the light begins to fail and when fragrance is often at its most pervasive.

Cutting Nine —

Trough Gardens and Tufa

It was sometime in the 1920s that old stone sinks and pig-troughs were taken up by the growers of alpine plants, mainly through the inspiration of one man — Clarence Elliott. He saw in them several important points: they would raise the tiny plants nearer to eye-level and away from pests such as snails and slugs and four-footed creatures — for they were normally placed on supports — and ensure controlled drainage; and, if this were not enough, they would enable the creation of imaginary miniature landscapes, for those susceptible to such things, in the same way the Japanese had for centuries been admiring the miniature

landscape in an area covering only a matter of square yards. We will leave such artistry to one side in this Cutting, because I am really concerned here with alpine plants and their cultivation, but in some tiny gardens — courtyards, patios, call them what you will — a trough garden can be a real asset. A great variety of tiny plants can be accommodated in a very small space to flower from earliest spring until the onset of autumn, and will always delight the plant lover.

Old stone containers are now very difficult to find. Shiny white modern sinks are of good depth but need their surface scouring or chipping in order to cover them with what is known as hypertufa—a mixture of cement and coarser materials: after a period of weathering the deception is often not apparent. With regard to slugs and snails, it is equally important to use supports which will tend to defeat these creatures. I have used land-drains and other pipes and dry bricks with equal success, but it is no use to build up a rocky platform; that is simply an open invitation for the creatures to climb. The support, of whatever kind, should be dry and sterile. After all, some of the little plants would only suffer one bite before expiring!

It is vitally important to ensure that the drainage hole be kept open, yet covered with overlapping crocks and perhaps a piece of perforated zinc. Even then, believe me, ants will sometimes find their way in, with dire results: there are various ant-killers on the market, to which recourse must be made at once. Where ants find their way, woodlice will be sure to follow.

The soil to be used should be a loose scree-mixture composed of about one-third of friable garden soil with some sharp sand, one-third leaf-mould, and one-third stone chippings of a small screening. This could then be planted, but the effect would be dull unless a trough was to be set aside for one sort of plant, such as *Gentiana verna* or some other captivating morsel. I think few of us could contemplate a trough without inserting a few pieces of rock to enliven the "landscape", and no rock is so good for the purpose as tufa.

Tufa is of two kinds, according to geologists. It is a name given sometimes to that strange rock used in late eighteenth- and also nineteenth-century grottoes, which looks as though stout fingers had been inserted into soft rock ages ago: it need not concern us here, but it is as well to know that there is this variant. What we are concerned with is the tufa which is the most recent "rock" formed in geological time: it is still being formed in caverns in seams of limestone through which water finds its way and trickles, dripping through mossy growths and eventually cladding them in limy sediment. This solidifies even to several feet in thickness, enveloping more and more moss as the deposit accumulates. When brought to the surface and exposed to the weather this substance is very soft, and is apt to powder away, but the majority hardens and after a few seasons is quite static. Some noteworthy facts emerge here. The first is that, though composed almost wholly of lime, it is in some queer way not inimical to plants growing in or near it which would otherwise die from excess lime. Another is that the "rock" is so soft that holes can easily be made in it to accommodate little alpines, which thrive amazingly and keep suitably dwarf. Moreover, that they are growing actually *in* the rock is an economy of space.

A hammer and chisel are needed to make the holes; the disintegrated tufa removed from them should be mixed with soil and used to surround the roots of plants to fill in the holes. It is clear that a nurseryman's potful of soil will not go into these little holes, which need not be more than an inch and a half in width and 4 or 5 inches deep: it is best to prepare rooted offsets in advance, established in tiny pots or in the ready-mixed soil. Sometimes potsful can be split, and most of the soil can then be removed. It is helpful to get the little plants accustomed to a spartan diet early in life. Keep the holes to a downward sloping or vertical angle; immediately give the plants a good watering to fill in the interstices, and all should be well. Spring is the best time to start this work; if the weather turns hot, some shade should be given during establishment.

Of course, small pieces of rock of any kind will suffice to build up an imaginary landscape, but I think tufa is best, and the most economical of space. Lumps of tufa used in isolation elsewhere are also highly desirable, but in order to ward off pests they should be surrounded by sharp, clean shingle. Even so I have lost plants through molluscs climbing up to the irresistable morsels. I have had one lump of tufa for at least ten years and some plants growing on it — notably *Daphne arbuscula* — are 8 inches across. Being somewhat concerned by the thought of greater expansion of the Daphne due to its roots getting into the soil, we lifted the whole thing — but no, no roots had emerged from the tufa. I therefore concluded that the little plants actually approved of the restricted diet and root-run, though there cannot be, I think, much nourishment in lime and decomposed moss and debris.

To complete the setting, many planters will be tempted to include one or two dwarf conifers or other miniature shrubs. My answer to this is — don't. All so-called dwarf conifers get alarmingly large over the years and their widespreading roots clog drainage holes and are very difficult to extract. In more sheltered districts *Crassula sarcocaulis*, which resembles a dwarf tree, can be enjoyed to the full; it also flowers in late summmer when alpine plants do not produce much in the way of blossom.

Besides *Daphne arbuscula*, which gives me so much pleasure in May every year from its bunches of deep pink little scented trumpets, I have that little broom-like plant *Erinacea anthyllis* (*E. pungens*) whose pale lilac pea-flowers, stemless, are followed by almost white pods of seeds. I suspect both these little plants will get too large in time, but who could grudge them their space? Another good small shrub is *Helianthemum lunulatum* with tiny leaves and tiny yellow flowers with orange eyes; it I *know* will become too large in due course. Besides such bushlets, which help to give the container some character, there is usually room for three types of plants: prostrate ones for hanging over the sides; a few for growing in the level area around the pieces of stone; and others to perch among the rocks themselves. Some good miniature prostrate plants are dwarf forms of the colourful *Phlox douglasii*, the froth of pale pink from *Gypsophila repens* 'Fratensis' and the yellow *Helianthemum alpestre* 'Serpyllifolium', and the blue *Globularia repens*. For the level areas one can tolerate a few incursive plants such as tiny campanulas: *C. excisa* is a joy, threading its way about, and three non-spreading species for late display are *C. tommasiniana*, *C. wockii* and *C. waldsteiniana*. *Asperula gussonii* and *A. lilaciflora* 'Caespitosa' usually settle in well and greet us with pink tubular flowers in June. A complete change of colour is the true blue of *Polygala calcarea*, a somewhat stoloniferous tiny plant which is a native of Britain's chalk hills; a good form is known as 'Bulley's'.

When it comes to planting among the rocks, it should be borne in mind that this has to be done at the time of building. European saxatile species of *Primula* are admirable and give a touch of quality to the work; they prefer the cooler aspects. I am very fond of Jack Drake's free-flowering form of *Potentilla nitida* whose rich rosy pink, almost stemless flowers stud the grey hummocks in summer, and also that very dwarf version of *Dryas octopetala* known as 'Minor'. But the greatest joy is obtained from the Silver or Encrusted saxifrages, headed by *Saxifraga paniculata* (*S. aizoon*). There are many forms: 'Rosea' has warm pink flowers and 'Lutea' pale yellow ones, but for yellow I should choose the unbeatable hybrid 'Esther'; it never fails to produce its lovely arching sprays of cool yellow. There is also a hybrid with pink flowers, again with arching sprays — 'Kathleen Pinsent' — but I have not found it robust. There is also little 'Baldensis'. They all make an entrancing effect in bloom. A pretty hybrid known as 'Canis Dalmatica' has good spikes of white flowers heavily spotted with crimson. *Saxifraga callosa* (*S. lingulata*) is a superior kind of the Encrusted Section (the group name refers to the encrusted lime deposits on the leaves — which will, oddly enough, be present even if the plants are growing in lime-free soil). Its well-known forms such as 'Lantoscana' and 'Bellardii' also prefer the cooler aspects of the rocky eminences, but are rather large for our purpose unless the container is really large too. The earlier-flowering members of the Kabschia and Engleria groups can also be grown in a container, but are better appreciated in the alpine house.

One of the most coveted plants for our mollusc-proof planting is *Physoplexis comosa*, long known as *Phyteuma comosum*. This is a campanula relative with the most intriguing heads of stemless flowers (often likened to soda-water bottles) in light lilac. But beware, if a mollusc gets so much as a whiff of this plant, it will climb almost anything to get at it.

Sempervivum arachnoides, with its silvery rosettes and starry pink flowers, is a "must" for driest top crevices; and one or two of the kinds with rich mahogany rosettes, such as 'Malby's Hybrid', add variety to the greenery though the flowers are brownish and rather dull. For years *Asperula suberosa* has survived in a dry hole in my tufa, and produces, in hot dry summers, those lovely heads of pink tubular flowers among its grey leaves, but as often as not it gets spoiled by rain, and one wishes for an alpine house.

It need not be thought that to achieve such plantings one must neces-

Saxifraga × kelleri

sarily have sinks and troughs. Any large container will do, so long as it does not look incongruous on supports. One keen gardener I knew had an old mill-wheel made of integrated pieces of stone. This was balanced on the top of a tree stump and in it alpines throve mightily, getting their roots into the jointing mortar.

It will be seen from the above few suggestions that a wide range of disparate plants can be grown, to the delight of the ardent plantsman. Because of the necessity of raising the containers off the ground, trough gardens are also of particular interest to the elderly and handicapped.

> At once, array'd
> In all the colours of the flushing year,
> By Nature's swift and secret-working hand,
> The garden glows, and fills the liberal air
> With lavish fragrance.
>
> — J. Thomson (1700–1748), *Spring*

Cutting Ten —

Dog's-tooth Violets

Although I devote a few lines to these quintessential spring treasures in the next Cutting, "The Lily-of-the-valley Bed", I feel their assets are well worthy of being set forth at some length. Not only are the flowers of dainty chiselled perfection, but their poise and colouring are all that one can desire, and they are held well clear of their foliage. The leaves of most species have mottled brownish tinting, earning them one of their sobriquets, "trout lilies".

Apart from the daffodils, I think the words of the old Madrigal, "The spring clad all in gladness doth laugh at winter's sadness", apply most closely to the species and forms of the *Erythronium* or dog's-tooth violets. Their nodding flowers have abundant charm and exquisite shape and tints, they are easy to grow, and the fertile ones spread abundantly by seed, when suited. A great stretch of the imagination must have been involved in arriving at their now accepted vernacular name; they are not even botanically connected with violets, and the only connection I can see with that flower is the crook in the tube of the corolla; as to the "dog's tooth", this refers to the shape of the bulb or corm. Nor can I see any real resemblance to an "adder's tongue", their other vernacular name. The leaves are broad and shapely, often prettily mottled, particularly in the European *Erythronium dens-canis* (also a native of Japan).

This species increases readily in the acid, light, loamy soil of my little garden. The bulb merchants separate different coloured forms, from rosy-white to quite rich rosy lilac ones; all are beautiful. One day the

Erythronium 'Pagoda' and *E. dens-canis*

mottled leaves will scarcely be showing, and three days later the dainty, nodding, starry flowers prettily marked within will be opening. There is nothing blatant about them; they do not look you in the face as does a daisy, but hide their charms in a bewitching way.

The first to bloom with me is *E. grandiflorum*, sometimes called *E. giganteum.* This is from what might be called the epicentre of the various species, western North America, in Oregon and British Columbia. It must be a great experience to see these early spring delights in their scattered thousands, even densely carpeting the ground. No sight other than the smaller species of *Narcissus* could rival them, such as *N. bulbocodium* var. *citrinum*, naturalised in their thousands in the Savill Gardens, Berkshire, with pink forms of *Erythronium revolutum* threatening also to become a weed not far away: the same may be said of the Royal Horticultural Society's Garden at Wisley, though here *Narcissus bulbocodium* is of the more typical dark yellow form

The *Erythronium* known as 'White Beauty' is a bit of a mystery. Being (presumably) a hybrid it is sterile and has to be increased by division, which it does not resent, quickly readjusting itself and soon becoming ready for division again. It occurs in the 1930 catalogue of Carl Purdy, from whose nursery at Ukiah in north California so many species were distributed in the early middle of this century. I am tempted to think that Purdy put this splendid plant on the market; he claimed it was a very fine form or variety of *E. californicum.* Its creamy flowers, zoned with yellow in the centre, are large, elegant and freely produced over the mottled leaves. By the time it is in full flower the queen of the race, *E. revolutum*, will be in bud, each stem a foot or more high bearing between 1 and 3 flowers of dainty perfection, from pearly pinky white to rich old rose. Years ago a very fine deep pink form was named 'Johnstonii', but today, wherever they thrive, they seed so freely that every tone of pink is found.

There are two stalwart late-flowering hybrids, increasing freely and thus useful for division, of soft sulphur yellow; they are 'Pagoda' and 'Kondo'. These may well be tetraploids, but I have no note of their origin.

And last but by no means least comes *E. hendersonii.* The petals are of soft lilac at the tips but white towards the centre, which is accentuated by a dark violet zone. You just *have* to bend down, lift the flower and inspect the wondrous colouring. As if the colours of the petals were not enough, the stamens and stigma are crimson.

All species and forms are enlivened by these central zones of colouring, perhaps just darker yellow or with a ring of orange or red. *Erythronium revolutum* has the effrontery to centre its pink segments with a dark orange zone, but all is forgiven in contemplating the extreme elegance and beauty of these blooms — the essence of spring — and they flower with the blue of *Chionodoxa* and *Scilla* and make us realise that whatever vagaries the weather may yet have in store for us, Spring has at last arrived.

As I have said, my soil is a fairly light acid loam; I have not seen dog's-tooth violets thriving on limy soil, though there may be examples. It is noteworthy that neither E. A. Bowles nor F. C. Stern mention them in their books, and both gardened on limy soils and loved bulbous plants.

A few weeks in spring see the erythroniums through the ground, in leaf and flower, and spent. Their life is full of glory, though brief. I have them growing in a bed of Lily-of-the-valley, whose beautiful leaves speedily cover up the fading tufts. It has become an accepted practice to divide snowdrops immediately after flowering, while "in the green", and the same procedure is approved by the erythroniums. Great care is necessary with the smaller-growing kinds; their thread-like leaf-stalks are easily broken, but if in dividing them you can ensure that each bulb keeps its one leaf, the newly separated individuals will usually flower in their second year, thus extending spring's miracle. The bulbs must be planted promptly, while still moist; bulbs that have become dry should be rejected.

All erythroniums seem easily satisfied in the garden, prospering best in moist soil with ample humus. Though they grow wild in the open sward they are surely most suited to moist open woodland or the scattered trees of the forest, where the annual fall of leaves will bring them the enrich-ment they so deserve — and with the scattering of trees and shrubs in our gardens, we approximate nature's open forests. They are said to grow in grass, but it must be of the less vigorous species, and not coarse tussocks. An interesting point is recorded by Purdy: there are several species native to the eastern United States, notably *E. americanum*, but apparently in cultivation these, like certain fritillaries, tend to split up into many small bulbs, with a consequent lack of flower.

> That they are perfectly hardy, thrive with no special care, and stay for years is certain, and especially in all of the country north of California and east of the Rockies.
> —Carl Purdy, Ukiah, California: 1930

Cutting Eleven —

The Lily-of-the-valley Bed

Reginald Farrer wrote in *The English Rock Garden* that "Lily-of-the-valley is the worst of all delicious weeds when it thrives". One might add that it is of little worth if it does not thrive, and probably as many plantings linger without thriving as brook no curbing. It would be a bold gardener who would put forth a recipe for success. I have seen Lily-of-the-valley run amok in sun and in shade, in heavy and light soils, even invading the interstices of paving and gravel paths. Yet in a luscious bed made up with leafmould it may refuse to increase.

I cannot imagine any gardener not making an effort to get *Convallaria majalis* established, even with the prospect of its running through every-thing in due course. It is worth trying it in several places at once — it will usually be found to thrive in one. I like to plant the common kind in sun and in shade; those in the sun will start the season's picking and be followed by those in shade, and all will be followed by 'Fortin's Giant', whose wide tubby bells appear about a fortnight later. It is a good plan to put some of this in shade as well. The strange little mauve-pink 'Rosea' is a mid-season flowerer; it is easygoing and prolific when suited, but is a very different type, with its long pedicels and reflexed corolla (when mature). I wish I knew where it originated.

Apart from the luxury of picking bunches of the flowers to enjoy indoors, there is also the experience of the waft of scent from a leafy patch. And the leaves themselves, mainly hiding the flowers, are of a rich green and make a dense ground-cover. It goes on and on, spreading in all directions until brought up short by a large dense clump of Hosta or some spreading dark shrub; one begins to wonder how much more ground to allow it.

But it need not be a carpet of one thing. I find the Lily-of-the-valley admirable for interplanting with small bulbs. Winter Aconite (*Eranthis*), for instance, should thrive in the same cool conditions, though they have never done so in my acid soil. By mid February the slim, grey javelins of *Crocus tomasinianus* will be appearing, to open into the most lovely little cups of lilac, light or dark, amethyst or purple, white or claret, all with orange stigmata. They seed themselves with such abandon that their thousands combine to offer a whiff of scent on still, sunny days. They are followed quickly by the big Dutch crocuses in white or purple or striped, also with vivid stigmata. I prefer to grow the well-known yolk-yellow Dutch crocus elsewhere, so that its colour can blend with the rich coral colour of *Mahonia* 'Moseri' or red-stemmed dogwoods and willows.

Crocus tomasinianus

No sooner are the crocuses over than the Dog's-tooth Violets appear. As noted in Cutting 10, the European *Erythronium dens-canis*, in pink or blush, is usually first, quickly followed by *E. gigantea*, from North America, in creamy tints. In spite of the beauty of early narcissi, I rate these the most exquisite of early flowers. Fortunately there is a succession of species to follow — palest yellow *E. citrinus*, pink *E. revolutum*, lilac *E. hendersonii* and the two valuable hybrids 'White Beauty' and citron 'Pagoda'. In his *Flowers — a garden note book,* Sir Herbert Maxwell observes that dog's-tooth violets thrive mightily after a forest fire in California; this makes me think a dressing of potash or bonfire ash would help them in our gardens. They have all happily settled down in my ordinary soil, though they may not thrive on limy ones, to which the Lily-of-the-valley are sympathetic. Meanwhile, snowdrops have come and gone with the crocuses, and the smaller species and cultivars of *Narcissus* increase steadily.

Before all these spring delights have faded, the lilies' leaves are well up. The month of May will see their successive crops of flowers; after them I have one more treat from the same patch, that of the blazing tomato-red *Tulipa sprengeri.* This grows to 18 inches or 2 feet with truly gorgeous flowers of a slim, refined shape; I find it thrives best in a cool, somewhat shady place and it seeds itself with abandon, each seed taking about five years to reach flowering size. With the tulip I like to arrange one of the hostas with pale yellow-striped leaves, which give just the needed complement to the red and rich greenery. A few white *Lilium martagon* complete the grouping later.

The *Convallaria* leaves die down in the autumn and the patch needs cheering up with something — an autumn-flowering bulb, for instance; not ardent sun-lovers, like nerines, but there are several autumn-flowering species of *Crocus* such as *C. byzantinus* (*C. iridiflorus*), a rich violet-blue species which increases readily in shaded places.

So here we have an area of garden with a succession of beauty from January onwards into summer and autumn, with no digging, staking or weeding. Is not this our aim?

A.T. Johnson, VMM

Nora Johnson

Cutting Twelve —

Arthur Tysilio Johnson and His Garden in Wales

Having lifted the latch of the small hand-gate in the low stone wall there was always a special pleasure when one walked down the sloping path to the back door of The Bungalow in the Conway Valley. Steeply up the tree-clad slope came the sound of the rushing brook, a sound which has always lived with me. Otherwise there was a silence broken only by the rustling leaves, birdsong and sheep on the distant hills, visible through the trees. The kettle would usually be singing on the hob and Mrs Johnson would call "Sara" to fetch A.T.J. down from his eyrie above. For it was not really a bungalow; another hand-gate led along a sunny path to the front door and the main rooms of the house. Above were two small rooms and below, the kitchen, which gave comforting warmth even in chilly weather. The whole building was set into the steep bank.

A. T. Johnson was born in the vicinity and spent his early years as a schoolmaster teaching, I infer, English, the Classics and perhaps what was then called Scripture. But his love of English led him to writing at an early age, with a leaning towards outdoor pursuits, all connected with wildlife. These and some poems appeared in various journals of the day. After his first, disastrous, marriage he met Nora Meek in about 1907 and they lived in close harmony until he died in 1956. To these early years belong his little pocket book *In the Land of the Beautiful Trout,* in which his love of the Welsh countryside shines forth. Shortly after, using the pseudonym "Draig Glas" ("Blue Dragon"), he wrote *The Perfidious Welshman*, which had its second impression in 1910. In spite of the pseudonym, the authorship leaked out and he and Nora spent a long vacation in California, getting to know much about the flora and fauna of that state.

Originally the little house had only the steep tree-clad slope as a garden, with a small area of flat, damp ground below, outlined by the curve of the mill-race from Bulkeley Mill a hundred yards or so away, up the valley. The steep bank was stony and rooty and sharply drained, but a surprising number of plants grew there thanks to the rainfall, which I judge to have been about 40 inches. The bank faced west and though well covered and surrounded by trees — mostly oaks, with a few ash trees and alders along the streams — it was a windy garden. The slope was threaded by narrow footpaths and steps. In fact the water-rounded rocks served as edging and walling stones, paving and steps; there was no shortage, and they gave the garden great character. One of the most pleasing effects in gardens in Wales, and indeed in the north of England, is the grey gravel as opposed to the yellow Thames gravel so prevalent in the south. The grey is so much more in harmony with flowers and leaves. For some of their wider planting areas on the flat the Johnsons hit upon the idea of making their own stepping stones, in the following way. First some small areas of spare ground had two inches of soil removed. The bottoms of these level hollows were sprinkled with the local shingle or gravel (usually granite), and over this was spread about two inches of concrete. When set the resulting slabs were lifted and turned over so that the surface presented the gravel and would not get slippery in wet weather. I understand many of these slabs are still in place.

In 1927 A. T. J.'s first gardening book appeared — *A Garden in Wales.* A few years previously the Johnsons had taken in a considerable piece of flat meadow, beyond the mill-race but bounded on the far side by the stream itself. Here was new scope for gardening, and the lease it gave upon a wider choice of plants prompted the book. There was room for a grass glade fringed by magnolias, firs, birches, *Nothofagus* and shrubs; it inspired me greatly when I first saw it in 1935 and continued to inspire me for twenty years of visiting it in alternate years. Much of it was shaded but a few years later the opportunity arose to acquire about a third of an acre of open ground to the south, including a place for a garage. This area was largely given to perennials and shrubs and *Magnolia* ✕ *veitchii,* which grew with great rapidity. By then his second garden book had appeared, *A Woodland Garden.* After the war the Johnsons purchased a slice of meadow leading to Bulkeley Mill itself, restored the Mill fit to be let as a small dwelling, and repaired the great wooden waterwheel so that its plash, plash added to the music of the stream. Thereafter the postal address was changed to Bulkeley Mill. The piece of land that came with it was gravelly and open and gave the opportunity to grow a number of old species roses, among other plants. *The Mill Garden* appeared in 1949, extolling many new plants. This was A. T. J.'s last major book, but he was kept busy on lesser publications by the successful little magazine called *My Garden,* owned and edited by Theo. A. Stephens. All this writing was done, not without great effort I believe, in the little top room; it was here that he conjured up those winning phrases and deep thoughts which have enchanted all who have read his words. There was no telephone to distract his thoughts.

With much of his time given to writing and photography, it is obvious that Mrs Johnson was also a great and efficient gardener. There were in all about four acres, and in its heyday the garden was always in first-class condition. I saw it in different seasons from spring to autumn. A very handy man with walling, fencing, mowing and all such jobs was he whom A. T. J. called "Prometheus" in his writings, who worked with them for some forty years, two days a week. I fancy that in view of his name he must have been good at keeping bonfires going even in that rather damp climate! There was also Maggie, a home helper. Until her sight weakened, Mrs Johnson did all the typing. It was a very happy working group and no time was wasted. His writing attracted visitors, who were not always welcome because of the time they absorbed, but they were always made to *feel* welcome. In a garden of that size, and run to such high standards, there were always pressing jobs to be done.

The Johnsons may be said to have grown with their garden. Their keen love of plants and avid desire for more and more of them as the total area grew meant visits to other gardens and nurseries, occasionally to the Shows of the Royal Horticultural Society, and travels to Scotland and distant parts of England. Among their fast friends were Walter Ingwersen and W. J. Marchant, two nurserymen of great repute and kindness from whom many nuggets arrived. But they knew and were known by many of the leading horticulturists of the first half of this century.

Both Ingwersen and Marchant were mostly occupied with and interested in the plants of the wild, the species, not the highly bred "grandifloras" of the nursery and seed trades. These plants of refinement gave the garden its whole character. And character it truly had. I think the word "gentle" sums it up as well as any. There were practically no straight lines or unnecessarily curving paths; all routes through the garden followed the contours, easily, gently, always leading one on to a fresh peep between shrubs up or down the valley. They also had an almost uncanny knack of placing plants, so that they would thrive and "look comfortable". There were no harsh orange or red colourings; the whole garden was filled with gentle tints from white to light yellow, clear and deep pinks, mauves and blues and dark purples, all backed by the native vegetation. The choice of colours was not always easy. To bolster his selection of plants for his writing A. T. J. needed great variety. Sometimes when tempted at a show or nursery he would be warned by Nora that "such a colour would upset your nightingales" — or, I might have added, the willow warblers.

The garden owed as much to William Robinson as to Gertrude Jekyll; there were no herbaceous borders or graded colour-schemes. It was perhaps the most important and original of what are called "ecological" gardens today, where each plant's preferences were studied, bringing into things a wholeness and a gentleness new to this century. There is no doubt that his outpouring of articles and many books exercised a great influence in their day. They were all illustrated by his highly skilled photography, close-ups of plants in the main and without, unfortunately, many views. While he gloried in the shrubs and trees and woodland plants — the rhododendrons, Ericaceae, birches, cherries, conifers and bulbs — "Herself" (or "The Lady of the Garden"), as he would call her in his writings, treasured everything including tiny shrubs, primulas, meconopsises, and alpines. Thus there was an exceptionally wide range of plants from aconites to *Arcterica nana,* from rhododendrons and hellebores to eucryphias and *Nothofagus.* And there was never a shortage of paths and views to be enjoyed, morning, afternoon or evening.

Perhaps after a long morning in the garden the weather would tempt a visit to nearby Bodnant — always a Mecca for gardeners — or the Happy Valley Gardens at Llandudno (full of good plants); or perhaps an expedition to Cemmaes Bay on Anglesey where the dunes were blue with *Scilla verna,* or a trek over the hills to the Auld Brig. And home in the early evening chill which falls so quickly in those damp valleys as soon as the sun sinks behind the hills — home to the quickly kindled range and a high tea, and long discussions about plants and this and that.

I heard the history of their *Daphne cneorum* 'Eximea'; *D. cneorum* was a well-known plant before the Second World War and used to be on every rock garden at Chelsea, but it suddenly lost its vigour. The Johnsons bought a plant from J. Stormonth's nursery at Carlisle which had been collected in the wild, and raised seed from it, and the result was this now well-known and brilliant clone enjoyed by all gardeners who can grow it. There were two self-sown plants in the garden which have achieved equal fame: *Cytisus* 'Johnson's Crimson', of intense colouring, no doubt inheriting its crimson tint and small flowers from *C.* × *dallimorei* which grew nearby. And the same was presumed about *Erica* × *darleyensis* 'Arthur Johnson', which might be described as a great improvement on the Darley Dale cross, with much longer flower spikes.

A booklet which A. T. J. wrote entitled *Labour Saving Plants* summed up for the first time how plants can be used not only to beautify the garden but, by virtue of their ground-hugging propensities, to avoid the use of hoe or spade. There is no doubt that much of the success and beauty of his garden was due to the use of these plants. Not only did they cover the ground to the exclusion of weeds, but the carpets and clumps of foliage and flower made the perfect complement and contrast to the dominance of shrubs in the scheme of things. Even today some of his plantings, notably of epimediums, remain free of weeds. Among these plants none was accorded more praise than the hardy geraniums. I did not discover how the pale form of *Geranium pratense* cropped up, but it was a favourite in the garden, and caught the eye of Mr B. Ruys of the famous Moerheim Nursery in Holland, who begged for some seeds. These duly germinated and among them was a stranger, a splendid lavender-blue of short stature which was put on the market in 1950 as 'Johnson's Blue'. It was probably a hybrid of *G. himalayense,* and has achieved great fame. Two selections of *G. endressii* were 'Rose Clair' in salmon-pink and 'A. T. Johnson' in pale silvery pink. They were listed by Ingwersen, as was *Mimulus guttatus* 'A. T. Johnson', a gorgeous seedling of wallflower-red edged with yellow which he had found in a boggy stream in the hills. A journey by car to south-western Scotland produced the pure pink *Geranium sanguineum* 'Glenluce', a welcome change from the normal "bloody cranesbills", and with extra-dark-green leaves. It is a favourite with lovers of lowly plants. We owe to the Johnsons, I believe, the many tints of columbines from white to pink and plum colour and to blue, self-tinted or perhaps parti-coloured, on which they exercised their skills as selectors and improvers of the 'Hensol Harebell' strain, influenced by the old Granny's Bonnets of the Welsh cottage gardens. It is worth noting here that *Ceanothus* 'A. T. Johnson' was raised by Burkwood & Skipwith at Kingston upon Thames, and named in his honour. One winter they went to the Riviera and found in bloom in February a form of *Calluna vulgaris* which they brought back and called 'Hiemalis' — a useful plant seldom seen today.

I consider A. T. J.'s was the outstanding garden of its kind and size during the second quarter of this century. As the years passed and towards the end of the planters' lives it became overgrown, without skilled staff to keep it in order. But such is the fate of most personal gardens. Among the principles they observed, the most sacrosant was "the preservation of a garden atmosphere which shall be, as near as is humanly possible, in harmony with the wild's uncultured beauty". Their garden achieved the nearest I have ever seen to this most difficult of all garden styles — that of being naturally beautiful and intriguing without ever being wild.

After Mrs Johnson's death Maggie and Prometheus married and lived at The Bungalow, which they called Oak Bank. Eventually Oak Bank and the Mill were sold, but I hear of the many fine specimen trees that still stand guard over the glade: *Aesculus neglecta* 'Erythroblastos', *Cercidiphyllum*, *Koelreuteria*, magnolias, birches, *Abies, Davidia, Metasequoia, Athrotaxis, Nothofagus*, and many rhododendrons and good shrubs. The owners keep the lawns well mown and must greatly enjoy each year's unfolding beauty. And still the chattering stream flows down the gentle meadow slopes.

Facing west, set into an ivy-clad bank halfway up the slope, is a small stone seat. At its back is a slab of stone with the lettering "In the garden of happy memories it is always summer". So it is with me.

Meconopsis chelidonifolia

Cutting Thirteen —

Perennial Blue Poppies
— and Others

The first Blue Poppy to flower in Britain was *Meconopsis simplicifolia*, in 1848. It did not make the headlines, being tricky of cultivation and in its original form of a purplish hue. Its variety *baileyi* is of a clearer blue but even less of a garden stalwart. Nearly fifty years later *M. grandis*, also of a purplish blue, was introduced and was grown in northern gardens.

This is really the crux of the matter, for all species and hybrids grow best in cool, damp climates, or in conditions such as those at the Savill Gardens in Windsor Great Park in Berkshire. There, fed by natural springs, in the shelter of trees and shrubs and with unlimited leaf-mould, they thrive heartily, probably as well as in the wild. Apart from the leaf-mould, which is so much more nutritious than peat, it is the cool air and partial shade that encourage them. In fact, in my own garden I have given up trying to grow any of them; we lack the cool air and moisture, whatever we may give them in the way of humus.

It was not until 1924 that blue poppies became a talking point among gardeners, due to the introduction of *M. baileyi*, later to be known as *M. betonicifolia*, the Betony-leafed Blue Poppy, which in some circumstances is a true perennial. By 1927 I had it in flower in my schoolboy garden, and it thrilled me beyond measure. Having been brought up on the common wild red poppy of the cornfields, and their selections the Shirley poppies in delicate tints, there was to me something almost magical in the words "blue poppy", fostered no doubt by the able pen of Kingdon Ward, that dauntless seeker after good plants to grace our gardens from the Far East. It is in fact from Nepal to Western China that most species come, from the woodland valleys and moist hillsides frequented by the best rhododendrons, where the monsoon spends itself and the air is cool.

In the hope, then, that some readers of these pages may be gardening in suitable conditions, I want to draw attention to some of these great glories.

Although it is the last, usually, to flower, we might as well start with the most popular, *M. betonicifolia.* It sends up from a goodly clump of basal leaves a stout stem bearing flowers in the leaf axils, and also one or perhaps three terminal blooms, which are usually the best in quality, size and colour. This is the species' most notable trait and is transmitted to most of its hybrids. The other very splendid species, appropriately named *M. grandis,* makes an equally fine or finer tuft of basal leaves and usually produces a short, stout stem which branches into several erect stalks, almost all from one point, each bearing one solitary flower. Purplish forms were first introduced in 1895, but in this century certain remarkable, glorious blue forms appeared, from such collectors in the wild as Frank Ludlow and George Sherriff, which surpassed anything in cultivation. In the Royal Botanic Garden at Edinburgh all the original collections may be seen, carefully segregated.

There are several good hybrids between *M. betonicifolia* and *M. grandis,* and their mode of flowering is often midway between the two. They are all known as *M.* × *sheldonii,* after a Surrey gardener who first made the cross. Under this name, then, is the magnificent 'Branklyn' (named after a famous Scottish garden, and with what is usually called "hybrid vigour" well represented). I have seen this not far short of 5 feet high. Its great flowers are of a rich blue tinted with purple in some conditions. But the cross was also made elsewhere in Scotland, and one of the most impressive selections is that known as 'Slieve Donard'. I remember seeing it in the company of Leslie Slinger of that famous nursery and there was no doubt, in his eyes, that it was the finest and most brilliant clear blue of them all. He had obtained it from Mount Stewart, and owing to Dr Charles Nelson's indefatigable detective work we now know that it was raised in Scotland by a Dr Curle, who also selected a paler blue seedling named 'Ormswell'. Besides 'Slieve Donard', others have been raised with equally brilliant blue flowers, such as Mrs Crewdson's hybrids and 'Archie Campbell'; 'Quarriston' was raised and named in Ireland. There is no doubt that these hybrids are among the most clear and dazzling blue flowers in cultivation, not excluding delphiniums and gentians. They must all be increased by division of the furry crowns in early September or early spring.

I have known and grown a very different species for nearly as long as *M. betonicifolia*. It is *M. quintuplinervia*, which Reginald Farrer dubbed the Harebell Poppy and described as "so beautiful that the senses ache at the multitudinous loveliness of its myriad dancing lavender butterflies over the rolling upper Alps of the Da-Tung chain in northern Kansu – Tibet". His enthusiasm can be well understood when we recall that each bell-like flower is poised on a slender leaning stem some eighteen inches high over a tuft of hairy green leaves. The flowers have a violet base and cream stamens. The clumps take kindly to division. A related species with wider, more open flowers of rich red is *M. punicea*, but it is temperamental in British gardens.

There are several species with clear, light yellow flowers, the best-known in Britain being the native Welsh Poppy, *M. cambrica*. It seeds itself freely wherever it is grown and seems always to be of two separate colour strains, which oddly enough do not hybridise. They are always either brilliant lemon-yellow or soft orange, and thus fit into different colour combinations. There is no doubt that the former colour blends best with all other *Meconopsis* species and hybrids. There are double orange ones, but I have never seen a double yellow. The doubling of so dainty a flower, over the divided filigree of its clear green leaves, is a doubtful advantage until one remembers that they are not likely to set seeds. They flower early, at the same time as the bluebells, with which the lemon poppies look delightful.

I think my favourite yellow species is the extra dainty *M. chelidonifolia*, a good perennial for a cool spot producing airy-fairy sprays of lemon cups on wire-fine branching stems. It has been known and grown since 1904 but is still comparatively rare. Pre-dating it by more than fifty years is the sumptuous *M. villosa*, which used to be called *Cathcartia villosa*. A hairy, stalwart plant of considerable charm and value with large flowers, it is easily raised from seeds but is not long-lived, and the same may be said of the so-called Lampshade Poppy, *M. integrifolia*, whose great nodding flowers have thrilled all who have seen it. Uniting with *M. betonicifolia* this species has given us *M. × sarsonsii*, a great treasure to be nursed in the softest of climates, where it will surprise with its ivory-cream flowers.

Devotees of these plants will also want to grow the several monocarpic species, *M. wallichii*, *M. paniculata* and *M. regia*. Apart from the magnificence of their golden- or silvery-haired winter rosettes composed of overlapping divided leaves, they produce stalwart stems bearing dozens of bell-flowers opening from the top downwards, in blue, yellow and coral-red, from every leaf axil. The fact that they open first at the top of the stems as in *M. betonicifolia* is a noteworthy fact and is unusual; there are not many such, for most tall spikes of flowers open from below upwards, witness delphiniums, lupins, foxgloves and eremuruses. It is not the only noteworthy point about the genus; it is nearly unique in hardy flowering plants to have species that embrace all three main colours of the spectrum, namely red, blue and yellow. *Delphinium* is another such genus, and *Lobelia* and *Gentiana* follow suit.

Cutting Fourteen —

The Pinxterbloom
and Its Relatives

I notice a tendency among some of the unfortunate folk who garden on limy soils to deny that rhododendrons have any attraction. It may be that they long for them very much and know they cannot grow them, or perhaps they simply don't like them, being much taken with the multitudes of lovely plants they can grow.

However, this tendency is not always felt for what we call azaleas (though botanically all are rhododendrons), and this is not altogether surprising. Apart from the highly bred strains of Mollis, Knap Hill and Exbury azaleas, with their large trusses of flowers, azaleas of the deciduous section — as opposed to the evergreen Japanese section — have not that rather overweening opulence of the greater rhododendrons. Theirs is truly a richness equalled by few other shrubs, and engenders as great a sense of loss when the flowers fall as that felt when the pink cherries spend their few days in glory and then decorate the ground with their petals.

Rhododendrons in their many kinds flower from January to August; the flowering season of the deciduous azaleas is from April to July, but as well as this long spell they often delight us with splendid autumn colour. They also have added attractions — most of them have a delicacy of line and a charm of small trumpet-flower, and a scent that makes a very special appeal. I think it is this set of characters which endears them instantly to all lovers of flowering shrubs.

The flowering season starts in April, daffodil time. It would not do to choose the strong yellow daffodils nor those with orange cups as companions for our early azaleas. (And here I must revert to the botanically correct name *Rhododendron*, instead of "azaleas".) The first is usually *R. pentaphyllum*, one of the few with five leaves in a whorl below each head of delicate pink blooms; its close relative *R. quinquefolium* usually has white flowers, and both have a charm all of their own and excel in autumn colours.

I lost my heart years ago to the charm of *R. vaseyi*, and in particular to a clear light pink form. Apart from the colour and shape, the stamens are long-projecting with a decisive upward curve which gives a special character to each flower, and indeed to the whole bush. Few azaleas can surpass it for sheer elegance. Soon after, two strongly coloured species flower, *R. albrechtii* and *R. reticulatum*. They need in particular white daffodils for companions, for they both have remarkable colouring in their richest forms — a vivid magenta-pink verging on crimson.

Perhaps the greatest joy with this group of plants is in the contemplation of a well flowered bush of the superb *R. schlippenbachii*. First of all, it has a majesty of broad rounded leaves accompanied by wide flowers of lovely shape, and of a most delicious pink in some forms. And it has some autumn colour, though not so brilliant as the others. These azaleas are seldom seen, though they have all been in cultivation since the end of the last century. All hail from Japan except the last, which is a native of Korea, and *R. vaseyi*, which comes from North Carolina.

It is usually in late April that the first really brilliant azaleas flower: they are called Mollis and embrace all the flame tints from yellow through orange to vibrant vermilion, some verging towards salmon and pink. They were selected by famous Belgian and Dutch nurserymen during the nineteenth century and took the greenhouse and the garden by storm, being easy to grow and hardy (except for the flowers). They are a mixed race, being descended from *R. mollis* from Japan and *R. sinensis*, supposedly from China. Apart from the strident camellias, no shrub at this time of the year has so gorgeous a colour. The flowers have no scent to speak of, but the stalks and foliage give off a rich musty odour; they do not excel in autumn colour. Famous old varieties are still grown, often owing some of their charm to the flush of green in the throat; but most may be said to give way to 'Koster's Brilliant Red', which has been bred over so many decades that seedlings often do not register much variation in colour.

And so we approach early May, when the most popular and flamboyant comes into flower, the familiar *Azalea pontica* or *Rhododendron luteum.* The splendid dark or pale yellow of the well formed flowers on rounded trusses is enlivened by a darker flare of yellow in the throat. They all exhale a most delicious and far-reaching fragrance which wafts through the garden. There is no doubt that this is one of the finest shrubs in our gardens, excelling in bloom, fragrance, hardiness and autumn colour. It varies when raised from seeds, both in flower-tint and in growth and foliage, and thus it is best to choose plants from a nursery in the growing season. Some have somewhat glaucous foliage, and these usually turn to beetroot colour in autumn, whereas most are some shade of flame or red. This azalea has for long years been used — owing to its easy growth — as an understock on which to graft others less vigorous; very often it produces suckers which overtake the scion. But wherever it grows it is nearly always welcome. I say "nearly", because it unfortunately flowers at the same time as the ubiquitous rhododendrons 'Cynthia' and 'Pink Pearl', whose flowers, on the blue side of red in the spectrum, clash horribly. But of course all strong yellows and blue-pinks should be kept well apart in planting; this is one of the first lessons one learns when considering colour.

After the Pontic azalea fades, the highly bred strains are upon us. A whole essay could be devoted to these, but I would rather leave them for another time in order to see whence they came: in other words, to trace their parentage and to look at the characters of the parents. Apart from the Dutch Mollis azaleas we first have the Belgian race of Ghent varieties. These resemble closely *R. luteum* in many ways and are just as hardy, but they have a wide range of colouring derived from *R. calendulaceum*, *R. viscosum* and others from the eastern United States, all with comparatively small flowers. These were all early introductions to Europe, but it was left to *R. occidentale* to bring size of flower coupled with hardiness and scent to lift the hybrid races to the pre-eminence of the Knap Hill and Exbury groups. There is no doubt that for quality in all respects, coupled with generous autumn colour, these superlative varieties go far towards rivalling in many ways the greatest majesty of the best rhododendrons.

It was in 1851 that *R. occidentale* was first introduced in Britain. Apart from the great influence it had in hybridising in this century, it came, in the hands of Anthony Koster who crossed it with some of his Mollis varieties, to produce my favourites among all azaleas, lovely things with lovely names — 'Exquisita', 'Graciosa', 'Delicatissima', 'Superba' and the rest — all of which have splendid growth and foliage, large trusses of large open flowers of surpassing fragrance, and autumn colour. Their tints are gentle and blend almost anywhere in the garden, whereas this century's efforts are often strident, hot, and make no blend except with coppery purple and yellow foliage-plants.

This little excursion into later hybridising has led us astray from our progression in season. Two species of mid-season flowering are *R. periclymenoides* (*R. nudiflorum*) and *R. austrinum* (*R. prinophyllum*, *R. roseum*). Both are natives of the eastern United States, and small-flowered, dainty, mainly white and pink respectively, fragrant, and provide good autumn colour. They prefer damp ground. Both *R. periclymenoides* and *R. canescens* are known as "Pinxterbloom", which is an old American name for Whitsun flowers. This has more significance than it might seem, for our next azaleas are the late-flowering species, flowering well after even a late Whitsun.

One of the noblest of these is *R. arborescens*. When the foxgloves are in full flower — which always seems to me to be the crown of the year, when spring is far behind — this gracious and free-flowering shrub is at its best, flooding the air with fragrance. The long-tubed creamy white blooms, often touched with rosy red in the bud, are enlivened by protruding stamens and by the leaves, too, which are of dark glossy green. Soon after, what is known as the Swamp Honeysuckle blooms. While *R. arborescens* is, as its name suggests, of good size, the Swamp Honeysuckle (*R. viscosum*) is more compact and is noted for its viscous blooms, pure white colouring and pronounced fragrance. It is brilliant in autumn. I think the most desirable form is that known as 'Glaucum'; the grey leaves add to the all-white effect.

It is worth noting that *R. viscosum* was the first azalea to be brought to Europe, in 1724, but it remained unnoticed and unassessed for most of the eighteenth century.

We shall go again to the United States for our latest-flowering species, but must make an excursion back to Eastern Asia for *R. amagianum*, a native of Japan. It is one of the large-leafed group which includes *R. schlippenbachii;* the flowers in some seasons last into July (but are not always freely produced), usually in some tone of orange red or salmon scarlet, not scented, and I have no note of its autumn colour. A relative, *R. weyrichii*, flowers earlier in a similar tint but sometimes flushed with purple. They both require careful placing in the garden.

So we come to two refined beauties that close the azalea season for us, flowering as they do even after *R. viscosum;* like that species they are deliciously fragrant, floriferous, and also noted for autumn colour, and for their ease of growth in moist ground. What more could one want? — and yet they are little known and planted. They are *R. alabamense* and *R. prunifolium.* The flowers of the first are, in cultivation, white or flushed with apricot or pink, dainty, long-tubed with projecting stamens, and will add tone to any assembly of shrubs. *Rhododendron prunifolium* is the last of all to flower, even when one has forgotten all about azaleas. The flowers appear amongst the leaves, when it is fully established, of a rich orange-red, frequently to be seen as late as July. For this reason and for its intense colouring it has been used to infuse lateness into some of the Knap Hill hybrids. Like the others mentioned it appreciates a moist soil — indeed, this cannot be stressed too often. It must be remembered that these plants all flower when spring is turning into hot summer, which causes the flowers to droop and go over quickly if the roots get dry. They suffer likewise in full exposure to the sun, and are best grown and displayed in broken shade.

Cutting Fifteen —

Mulches and Mulching

Mankind spends an immense amount of time and energy in his gardens and fields in an attempt to beat Nature at her own game. In fact, if the earth were left alone it would certainly become covered by what we call weeds, and they in turn would be superseded by trees. The result would be a self-perpetuating forest, some thick, some sparse, but in either case upholding a surface fertility which would be just right for the prevalent mixture of trees, shrubs, perennials (including bulbs) and annuals. The fauna would provide necessary enrichment to the accretion of leaf-mould. Even the floor of the sea is covered with what we may call water-weeds, some of which achieve the height of our highest trees, and they are also "manured" by fauna.

I have long been of the opinion that this is also one way of gardening successfully. Our scattered trees and shrubs — and of course the plants — all provide a covering of the soil with eventually decomposing matter which is in part buried by worms. Thus is humus ensured, a prime ingredient of fertile soil when once it is deemed adequately drained for what we want to grow in it. But in our gardens and indeed our fields we need the addition of certain fertilisers of a "balanced" kind to replenish the important elements taken up by the plants.

Having dug over our plot of land and done the initial planting, there is a period of a few years while the soil remains uncovered, awaiting the growth of shrubs and plants. This is the time during which we need additional humus and fertiliser to prevent the sun from scorching the soil.

And it is important to apply the mulch while the ground is still moist from winter rains, thus protecting the moisture from early evaporation. It is a mistake to apply a mulch when the ground is dry; this prevents what rain falls from getting into the soil, and speeds evaporation. Except where a carpet of dead leaves would inhibit the growth of plants like heathers, aubrietas and similar lowly species, I have been in the habit for many years of sweeping all fallen leaves under shrubs and trees, thus improving fertility in the easiest way, preventing weed emergence, and saving labour.

But some of our gardens are not thickly planted and could not be expected to supply a covering of fallen leaves. Moreover, perhaps the selected style of cultivation is of a type — for vegetables or roses or annuals — which necessitates cultivation, digging and the rest: then the humus, fertiliser et cetera have to be dug in. Elsewhere, the humus we have to acquire is such as leafmould, peat, rotted sawdust, wood or bark chippings or spent mushroom compost. (Leaf-mould from trees on limy ground will contain some lime, likewise the mushroom compost.) It should be borne in mind, too, that undecomposed natural materials such as sawdust and wood or bark chippings use up nitrogen in the process of decomposition and this food has to be put back into the soil by applying fertilisers.

There is yet another material that can be used for mulching, for we have recently acquired a new noise-making aid in the form of "shredders". These will gobble up and shred twigs and all garden refuse and make it suitable for application to the soil. They are, no doubt, a useful invention for districts where bonfires are frowned upon, saving the expense of bagging the refuse and the trouble of disposing of the bags. But is there to be no cessation to the production of noisy garden machinery — mowers, clippers, power-saws, sweepers and now shredders? Weekends are no longer peaceful in a built-up area. I think there ought to be a law passed prohibiting the use of noisy machinery, at least on Sunday afternoons.

There comes a time when the beds and borders are so well covered by shrubs and plants that there is little space for the application of mulches.

This is a very desirable state of affairs, but it is not the end of the story. Weeds may well be defeated, but fertility will decline because the plants themselves do not provide enough rotting leaves. These areas need a dressing every spring, in showery weather, of a granular, balanced fertiliser. By this means I have had areas covered with plants in a healthy state for many years.

So far I have been advocating the use of mulches which decompose (on limy soils they will disappear very fast). Besides their other advantages, mulches enable one to set foot among the plants without flattening the surface and leaving tread-marks. This reminds me of a keen grower of alpines who gardened on heavy clay — not the sort of medium enjoyed by the plants, which suffer in such a soil from too much richness and mois-ture, and from wet "necks", something which they cannot tolerate. He solved the problem by covering the area where the alpines were to grow with two inches of pea-shingle: I have never seen more healthy or robust alpines. The same ruse was adopted at the Savill Gardens, Windsor, where about an acre of light sandy soil was so covered and now grows a fantastic number of dissimilar plants, from trees to shrubs. Another example, even larger, is to be found at the Hillier Arboretum, in Hamp-shire. The bulk of the plants here are dwarf woody plants, including pros-trate junipers whose steely blue-grey looks particularly well against the shingle. Indeed, it makes an excellent mulch, allowing the rain to go straight through,   preventing evaporation and weeds and effacing foot-falls.

We all know how, when gardening, one job leads to another; one touch of maintenance here will make us feel the necessity of another touch there; that is how I feel at the moment, and I am now going to extol the virtues of shingle in the garden landscape. It lends itself especially well to the bright light of dry coastal areas, where certain plants thrive in the full exposure to wind. I am envisaging a garden near the sea where, unless covered with growing plants or several inches of shingle, light soil would blow away. After all, some of us *have* to garden in such conditions, and to make the best of given conditions and create a triumph out of necessity is surely one of the first lessons to be learnt in gardening. Plants that thrive in certain conditions are better, by far, than unsuitable plants pining for different surroundings.

I think I should start with placing some yuccas and phormiums (if it were warm enough for them) in strategic positions, to give a unique feeling to the garden. Particularly should I use the short-growing yuccas *Y. flaccida* and *Y. filamentosa*, whose splendid spikes can be expected to appear from a clump almost yearly. The former is the more elegant. For majesty we can hardly beat *Y. recurvifolia*, which in some years throws up hefty spikes of cream bells among the great drooping sword-like leaves. I do not recommend *Y. gloriosa* because of its tendency to flower at the approach of frost, thereby forfeiting one of summer's glories. But the notable hybrid of *Y. recurvifolia* called 'Vittorio Emanuele II' is red-budded and extremely handsome, early and free-flowering, a plant that has lingered unobserved for too long. Although they are not quite so hardy the phormiums also give a striking effect, their long blades often topping 5 feet in *P. tenax*, the so-called New Zealand Flax. It is worth noting that old or split leaves make admirable *ad hoc* tying material in the garden. "Leaves five or six feet long divide easily into serviceable strips of extraordinary strength." The shorter species, *P. cookianum* (*P. colensoi*), is hardier and more graceful. Many forms with leaves striped in a variety of colours have been selected in New Zealand.

As a complete contrast to these great sword-leaves we need some shrubs of dense, comfortable, rounded habit, such as the many hebes and hydrangeas (*H. macrophylla* and all the hortensias will not take chalk or lime), *Brachyglottis rotundifolius* and 'Sunshine' — they used to be called *Senecio* — olearias, various cistuses, *Euonymus fortunei*, *Phlomis*, *Cassinia*, *Corokia*, many compact species of *Cotoneaster* and *Escallonia*. These are all evergreen, while *Hippophaë*, *Tamarix*, *Atriplex*, small-flowered fuchsias, *Rosa rugosa* and *R. pimpinellifolia* are deciduous. These will all take salt-laden winds and would give a long period of beauty between them. Some netting, strong-growing *Escallonia* 'Red Hedger' and 'Crimson Spire', *Griselina* and *Salix caprea* would provide some shelter. Nestling among the shrubs would be plenty of nooks for bulbs and many of the shorter herbaceous plants, such as *Erigeron glaucus*, osteospermums, armerias and eryngiums. This may seem an intimidating list, but I have barely touched upon the extremely varied assembly of shrubs and plants for a seaside gravel garden. And, I may add, all these plants with their glossy or matt evergreen leaves will be found to be the perfect contrast to shingle, whether it be at the seaside, or on the top of a chalk hill or a sandy moor — only for such sites, further advice would be needed as to which would be hardy. And I could hardly do better for this purpose than recommend my own books!

I repeat what I intimated earlier, that a plant growing well is worth far more than a plant struggling to keep alive in alien conditions.

Cutting Sixteen —

The Laburnums

The Golden Rain trees — so they are appropriately called — are one of the highlights of late spring and early summer. Most people, and certainly all gardeners, know a *Laburnum* when they see it, and either love or loathe it. Probably the loathing springs from seeing it in harsh association with crimson thorns and *Rhododendron* 'Cynthia', or because they know its seeds are poisonous. But there is no doubt that together the species and hybrids make a highly effective incident in the flowering year, and they are all of easy growth in any reasonable well drained soil, including those on chalk; in fact *L. anagyroides* in particular is almost naturalised in various parts of Britain, introduced from southern and eastern Europe long ago.

Sometimes before the end of April the flowers appear of *L. anagyroides* (*L. vulgare*), the Common Laburnum, a lovely contrast to bluebells. Unless trained up in infancy to a tall stem, the species and hybrids are apt to make short trunks and develop into many-stemmed specimens. This species, though early, is inferior to what is erroneously known as the Scotch Laburnum, *L. alpinum*, a native of much the same region; there is only a little botanical difference between them, but the flowers of the latter are borne in longer racemes. Either may have racemes up to 10 inches long, though often they are shorter.

If we are intending to plant a *Laburnum* in our gardens it is best to choose one of the hybrids, which in the best form, 'Vossii', has racemes sometimes as much as 2 feet long. A tree well hung with this astonishing display eclipses all ornamental trees of its period of bloom, and it will be evident that a stem or stems of 6 feet or more will show to best advantage the hanging, scented profusion. Its correct name is *L.* × *watereri* 'Vossii', the first hybrid recorded having been raised by Mr Waterer at Knap Hill Nursery, near Woking, during the first half of the nineteenth century. Another form, 'Parkesii', is equally beautiful, with a rather more graceful outline, for it must be admitted that most laburnums are somewhat stiff in growth. These superlative hybrids carry on the flowering period often into June, and usually the best flower last. Possibly the last to flower is an obscure seedling, very near to *L. alpinum,* called 'Newryensis'. It was raised at Tom Smith's famous Daisy Hill Nursery in Northern Ireland in the early years of this century. Fortunately an original gift to Glasnevin, Dublin, survives, for not only is it late-flowering, but the flowers lack the small brownish throat-marks and thus the yellow is pure and bright.

Apart from this last form, most cultivated laburnums are of much the same colour. It is a slightly greenish light yellow and the trees are usually so free-flowering that they make a strong display and are not always easy to place. There is no doubt that their insistent yellow is happily blended with the orange and flame Mollis azaleas, but it is not every garden that can accommodate such a fierce grouping. To me spring is a period of cool colours, the creams and whites and various tones of blue found in forget-me-nots, *Brunnera macrophylla,* certain lavender-blue rhododendrons and, of course, bluebells. There is also *Wisteria sinensis* to be considered, which makes a delightful contrast in several famous gardens when grown with *L.* × *w.* 'Vossii', trained over arch or pergola. For laburnums, despite their stiff stems, can be made to assume a graceful habit by judicious pruning in early summer.

Laburnums do not, to my mind, assort well with pinks and reds. White and near-white are the safest tints, and light green, which sharpens the clarity of the yellow. I shall always remember a garden where a tree of 'Vossii' had been given a shady position under trees, which had caused it to arch gracefully towards the light. I came upon it on a clear day; the sunlight was filtered through the canopy of a nearby Beech tree. No other greenery would have been half so effective, for young beech leaves are of a tender light tint and the mode of branching of this particular tree was gentle and persuasive. The breeze caused the sprays of silky foliage to rise and subtly fall while the laburnum's flowers waved and shook. Nothing could have been further from the stiff blatancy of a 'Vossii' grown in the normal way. White is prevalent at the laburnum's season: the Horse Chestnut, the Rowan, the Wayfaring Tree (*Viburnum lantana*) and the Cow Parsley are all ready to bear it company in our countryside, while in our gardens no shrub so appropriately complements it as the Whitsun Boss, or Guelder Rose, *Viburnum opulus* 'Roseum' — it used to be called 'Sterile', which was a much more suitable epithet: the rounded heads of flowers are not pink but white, emerging so attractively from their early green tint.

I have stressed the lack of grace of the branches of almost all laburnums, but there is a truly weeping form of *L. anagyroides* called 'Pendulum'. It is a very charming tree but unfortunately has rather short racemes. Hanging over water it can be very elegant in reflection.

There are several other forms of the Common Laburnum with strange foliage, of no value in the garden except for 'Aureum', which augments the yellow of its flowers with leaves flushed with yellow where they are exposed to the light. It is thus of use in colour value later in the season. All of these, and other, forms are propagated by grafting onto seedlings of the common species. 'Aureum' has a most peculiar habit of producing its yellow leaves sometimes well below the point of grafting, and in this it echoes the extraordinary prowess of the graft-hybrid + *Laburnocytisus adamii*. This originally arose through a Monsieur Adam having grafted a scion of the mauve-pink, low-growing Broom, *Cytisus purpureus*, on to a stem of laburnum. The surprising result was a tree bearing a mixture of yellow and particoloured Laburnum flowers and mauve-pink Broom flowers spasmodically along the branches. It is what is known as a 'chimaera', or graft hybrid. Years ago it was the custom in many nurseries to propagate hybrid brooms by grafting onto seedling laburnums, but despite countless thousands being so produced, so far as I know the strange result has never been repeated; + *Laburnocytisus* is a curiosity, and an ornament of doubtful attraction in our gardens.

Those who garden in warm sunny districts may like to experiment with another curiosity, *Laburnum caramanicum*, which is a somewhat tender shrub, producing its upright terminal spikes of flowers in late summer or early autumn.

> A warp'd wicket hidden in a flowery Privet hedge
> admitted to her mother's along a pebbled path
> between two little squares of crowded garden framed
> in high clipt Box, that blent its faint pervading scent
> with fragrant Black-currant, gay Sweet William and Mint,
> and white Jasmin that hung drooping over the door.
>
> — Robert Bridges

Rosa brunonii

THE
LARGE DAYS

Cutting Seventeen —

Just Leaves

Nine-tenths of the garden's yearly beauty is from leaves, yet we accord our fullest attention to flowers. Leaves are not only a background to flowers but an integral part of garden design and management; the evergreen shrubs control our views, and without ground-covering plants we should have to resort to hoeing or hand weeding, or even digging. Now, I have no objection to digging: it is a satisfying and excellent exercise; but if one is to have a well filled garden the spaces needing digging will not be great, and the lowly spreading plants will resent it.

Careful choice of plants with due regard to their leaves will be found to accentuate perspective if it is borne in mind that larger, glossy-textured leaves should be placed to the fore, with small, matt leaves farther away. The same applies to the tints of the leaves, using the bright, light greens in front with dull and sombre greens beyond. The extreme would be to use yellow flushed or variegated leaves nearby, leading through white-variegated to greyish and blue-greens beyond. It has been said that "art consists in disguising art", and these sentences prove it. The variety and the possibilities are endless if one has a mind for it, for it is not generally realised that among leaves are *all* colours which are found in flowers except true blue. There are not only the usually accepted variegated leaves and those of greyish and glaucous tones, coupled with the dark brownish purple which we loosely call copper, but pink, orange and red. The last three are especially present in the brilliant varieties of *Calluna* (Ling or Heather), *Mahonia* 'Moseri' and certain cultivars of Acer, to mention just a few. It is a good exercise to wander round an established garden, closing one's eyes to the flowers and studying the leaf-value of each plant in each garden setting.

Considering leaves from a scientific point of view brings entirely different thoughts. They are purely functional, performing their duties in different ways, but always bound up with the health of the plant, the taking in of light and the giving forth of moisture and gases. One might think therefore that they would all be of similar shape and size so that they might absorb the maximum benefit to the greatest advantage of the plant. It is here that the student of evolution may well be confounded by the infinite variety of shape, size, texture, composition and poise, and all other facts and factors that go to make up Nature's bounty. We may conclude that each plant's foliage is performing the same job in the way most suitable and helpful to that plant.

After these broad outlines of the subject comes the equally great and imponderable realisation that there is no answer to the query as to differences in shape or the presence or absence of serrations, hairs, prickles and the like. Some features have more or less obvious uses; one is taught to think of prickles as a means of defence, for example, and of long terminal points to the leaves as of assistance in removing surplus moisture. But the more one thinks about leaves, the fewer conclusive facts emerge; there are exceptions to every rule, and it is, of course, this incredible variety in every respect that serves us gardeners so well.

Leaves have much to tell us. They provide broad lines of guidance which help us in cultivation. For instance, almost all grey, woolly leaves or those of glaucous hue demand, or are best in, full sun. All yellow-variegated leaves have the same preference but white variegation is usually most pronounced and lasts best in full or part shade. Yellow-flushed evergreens are best in sun, whereas yellow-flushed deciduous shrubs retain their colouring in part shade. All coppery leaves reveal their richest colouring in sun, tending to be a dingy green in shade.

Foliage also gives us guidance in arranging our plants to provide the best effect in the garden. There are certain unwritten rules that govern the segregation of plants, if the garden is to be considered anything other than a mere hotch-potch.

The generally mixed garden of today, comprising trees, shrubs, plants and bulbs, is often given the title of cottage-garden; it would be against the rules to include in it heathers and conifers, but in the same way, one could not well tolerate roses and annuals in a garden of sweeping groups of these.

Heathers and conifers — low-growing — go with grasses and dwarf shrubs. Likewise, in a piece of thin woodland one would plant shade-loving shrubs and plants, not border flowers, Floribunda or Hybrid Tea roses. Another of today's fashions is to make gravel beds to take yuccas, grasses and glaucous and grey-leafed plants; a good idea in the right place, and the gravel provides a mulch against excessive heat and unavoidable foot-falls.

In all these schemes it is the leaves that do the work, form the picture and tell us what to use. Where we have chosen wisely we shall find that the leaves tell us whether a plant is healthy. And if it is healthy the flowers that result will be of good and lasting quality. It is a good plan to seek out those plants whose leaves are attractive, if possible, both before and after flowering; this will make for lasting beauty in a garden. A few that come to mind among hardy perennials alone are Japanese anemones, some grasses, geums, *Iris pallida dalmatica*, *Phlomis russeliana*, heucheras, bergenias, *Brunnera macrophylla*, the larger sedums, *Campanula latiloba*, and of course most ferns. Exquisite though they may be in flower, the following plants become disreputable afterwards: bearded irises, *Papaver orientale*, *Dicentra spectabilis*, *Ranunculus aconitifolius* — and yet, how can we do without them?

Cutting Eighteen —

Variegation

During the half-century since the end of the Second World War, commercial horticulture has sustained a remarkable resurgence. Many factors have contributed to this. As the years passed and more nursery stock became available, mechanisation increased in every department of the nursery world, from field cultivation to transport and salesmanship. Prices became realistic, enabling the hitherto down-trodden nurseryman to make a respectable living. Garden centres fairly quickly followed, and containerisation became the norm. Transport and cars on the one hand and mail order on the other have completed the revolution.

When the history of this phase of nursery work is written, I think two things will be outstanding: the search for tempting novelties, and the popularity of plants with variegated leaves. I use the term variegated in its broadest sense: perhaps "with leaves other than green" would be more appropriate. A plant may produce good flowers for a few weeks, but if in addition to flowers it has colourful foliage its selling life in plant centres will be lengthened, and of course it will have an equally long period of appeal in the garden. And this is where the danger starts.

I do not think that anyone is going to dispute the oft-repeated fact that green is the most valuable and necessary colour in the garden. It is impossible to have a garden without it. At the same time, in these days of striving to be "different" and yearning for brightness and novelty — perhaps as an antidote to the repetitive bad news and the ever-increasing prices of commodities in general — we must not forget that good greenery has a soothing effect. There is no doubt that the inclusion in our gardens of too many variegated plants can have just the opposite result. In fact, I would go as far as to say that the placing of colourful leaves is as important as the choice of colourful flowers. It has been said many times that leaves are with us for six months of the year if deciduous, and for the whole twelvemonth if evergreen, whereas flowers come and go in a few weeks at a time. How much greater an impact on our gardens is made by a variegated plant, especially if it is evergreen!

I know of a garden planted late in the nineteenth century which has so many variegated shrubs that it gives the impression that the sun is shining, even on a dull day. This is the kind of thought that should be in the back of our minds when siting a variegated shrub in our gardens, and particularly applies to plants with yellow variegation or wholly flushed with yellow. You will note I use the term yellow rather than "golden", though the latter is in general use; but no hint of gold can outshine a strong yellow. And yellow is one of the most telling of colours in the garden, only outdone by pure white and blazing scarlet. (In passing, I would mention that even blazing scarlet can be made to recede if accompanied by dark coppery purple foliage.)

There are many things to be considered before placing a variegated tree, shrub or plant. There are the practical things, such as suitability of soil and site and size, and there is the flower colour, if any, and the type and style of the leaf coloration. It is not generally realised that leaf-colour has its own set of rules when it comes to siting a plant. Let us leave trees aside for the moment and consider shrubs, which form the backbone of all but the smallest gardens. They fall into distinct groups.

Yellow-variegated evergreen and deciduous shrubs need full sunshine to give of their best. In shade the yellow becomes less distinct.

Yellow-flushed evergreens require full sun. They tend to flush with green in shade.

Yellow-flushed deciduous shrubs "burn" in full sun and should be placed so that they are shaded from the sun's rays during the middle of the day. If the plants are grown in continuous shade the yellow will become soft lime-green — a valuable tint in colour work.

White-variegated evergreen and deciduous shrubs will thrive in full sun, seldom "burning", but shade encourages the white areas of the leaves to increase.

Grey-leafed shrubs, whether glaucous or felted, are at their best in full sun.

Coppery-purple shrubs, deciduous or evergreen, are only at their best in full sun; the lighter tones, coral pink, et cetera, likewise, but instead of intensifying during the growing season they tend to pale and become almost green with the passing weeks.

With regard to trees the same set of rules applies, but there are exceptions. For instance, *Robinia pseudoacacia* 'Frisia' does not burn in full sun but becomes richer and almost overbearing towards autumn, losing the delightful lambency of early summer. In planting shrubs in woodland gardens I have sometimes felt the need of a grey-leafed specimen, which is difficult until we remember *Rosa glauca* (*R. rubrifolia*). It will thrive in part shade from trees or full shade from buildings, the foliage losing its sun-induced coppery tones and becoming light jade-green. Its companions among herbaceous plants in the same circumstances are the various hostas, and also, in part shade or in cooler regions, *Anaphalis triplinervis* — about the only greyish perennial that will not tolerate dryness and hot sunshine. Otherwise the rules given above apply to perennials as well as to trees.

My front garden, only a small portion of my quarter-acre, is devoted to shrubs and bulbs for winter effect. There are heathers, rhododendrons, skimmias, mahonias, sarcococcas, a few small conifers, and hebes, most of which produce flowers during the dark months. They are enlivened by red Dogwood and a scattering of variegation: *Aucuba japonica* 'Sulphurea Marginata', *Elaeagnus* ✕ *ebbingei* 'Gilt Edge', *Euonymus fortunei* 'Emerald Gaiety' and 'Emerald 'n' Gold' and a few ivies. The two most noticeable shrubs are the coppery dark-leafed *Rhododendron ponticum* 'Foliis Purpureis' (var. *purpureum*) and the astonishing coral-red leaves of *Mahonia* 'Moseri'. Amongst all these are little bulbs and hellebores which flower from November onwards. The area was deliberately planted for winter interest because one goes in and out from it daily, whereas the back garden is pleasing for the rest of the year, when one can sit around on a choice of three seats.

The best character of the wintry front garden is that, being almost entirely filled with evergreens of one sort and another, it needs the minimum of attention and remains respectable throughout the year. It certainly takes much less work in maintenance than a similar area in the summer garden. And its sober evergreens are lit by the variegated plants through the year, so that it is not dull at any time. This, then, is one of what I should call the prime uses of variegation. The tinted leaves do not jar at any one time and are kept in their place by the darker evergreens, without which they would appear garish.

This is the danger to which I referred in my opening paragraphs. In the summer garden, bright foliage must augment flower colour and not set itself up in opposition. Since the summer garden depends so much for its beauty on flowers, which come and go weekly, it stands to reason that a plant with yellow foliage will have great and lasting effect, both before and after its yellow-flowered neighbours have come and gone. The fact that yellow variegation is at its best in full sun emphasises this, whereas white or cream variegation will tend to add lightness to any assembly of colours in the shade. Likewise, assortments of soft blues, lavenders and pinks can be augmented with grey foliage as well as with white and cream variegation. Used in these ways, subservient to flower colour, variegation in the garden can be of long-lasting value. When the combination of flower- and leaf-colours is right, a shrub or plant of the appropriate tint of leaf can set the tone of a whole border; a new note of foliage can be the dominant factor of a change of colour at the turn of the path. The opportunities are endless when one considers the varying merits of flowers, berries and the all-pervading foliage.

We have only touched on other leaf-colours in an earlier paragraph. There is no doubt that what for want of a better term we call "coppery purple" is popular today. It requires careful thought in placing. As I have said, it must have full exposure to light to reach its richest colour and greatest value. It would be pointless, for instance, to use a Copper Beech in a wood: moreover I think, not only that such trees and the various coppery-leafed maples and prunus trees should be used in the open, to develop their best colour, but that they are only appropriate in gardens, near buildings, and not in the natural scenery of the countryside. But they cast dark shade and do not reflect much light. They thus darken our rooms. I expect there are positions where a Copper Beech could be used with distinction, but there are not many such opportunities. They and the dark-leafed Norway Maple, Cherry Plum and Bird Cherry are all trees that have their great glory in late spring and early summer, but then tend to be dark and unattractive until their autumn tints enliven them. An avenue or a cluster of coppery-purple trees is a dead loss because their own growths absorb the light.

With coppery shrubs it is a different matter. They are, once again, useless in the shade in any circumstances, but they are of real value when used as dark contrast to show up flowers of pink and pale yellow, also white, and silvery grey foliage. They can be the deep Brahms-notes of assemblies of various colours and almost alone — apart from sallow greenery — are they to be used with great aplomb to contrast with and augment the hottest tones of the spectrum — the scarlets, oranges and flames found particularly among azaleas. These remarks apply especially to *Berberis thunbergii* 'Atropurpurea Nana' and its relatives, and also *Cotinus coggygria* 'Royal Purple'. Anyone who has been to Crathes Castle (Kincardineshire, Grampian Region, Scotland) cannot fail to remember the stunning use of this plant with a wide variety of flowers of various — even warring — reddish tones, backed by the soft rosy brown stone of the surrounding walls. The coppery shrubs mentioned are of a dense habit and always dominate their neighbours, whereas the many Japanese maples, varieties of *Acer palmatum,* have a lightness and elegance which fits them for a subsidiary role.

It remains to consider those extraordinary trees and shrubs which shock by their vibrant shrimp-pink or salmon-orange young foliage, such as *Acer pseudoplatanus* 'Brilliantissimum' and 'Prince Handjery', *Aesculus neglecta* 'Erythroblastos', *Spiraea japonica* 'Goldflame' and various callunas. They are at their best in early summer, fading to paler greenish tones later, except the callunas which excel in autumn and winter. I find the *Spiraea* particularly difficult to place because of its summer crop of puce-pink flowers; this same trait is inherent in the callunas. Otherwise it is obvious that these remarkable "sports" can only be used with white flowers or those in the orange, salmon and flame group, with the improbable exception of the lavender-blue of *Rhododendron augustinii* and its relatives. I have resisted ever using any of them myself, finding that good light greenery takes a lot of beating.

The Influence of the Rose
on Garden Design

It is usually stated that there are about 150 species of *Rosa* wild in the Northern Hemisphere. Of these only a handful have been interbred to create our modern garden roses. It is probable that two species, perhaps more, laid the foundation of the garden roses treasured from ancient times in China, but so far little information has reached us about them. We are on slightly firmer ground when we consider the ancient European roses, thanks to the work done earlier in this century by Dr C. C. Hurst. These roses — our ancestral hybrids derived from *Rosa gallica* and others — form a fairly compact group from which, linked with the ancient Chinese roses during the last two centuries, most modern roses have been bred, though the earlier ones were chance hybrids.

I do not think we can claim that a five-petalled single rose has exceptional beauty of form when compared with an orchid, a daffodil or a dicentra. We have to look beyond this for the reason that *Rosa gallica* itself was a sacred emblem of the Medes and Persians in the twelfth century BC. It seems to me that it was the officinal qualities of the flower, real or supposed, that made it worshipped and sought after. We do not know with any certainty when rose-water was first distilled and used with so much delight, but we do know that petals of *Rosa gallica* have always retained their fragrance even when dried. For this reason it was treasured for scenting rooms, making conserves and other commodities, and would have been transferred from the wild together with other herbal and medicinal plants to the earliest gardens.

Early pictures in tapestries and herbals depict gardens hedged about with roses, containing fruit trees and various flowers, but I should not call these rose gardens. We have to look long and hard at the history of garden design to find the beginnings of design in plantings of any kind, for art came to gardening very late. Through the centuries plants were looked upon as interesting individuals, and as such were they used to fill the intricately outlined beds, edged with bones, stones, boards or dwarf plants. Thus was a mixture of fruit trees and bushes, plants, bulbs, vegetables and herbs used and cultivated in the ever-increasing craft of gardening in cottage gardens and in the great walled gardens of the wealthy. This craft went on while the fashion for formal avenues and gardens was brought to remarkable exactitude by great landowners, just as in the next fashionable period, the eighteenth century, all was swept away and the "landskip" or landscape garden reigned supreme. From the early seventeenth century, however, plants began to be viewed with new eyes, and were being grown as much for their beauty as for their curiousness and medicinal values, or for food. This was the turning-point, but little progress was made before the realisation came to people with large gardens that, having spent their time in pursuit of all that trees and native bushes could give them, it was time to bring the joyous flowers to the immediate environs of the dwelling. And what should be more appropriate than to describe on the sweeping lawns a pattern of beds derived from schemes of two centuries earlier?

But meanwhile a noteworthy happening needs to be recorded. Napoleon's first Empress, Joséphine, at her château of La Malmaison, had developed an entirely new style or design of gardening whereby, in the setting of a lawn, paths were made to bring the visitor to bed after bed filled with the new plants that were pouring in from different parts of the world. We know that one of her first loves was *Rosa*, of which she collected about 250 sorts. The design of her garden was abstract; it embodied

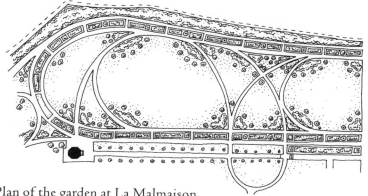

Plan of the garden at La Malmaison

nothing of the mediaeval knot, the seventeenth-century parterre or the eighteenth-century landscape. Large-growing shrub roses (which is what they were at that time) could not well be accommodated in the first two styles, and were not really welcomed in the third. Joséphine's effort must be ranked as a new departure in garden design, and I think it must also rank as the first garden designed to grow one group of plants, roses, though it is likely that many bulbous and other plants were also there.

The design of her garden was what J. C. Loudon designated, some years later, the "gardenesque", and was the foundation on which most garden designing has been based up to the present day.

The nineteenth century saw a great upsurge in rose growing. The old European shrub roses became hybridised with the ancestral roses from China from the last years of the eighteenth century onwards. This resulted in recurrent-flowering roses, often of small stature. These were just what was wanted to help to fill the borders round the house, the summer-house and elsewhere, and the new beds described on lawns with compass and set-square. While the new greenhouses permitted and encouraged gardeners to work out elaborate plans for bedding-out tender annuals on the lawns, the new roses were viewed with ever-increasing admiration. Though most nineteenth-century roses have French names, as the years passed increasingly were English rose breeders at work, and they published not only descriptions of the new roses but also designs for rose gardens.

It was William Paul, the famous rose grower at Cheshunt in Hertfordshire, who advocated formal designs, to be appreciated the more by having in their midst a mound, also planted with roses, from which the pattern of the beds could be surveyed. This was harking back to ancient garden concepts, as was the sunken garden, a means of appreciating the design to the full recommended by the Revd Dr Shirley Hibberd in 1874. Many of the new roses were weak growers and could be planted a foot or even less apart. They were, with their fairly recurrent flowering, rivals to the bedding plants. The only other group of shrubs of any standing were the newly introduced rhododendrons, but these were large-growing and out of flower by about mid June.

The rose was thus established towards the end of the century as a colour-giver over a long period. The short-growing hybrids were augmented by grafting upon them stems of varying height, making veritable banks of colour. No other kind of shrub has been produced in any quantity by training into standards: this is another unique use of the rose in garden design.

With the decorative patterns of beds in the lawn went the embellishment of the whole design by the inclusion of ornaments in stone or metal, seats in bowers and arches over the paths. A few roses were at hand to decorate these structures, the Ayrshire and the Boursault roses and early hybrids of *R. multiflora.* Here again the rose was to the fore in encouraging, with honeysuckles, this new decorative use of plants in our gardens.

There is no doubt that to get a picture of the ideals of late nineteenth-century rose garden design one should pay a visit to the Roseraie de l'Haÿ at L'Haie-les-Roses near Paris. Here is the fullest use of beds and borders, *treillage,* pillars and arches, swags and standards, laid out in 1893. It is well tended and a perfect historic piece, filled to overflowing by mankind's efforts at rose breeding.

After over a hundred years of rose inbreeding, our garden gates have opened to embrace large and small roses as shrubs, not only bedding plants, and the vast array of new hybrids of climbing and rambling roses. Together they form a brilliant assembly, producing beautiful blooms for four or five months, to fit into almost every kind of garden.

Of no other genus but *Rosa* can this be said.

Cutting Twenty —

The Brown Border

One day I had a special invitation to go to a garden in July "because the brown border then looks at its best". I was not sure that I wanted to see a border predominantly brown in summer; would it not presage autumn? However, I went, and on a bright day. The dull filigree of wrought-iron gates painted in matt black, between dark-tinted brick piers, gave on to a gravel walk. On one side was a strip of mown lawn and trees, and on the other the brown border.

But what a galaxy of interest and colours was contained in those two words! First there was a background hedge of dark blue-green *Chamaecyparis lawsoniana* 'Allumii', which was a full statement of contrast to the many tones of the border. At the far end was a group of bronze-coloured lumpy *Thuja occidentalis* 'Hoveyi' with the dark mahogany tint of *Gleditsia sinensis* 'Brussels Lace', a tree which would get fairly large in time. This lumpy effect was augmented by a large bush of *Berberis thunbergii* 'Atropurpurea', having a very subdued colouring with less of the purplish tint than many, and in full summer giving a maroon touch.

To offset this distant heaviness was a large clump of the airy-fairy perennial oat, *Stipa gigantea,* whose stems never need staking and which reaches some 5 feet high and wide. It is so open and light that you can see through it, of a bronzy cream turning later to straw-yellow. A further dark note was provided by *Pinus mugo,* the bushy Mountain Pine: this was a leaf out of the Red Border at Hidcote Manor in Gloucestershire, obviously. Scattered and grouped in the foreground were *Sedum maximum* 'Atropurpureum' in dusky mahogany tone with strange coppery flower heads, and the striking dark *Heuchera micrantha diversifolia* in the strain known as 'Palace Purple', again nearer to mahogany than to purple. The leaves have a metallic glint and the dainty flowers are of a pinkish brown. As a further jolt to the senses, a few *Viola* 'Irish Molly' mingled with *Ajuga reptans* 'Atropurpurea' in front.

Now for the complete contrast of four plants which dominated the border. Bolt upright at the back was a six-foot group of a cream *Delphinium* with black eyes to the flowers. They peeped between the six-foot sword-like leaves of *Phormium tenax* 'Purpureum' in subdued browny purple. In the foreground, to lighten it all, was a good shrub of the Rose 'Penelope', which has a delicate mixture of salmon, cream yellow and flesh pink in its make-up. The whole remarkable grouping was given sumptuousness by two groups of the incredibly red annual Poppy, *Papaver commutatum*, enhanced by their large black centres; they were, when all was seen and said and done, the ultimate delight. Theirs is not a staring hard red like that of some Oriental poppies, but a full tone near to the spectrum centre.

Some lesser plants were there: the dead-brown wispy grass leaves of *Carex buchananii* and the waving mass of *Stipa calamagrostis*, light green but turning to parchment brown as the summer advances; also the hairy caterpillars of *Pennisetum orientale* (*P. setaceum*). It was obvious that grasses were needed in plenty to alleviate the sober tones and shapes.

One never sees an exposition like this without thinking what would augment it from plants on one's own palette. I was thinking of the coal-black Hollyhock, a favourite of Constance Spry and now so seldom seen. *Crocosmia crocosmiiflora* 'Solfatare' would not come amiss; while its flowers are of soft apricot-yellow, its leaves are bronzy brown. And what about a few of Le Grice's brown roses? I think I could fit in 'Café', 'Amberlight', 'Brownie', 'Tom Brown' and 'Vesper', lauded for use by floral artists. Their flower tones, all of varying shades of brown, would be very useful, though their green leaves might be a trifle upsetting. And I should like at the back the Fennel, *Foeniculum vulgare purpureum*, with that feathery mass of brownish green and dull yellow flowers, rising to five feet. But cut off the seed heads early, otherwise your garden will be full of its progeny.

Gwendolyn Anley, VMH

Cutting Twenty-One —
Gwendolyn Anley

Gwendolyn = Anley (this was how she always signed herself) presided over and worked in a well designed garden for about forty years, devoting her considerable energy and skill to the welfare of a great assembly of plants. For much of the time she had the help of a full-time gardener, who in turn had the help of a lad, who eventually became the only garden staff. Brigadier General Barnett L. Anley did nothing to speak of in the garden until he retired, and then he took up growing hardy border carnations.

I think the garden had been laid out, if not designed, by a landscape firm. It had all the recognised different compartments: a short drive with a rambler rose screen and espalier apples on one side, on the other side beds and a lawn with fine trees and a tennis court. The levelling of this area resulted in a cool shady retaining wall at one corner with supporting walls opposite, flagged path and a herbaceous border backed by cypresses. Around the house were paved terraces, more trees in grass, a rock garden, a vegetable garden with cordon fruit trees, a pergola, and more beds. Then there was within easy reach of the back door a garage, potting shed, alpine house, lath houses, and beds for irises. Later a further strip of garden was acquired; it ran the length of the ground and was given to ornamental trees and shrubs — in all, perhaps two and a half acres. It was all laid out on a slight eminence on very sandy soil, known locally as Bagshot Sand but without the inhibiting iron "pan" of many lower areas in the neighbourhood.

Mrs Anley gardened with great skill almost to the end of her life and was always armed with secateurs, raffia, labels and other tools of the trade. I was taken to see her by John Wall, Curator of the rock garden at the Royal Horticultural Society's Garden at Wisley. Alpines and rock gardens were their keenest interests, as they were, at that time, one of mine. It was somewhat daunting to read a notice on the front gate: "Considerate people will shut this gate; others are requested to do so." The notice was mainly because of her pet dog, a Peke, of which over the years she had several. It was a very good notice and had the desired result, but my feelings were somewhat perturbed by another notice over the fireplace in the study: "If you have nothing to do, please don't do it here." I need not have worried, however; we were welcomed with great kindness, and a long subsequent friendship confirmed that she lavished kindness and consideration all her friends. The notice merely intimated that — in spite of house and garden staff — she lived a very busy life. She took immense trouble to see that her plants were in the best of health and attributed much to the beneficence of leaf-mould of which there was always an ample supply available from well-constructed bins. There was no doubt that her outlook was soundly practical, though tempered by a deep appreciation of beauty. Indoors she was preparing her book *Alpine House Culture for Amateurs;* it appeared in 1938 and remained a standard work for a long time.

As the years passed Mrs Anley's interests varied and her energies became concentrated on her new plantings of shrubs, snowdrops (of which she amassed about forty kinds in the 1950s), peonies, including some of the Saunders hybrids from New York, sent over by Miss Sylvia Saunders who was an old friend, and of course irises, of which she maintained a large collection of the most up-to-date of the Bearded section. These were I think her first and last love. I remember her on almost all fours replanting different sections of the beds in the hottest of summer weather. At the end of one of the beds was a large group of self-sowing *Tulipa whittallii* which made a splendid display in spring. It was her wide-ranging enthusiasm that made a visit so interesting and also kept her occupied from snowdrop time until autumn, when *Campsis grandiflora* made a spectacular display on the dovecote.

A collection of *Iris* species was gradually accumulated after the war, a job most carefully done in preparation for her second book, *Irises, Their Culture and Selection*. Like her former book it was prepared with great care and expertise, and I had the honour of doing some drawings for it. A revised edition was brought out in 1948.

But we must go back to the late 1930s, when Mrs Anley made a trip to Japan. She went with the idea of seeing Japanese gardens and of absorbing Japanese methods with alpines, but came back with a treasury of Japanese thoughts which altered her outlook in many ways. The growing of dwarf conifers had always been one of her enthusiasms; a considerable collection was maintained at one time, and as they were pot-grown she was able to exhibit them at one of the post-war Chelsea Shows. They covered a large table and gained a high award. To them she added imported specimens of bonsai, and started growing her own, under specially constructed lath shelters. I think it was the discipline and economy of cultivating these characterful pieces that proved the great attraction. But the Japanese economy of line was also apparent indoors, where there was often a single shapely branch of shrub or tree placed on table or mantelpiece for appraisal. Japanese prints replaced Crimea War scenes on the walls, and all her skills were brought to bear on thinning and shaping the trees and shrubs in her garden. No tree received more care than *Pyrus salicifolia* 'Pendula'. From an overcrowded huddle of drooping branches it became a sheer masterpiece of elegance.

Hostas became an enthusiasm, fired partly by her visit to Japan, and these and hardy orchids grew well among the shrubs. Shrubs were taken to heart with the assistance of Walter Bentley, a famous gardener at Newbury, Berkshire, and Hugh Armytage Moore of Rowallane, County Down, Northern Ireland. They both specialised in the best shrubs and trees. Sir Cedric Morris brought other enthusiasms forward.

The lawns sloped down from the house on all sides except by the garage, which had on its west wall the delectable Fig 'White Marseilles', than which none melted faster in my mouth. A lovely young specimen, already white-barked, of *Betula papyrifera* grew near to a Blue Cedar; Rose 'Mermaid' flowered well on the north of the house until a severe winter killed it to ground level. It survived and grew again. In the shady corner by the tennis court grew a huge clump of *Hepatica* × *media* 'Ballardii' and various ramondas and haberleas, but as a general rule it was a sunny garden and *Pulsatilla vulgaris* seeded itself with abandon. Alas, this did not apply to the forget-me-not-blue 'Budapest' form, of which there was a good clump, a present from Hew Dalrymple, famous for the Bartley strain of primulas.

I am sure Mrs Anley was innately a happy person, despite three great sadnesses — the death of her only daughter at an early age and the loss of her god-daughter, who was her house staff, and of her husband later on. She also had the misfortune of watching her garden being invaded by *Equisetum* or Mare's-tail. Her house looked over a field owned by Jackman's nursery. Rowland Jackman told me that in an effort to get rid of the weed he had the field scarified every month for two years, but it made no difference. It is known that the roots go down at least sixteen feet. The weed gradually spread over the borders at St George's, went under the house and proceeded to engulf the tennis court and in fact the whole place. It was this gradual disaster that drove her away from the main garden to the areas around the potting shed and alpine house where everything was in pots and containers of one sort and another.

Apart from many visits to her garden at all times of the year, where I knew that a warm welcome awaited me, some of my happiest memories of Gwenda are of music. We both shared a great love of this, and in the 1960s she managed to get four tickets every summer for Glyndebourne, right in the middle of the stalls. While she provided the tickets and supper, I provided the car and we each took a friend. It was a wonderful experience and each evening seemed to be more summery than the last.

CUTTINGS FROM MY GARDEN NOTEBOOKS

It was a perfect blending of gardening and music, those two recreations which are so different yet so complementary.

She enriched my life with gifts of several books and much kindness, refuting to the full whatever impression might have been gained by the two notices in early days!

She also enriched our gardens, not only with plants that she so generously gave away, but with plants of her own raising. Many irises were raised but, her usual high standards to the fore, she only named two. One was the splendid dark violet-blue 'Arabi Pasha', which is still to be found in nurseries, and the other 'Mirette', named after her little dog — who would only eat a piece of chocolate if she got down on her knees and gave it to her. This iris is a refined and elegant pale lavender-blue. It is no longer in catalogues, but I still grow it. There were also two plants named after her husband: *Calluna vulgaris* 'Barnett Anley', which is found in many lists today, and a lavender of the same name which seems to have disappeared. Messrs Burkwood & Skipwith of Kingston upon Thames, Surrey honoured her by naming an *Escallonia* 'Gwendolyn Anley', and this is still grown in many gardens.

Cutting Twenty-Two —

The Narrow Border

In these days of restricted building space coupled with the high cost of hired labour, it is inevitable that our gardens tend to be small. With the overall area being restricted, it follows that the separate features are generally small also. One feature of English gardens remains, that of the ever popular border, though that too has shrunk over the decades. Gone are the days when a border, say, 10 feet wide can be contemplated; there is no staff available and insufficient space, and even if there were enough space, a wide border would upset the overall design. It follows, therefore, that our garden design must be adjusted, and one of the immediate results is that borders tend to become narrower. This is unfortunate because, seen frontally, such narrow borders lack solidity, and the plants do not form massed groups. On the other hand, those who keep the border in order will find it much easier to cope with, reaching with ease among the plants to grasp the inevitable weed or fallen stem.

There are, I think, two distinct ways of getting the most out of our narrow border. One is to forget the restrictions and plant in long lines of plants in season. The other is the direct opposite: to plant shrubs to break up the length and create different compartments of planting. In most cases it is a help, in enjoying the beauty of the plants from end to end of the borders, to be prevented from viewing them in any other way; it is surprising how effective a long narrow border can be if the viewing is thus restricted, by hedge or isolated shrubs or bushes, or even a low wall, supporting climbing plants.

I have in mind a long narrow border of which the only views are from end to end because, although there is a grass walk to stand on while appreciating it, there is also a  hedge completely sealing off all frontal views. Passing behind the hedge, therefore, one uses the grass walk as a means of viewing the border from end to end. Along the front is an edging of Catmint (*Nepeta* ✕ *faassenii*), which if clipped over in July will remain in respectable bloom until the autumn, contributing its greyish leaves and soft lavender flowers to almost any colour grouping. Behind it are pyrethrums, irises and lupins, all for June display. Pyrethrums (*Tanacetum coccineum*) have good parsley-like foliage until autumn and likewise, with a good cut-back after flowering, the lupins produce excellent leaves; the irises, on the other hand, are apt to become tatty by August unless *Iris pallida dalmatica* be chosen.

These two lines of plants therefore provide us with June colour and effective greenery until autumn. Behind them is the main mass of summer flowers, which with careful choice can include items for flowering into September. The real luxury to be aimed at behind all this is a wall on which can be trained climbing plants. While the wall may be said not to decrease the area available by much, it will lessen the width of border available for herbaceous plants by at least 2 feet — for the climbing plants, and space to tend them. But even a narrow border planned with these restrictions can be very satisfying. In a border such as this the full enjoyment is from the long lines of flowers and foliage; perhaps it may be likened to a form of old-style bedding, though done with perennial plants, carefully graded for height and season.

My other approach is to break up the border into compartments, with large shrubs. How often in old gardens one comes across a shrub that has grown with age into a much larger specimen than was visualised at planting time, but now in its full grandeur is too good and valuable to be scrapped. On the contrary — it makes an imposing division and creates a cul-de-sac behind it for a new scheme of colour or selection of plants. If this effect can occur by chance, it can also be designed, and I know one long narrow border not more than 5 feet wide, with a wall at the back; in front is a narrow pathway, and a low wall with a sheer drop to lower ground. So there is no chance to view the border frontally, except in short strips.

As it is in full sun on well drained soil, it was decided to plant the entire border in pastel shades with lots of greyish foliage. The large shrubs used for breaking the continuity of the planting were *Hippophaë rhamnoides*, *Buddleja fallowiana* 'Alba', and roses 'Golden Wings', *fedtschenkoana* and 'Souvenir de St Anne's'. An important point was the inclusion of one male plant of

the *Hippophaë* or Sea Buckthorn to pollinate the others, which were female, so that their orange berries were produced in autumn. The foliage is of a dark greyish green while that of the *Buddleja* is grey-white; it lasts in flower far longer than the usual *Buddleja davidii* hybrids. When the  buckthorns were fully established *Clematis* 'Huldine' and 'Mme Le Coultre' were added to increase the flower display for summer. The species rose *Rosa fedtschenkoana* is noted for its grey foliage and its welcome habit, not only of producing new shoots through the growing season, all bearing single white flowers, but of turning the earlier crops into red heps at the same time. It is totally hardy, whereas the *Buddleja* is apt to suffer in cold winters. Both of the hybrid roses — in pale yellow and blush white, respectively — are recurrent flowering until October calls a halt.

With these shrubs providing colour and interest from late June onwards, it was a simple matter to plant on the wall some climbers and shrubs which could be trained flat in between the major shrubs, thus achieving a continuous display before perennials were even contemplated: such is the value of a mixed planting of climbers, shrubs and roses coupled with perennials for all the months from June onwards. And it is not difficult to insert, around the shrubs, such things as peonies and groups of early bulbs, to complete the eight months' display which should be the aim of all small-garden owners.

As to the spaces between the irregularly placed major shrubs, these were each given a different selection of perennial plants to fill them, though each grouping was expected to provide some flower at view as one progressed along the path. The June display would give way to July, August and September for each successive flowering; Catmint and erigerons, peonies and irises met sidalceas and phloxes, agapanthuses, asters and schizostylises, until autumn finally drew the curtain. A painting of autumn colour as well would be too much to expect, though the inclusion of *Berberis dictyophylla* would add to the grey in summer and also provide an autumn flame. But it is a prickly friend.

All this needs a deal of thought and a knowledge of how plants are likely to grow. In fact, I believe careful integration of climbers, shrubs, perennials and bulbs is not only one of the great arts, but one of the most difficult. Seldom does any plant do exactly what is expected of it; one often has seasonal difficulties to contend with, and no two years' growth or experience are the same. While the cultivation of unrelated plants may be fundamental and comparatively easy, the grouping of them for definite and artistic effect will test the powers of the most experienced and ardent of gardeners. Truly may it be said that gardening is one of the most demanding of arts.

> Flowers gathered in this world, die here; if thou
> Wouldst have a wreath that fades not, let them grow
> And grow for thee. Who spares them here shall find
> A garland, where come neither rain nor wind.
>
> —Henry Vaughan (1622–1695); from *The Garland*

Cutting Twenty-Three —

Sweet Instructions

It was John Parkinson who in 1629 wrote about certain plants which "send forth a pleasing savour of sweet instructions". This was his elaborate way of saying that they smelled sweet. There is always something smelling sweet in my garden, and in fact one of the first things I do on meeting a flower new to me is to let the nose as well as other senses assess it. That is the way to know plants — by the smell of their flowers and leaves. It so happens that many of the smallest flowers have a delicate fragrance, and they are ideal for those little vases or goblets which will take, say, a brace of blooms, to be placed on one's work table. It is not really difficult to keep up a succession of delights for this purpose. Where should we be in March, for instance, without our bunch of violets, or in April without that soft fragrance of primroses?

By planning carefully one can start the year with a sprig of Witch Hazel (*Hamamelis mollis*) followed by, or concurrently with, Winter Sweet (*Chimonanthus*), two of the sweetest things of the whole year. Although *Lonicera* ✕ *purpusii* is equally sweet, it drops quickly in our heated rooms. To me the various species of *Sarcococca* are appealing, but some friends find them offensive; they are very free of their scent in the garden and if you plant them near the door, a sudden sweet aroma will greet you. I suppose few people pick little *Crocus tomasinianus* — it is so short — but one of the miracles of the early spring is to gather a few buds and watch them rapidly unfolding in the warmth and light, giving forth their "sweet instructions".

By my door, too, I have *Skimmia* ✕ *reevesiana* 'Rubella', perhaps the most reliable of the male kinds grown specially for their penetrating sweetness. Just a twig or two will scent a room. Daphnes are to be treasured for these little vases, particularly *D. odora*, which flowers very early in the year; and also, rather later in spring, the intriguing shade-loving *D. pontica.* The dark shining leaves offset the pale yellow-green bunched flowers, which do not release their delicious odour until the evening. It is a "must" for a shady garden, and for its scent.

In the spring, flowers crowd upon us. Lovely though they are, wafting their fragrance through the garden, I have not found the varieties of the Japanese *Prunus mume* much use for cutting; they wilt in centrally-heated rooms. Even three flowers of *Cyclamen repandum* will scent a small room and

Chimonanthus praecox 'Luteus'

please us with their rich warm crimson-tinted flowers, and if they can be in the same little vase as Lily-of-the-valley, the contrast of colour and shape will augment the fragrances. *Cyclamen repandum* is not reliably hardy in my garden but does well in slightly warmer climates, seeding itself with abandon in border or turf.

When it comes to *Narcissus* the choice is wide, so many being exquisitely fragrant; in general, the short-cupped ones are more fragrant than what we call daffodils. I remember being enthralled with the scent of *N.* 'Barrii Conspicuus' when, as a boy, I was only used to the faint scent of ordinary daffodils. The glistening texture of the perianth, thin though the segments are, is an added joy. It is today considerably outclassed in many ways, though not for scent. The well-known Paper-white (*Narcissus papyraceus*) of the florists has surprised me by its success as a garden plant, and it is very sweet; likewise all the jonquils and the varieties bred from them, such as 'Cheerfulness', and most have the bonus of two or more blooms per stem. As he revealed in his writings, E. A. Bowles, whom some of us knew as Uncle Gussie, would always have several vases on his table, each with a different daffodil variety, the better to get to know each flower intimately.

Tulips are a bit large for little vases, and most have a rather strange, heavy odour, but I give full marks to the yellow 'Generaal De Wet', an early-flowering variety, pure yellow without a black centre. Lilacs are mostly too big and heavy for small vases, but usually a delicate piece can be found on the Common Lilac (*Syringa vulgaris*) or its hybrid *S.* × *chinensis*. They are as fragrant and appealing as any and more graceful than the large hybrids, which, oddly enough, have not lost the wonderful lilac scent. It would be a poor year for me if I did not inhale just once that heady, rich perfume. With them flower the Guelders of the *Viburnum carlesii* breed; no whit less fragrant is the hybrid 'Fulbrook', and in addition I find it to be the best garden plant of the lot. There is something particularly charming about this group of shrubs with their rose-pink buds and crystalline white blooms in compact, scent-filled heads amongst the unfolding downy leaves. Soon after opens the plum-tart *Iris graminea*. You are apt to miss its flowering because the blooms are held on short stalks among tall, narrow, green leaves, but there is no chance of not enjoying the intriguing perfume and unique coloration when once they are sought and picked.

Many rhododendrons and azaleas are refreshingly fragrant. If you garden in a warm district you will be able to grow those almost overpoweringly fragrant tender species and hybrids typified by 'Fragrantissimum'. Much later, towards the end of the rhododendron season, some American species flower, such as *R. arborescens* and *R. viscosum*, creamy and white respectively, and both have far-carrying aroma. Furthermore, it is almost impossible to pick a spray of these deciduous azaleas without making an effectively balanced little display.

One of the most intriguing scents of the whole year is found in two primulas, both of which need damp sites: *P. sikkimensis* and *P. alpicola*. The first is always of clear cool yellow; the second may be creamy, in var. *luna;* or, less appealing because of its inconsiderate way of fading to grey, violet. Both bear their flowers at the top of a tall stalk, and they are drooping and bell-like, with a ring of farina in the throat. I know little else with their strange scent.

With the approach of full summer we have *Philadelphus microphyllus* and roses upon us, and the choice among the latter is endless. I stress this particular species of *Philadelphus* for "diffusing a pineapple fragrance to a distance of several yards" and for its miniature blooms, though such as *P.* 'purpureo-maculatus' and 'Sybille' make more effect in the garden. These two, and others, are decorated in their centres with a suffusion of mauve — always a sure indication of scented excellence.

Honeysuckles of various kinds are markedly good of an evening — their long-tubed flowers are specially adapted to the visitation of evening moths, and their scent is as pervasive as any other flower, and as sweet.

I do not feel it necessary here to record numerous roses for our purpose. However sweet they are when held to the nose, many do not release their scent in the garden. Good exceptions among modern roses are 'Whisky Mac' and 'Fragrant Cloud'. Otherwise I think it best to seek

those not far removed from *Rosa moschata* (the Noisettes in particular) and
R. multiflora, among climbers. The reason is that these two roses belong
to the Synstylae Section, whose species let flow abundantly their essence
from the stamens, not from the petals. An interesting example is 'Souvenir
de St Anne's', a semi-single sport with good stamens, from the very double
'Souvenir de la Malmaison'. While the latter has little scent, the former is
well endowed; it is always in flower, until late autumn, and belongs to the
Bourbon group. The original was named in 1843. A spray of purple
Heliotrope, itself a treasured scent-giver, would go well with the gentle
blush of the rose.

In their different ways, scents and colours, roses carry us through the
summer days without cessation, and I challenge anyone not to realise the
beauty of a rose bloom given the table to itself. That is the way to one of
summer's great blessings. But during the hot weeks we may perhaps be
content to enjoy the scents of the garden, until one day in late September
or early October we suddenly detect a new whiff from the *Elaeagnus*. Those
silvery little bells, hidden beneath the leaves on the shortest of stalks, have
a surprising carrying power. The resplendent yellow variegated shrub, *E.* ✕
ebbingei 'Gilt Edge', is a thing of delight for its colouring, but perhaps its
parent, *E. macrophylla*, is the more free and potent in scent. They both make
large shrubs, likewise *Osmanthus ilicifolius*, whose tiny white stars are again
often rather hidden amongst the holly-like dark green leaves.

In August and September, apart from roses, there is really nothing to
touch the clethras. I only grow the pink-tinted *C. alnifolia* 'Pink Spire' and
the later *C. tomentosa*. Neither is as invasive as *C. alnifolia*, and both need
lime-free soil in a cool position. They have long flowering periods and for
several weeks will furnish ample small sprays which will fill a room with
fragrance.

In these late summer days *Buddleja fallowiana* 'Alba', a lovely silvery-
woolly-leafed kind, has as long, or longer, a flowering period. The white
form has orange eyes, which are not quite so acceptable in the normal, but
rarer, light mauve type. They need a warm sunny position and sometimes

will even then be killed to the ground in winter; but they usually regenerate, providing us with comparatively small nodding flower sprays. For an even warmer position I hand the palm to *B. auriculata,* which is not usually at its best until November. The small creamy grey sprays of tiny blooms are particularly remarkable in that they retain their fragrance even when dried.

So we have come full circle with our flowers of the year, although I forgot that lovely cream goblet of lemon bouquet for high summer, *Magnolia virginiana.* Bulbs opened this Cutting and with bulbs we will finish. I doubt whether any flower of the year can surpass the veined, open beauty of *Crocus speciosus,* and in the extra richly coloured 'Oxonian' or 'Artabir' the amazing contrast of the flaming orange stamens and stigmata accentuates the predominant violet-blue, the overall colour enhanced by copious darker veins. And a rich, warm scent pervades them. Last in the year shall be another species, diminutive, of lilac tint, elegantly veined outside: *C. laevigatus* 'Fontenayi.' Just three in a wine-glass are adequate to waft sweetness to our noses. It has a long flowering period, spanning the winter during mild spells and increasing freely in any sunny border in friable soil. All such frail crocuses are best grown between stocky foreground plants, or dwarf shrubs, to protect them from boisterous winds. They will not fail you, yearly.

Cutting Twenty-Four —
Sidelights on Rhododendrons and Laurels

In Britain we had been yearning for evergreens to use in our gardens ever since it became apparent that there were some foreign species hardy enough to grow in the open air alongside our own native holly, yew, box and ivy. The "greenhouse" had been invented to care for those that were considered tender. Into our parterres were placed small plants of "greens" to give a lively air to the beds for the winter. Many lesser hardy shrubs came into cultivation over these years, but none made so great an effect as the Common Laurel, *Prunus laurocerasus*, in the early seventeenth century. Here was a noble evergreen, easily propagated, hardy throughout most of Great Britain. The first plants were brought to Britain in 1576 from Eastern Europe and Asia Minor, and it has become part of our way of life.

Although this prunus was — in part of its native territory — growing with a more spectacular flowering evergreen, namely *Rhododendron ponticum*, the latter did not grace British gardens until about 150 years later, and then not from its similar eastern distribution but from its extreme western limit.

It so happens that *Prunus laurocerasus* has a close relative, *P. lusitanica* — the Portuguese Laurel — which hails from the extremes of mainland Western Europe, with a superior form in the Azores, *P. lusitanica* var. *azorica*. The Portuguese species was in our British gardens by the middle of the seventeenth century, whereas that from the Azores did not arrive until the second half of the nineteenth century. It is, I think, worth noting here that anybody who has room for either of these two superlative shrubs should prefer the Azores form for its superior growth and foliage. It appears to be perfectly hardy.

But let us get back to *Rhododendron ponticum*. This reached British gardens in 1763, not from Caucasia (Pontus), but from south-eastern Spain, in the form known as *R. p.* subspecies *baeticum*. There are only minor botanical differences between this and the forms from the Black Sea regions, but it is curious that there are not other habitats known between these outposts. The subspecies is of more compact growth than what we call *R. ponticum* in our gardens. It is probable that the innumerable seedlings around are somewhat hybridised with *R. catawbiense* from the South-eastern United States. This is a doughty species with good foliage and a fine truss of bloom, and it is indeed the grandparent of many of the Hardy Hybrid rhododendrons which dominated English rhododendron gardens until the influx of vastly different species from the Far East, mainly in this century. When it was introduced, *R. ponticum* made a great impact, and was soon chosen for a coloured painting in the celebrated *Temple of Flora* by R. J. Thornton, of which parts appeared from 1799 to 1809. In those days the fine truss of large blooms was well above the average, in size and beauty, of the selection of plants depicted.

In our gardens *R. ponticum* is best classed as a weed — and a weed it can well be, from self-sown seedlings or self-layering shoots from the root upon which choice hybrids have been grafted. We cannot tolerate, in any case, its lanky, spreading growth. In western, damper, districts of the British Isles it has established itself as a rank alien growth, to the detriment of almost everything it engulfs. I remember once seeing a single plant which had grown to about a hundred feet in diameter across the lawn. There are times, however, when I bless it for its lovely sea of soft mauve which, with bluebells nearby, decorates the floor of many an oak wood. There is to my mind no other June joy to equal that particular contrast of soft tints on the verge of summer. It may be noted here that the Common

Laurel is just as all-embracing and a much more attractive evergreen, which unlike the Rhododendron will also thrive on limy soils. Its spikes of small white flowers have a rather objectionable odour.

We have come a long way in the importation of hardy evergreens since the early days of the Laurel and the Pontic Rhododendron. While the Laurel conquered British gardens despite its flowers, the Rhododendron did so because of its flowers and despite its unremarkable foliage. There is, however, one remarkable leaf form which I should like to see more grown, and that is the ancient *R. ponticum* 'Foliis Purpureis'. It is a compact plant: mine after some thirty years' growth is still only about 6 feet by 6 feet. Though the young foliage in summer is the normal green, with the approach of cold weather all exposed leaves turn to the rich colour of a Copper Beech; it makes a wonderful contrast to the pale flowers of midwinter. I obtained scions years ago, from Kew. It gained a First Class Certificate in 1895 when shown to the Royal Horticultural Society by William Paul, the celebrated rose grower of Cheshunt, Hertfordshire, and was given to Kew in 1897. The flowers are of course the normal mauve-pink; even so, it is a very superior shrub which is slowly gaining recognition.

It may be as well to recall some other rhododendrons with coppery purple foliage. There is the lanky grower 'Moser's Maroon' whose flowers are also maroon-crimson, complementing the young foliage. (Monsieur Moser, a nurseryman of Angers, France, seems to have been very alive to foliage colour; one recalls *Prunus sylvestris* 'Moseri' and *Mahonia* 'Moseri'.) The most spectacular among coppery leafed rhododendrons is probably 'Elizabeth Lockhart', a sport from 'Humming Bird', itself a hybrid of *R. williamsianum* and inheriting therefrom a compact rounded habit and wide bell-shaped flowers of crimson-pink. Totally different is *R. lutescens*, a small-flowered species in light yellow. It flowers in earliest spring and the FCC form in particular contrasts the blooms with coppery brown leaves which remain in beauty all the season. Quite small-growing is yet another with shining dark coppery small leaves in winter — the best form of *R. saluenense*, now known as *R. s.* subspecies *chameunum*.

Among the Hardy Hybrids there are many of a heavy, lumpy covering of dark green that need the airy grace of the finer bamboos and ferns to lighten them. Not so if one selects carefully from species and forms that have mostly been introduced from the hinterland of China, such as *R. concatenans* and *R. xanthocodon*, both with comparatively small oval leaves, of greyish green throughout the year but starting with a brilliant glaucous tint in early summer. They are manageable shrubs for cool sheltered gardens and are of more recent introduction than the group species *R. cinnabarinum*, introduced to Britain 150 or so years ago, with similar foliage.

I rank these glaucous-leafed species very highly in planting with colour sensitivity. We used them with *Hosta sieboldiana elegans* and flowers of salmon, pale yellow and rich claret as a complement to the blue-green tiles of the Spanish House at Mount Stewart, Northern Ireland. There are two other very delightfully glaucous-leafed species: *R. lepidostylum* is one, a low-spreading bush whose young hairy leaves are a glaucous jade green in early summer. Its pale yellow flowers make a wonderful blend. The other is *R. campanulatum* subspecies *aeruginosum*. A compact plant, this is noted for the brilliant verdigris-blue of the young foliage, unexcelled by anything in the garden. Then there is the dwarf-growing *R. calostrotum* — a close relative of *R. saluenense* mentioned above — with typical pansy-shaped flowers of rich cherry-colour over neat glaucous foliage. This applies to the form which has been called 'Gigha', originally raised by Harry White at Sunningdale Nurseries and now known as 'Harry White'.

Many — or most — of the dwarf rhododendrons have an additional attraction to the colours of their flowers and leaves: when handled they give off a rich aromatic odour, which is also apparent in warm weather. The one thing we haven't yet been cursed with are many variegated forms. The genus does not seem prone to such extravaganzas, though it has every possible variant in leaf-size, tint and texture. In placing species in the garden it is well to remember that the larger the leaf, the greater is the amount of shelter from wind and direct sunshine needed. Many of the choicest species introduced during the last hundred years or more are tender and in Britain thrive best up and down our west coasts. The earliest crimson-flowered species to come into our gardens was *R. arboreum*, which first flowered in Hampshire in 1825 and was immediately hybridised with a *R. catawbiense* × *R. ponticum* hybrid. The results were variously called *R.* × *altaclerense* (commemorating Highclere, the seat of the Earl of Caernarvon), *R.* 'Smithii' and *R.* 'Russellianum'; they decorate all our biggest western gardens in the British Isles with giant bushes up to 40 feet or so. As *R. arboreum* is not generally hardy in these islands except in sheltered places, it is remarkable that these hybrids have proved, increasingly with further hybridising, more and more hardy. The same thing has happened with hybrids of the delicate *R. griffithianum*, a queen among the whole range of beautiful species, excelling in beauty of bark, foliage, flower and fragrance. Its hybrids, typified by the over-celebrated 'Pink Pearl', are progressively more hardy. But you would have to garden in the coombs of Cornwall or in sheltered valleys of western Scotland to achieve success with the noble species itself.

As one moves up into the greater-leafed rhododendrons one is struck yet again by the singular and varied beauty of the genus; we do not have to wait for flowers but can glory in the bark and stance, and the beauty of the leaves, all with us for the whole year. They are at their best in mild damp weather, before the leaves begin to fold backwards with cold drying winds. A whole year's appreciation can be given to the rounded bushes of *R. bureavii*, *R. callimorphum*, *R. souliei* and *R. thomsonii* and their immediate relatives: lovely rounded blades of smooth, dark or glaucous colouring, dislaying their matchless bells in due season. "The finer species of rhododendrons exact admiring attention at all seasons."

So far, in size of leaf, the laurels mentioned earlier can hold their own with the rhododendrons. In fact, only the largest-leafed rhododendrons can compete with that great dignity, *Prunus laurocerasus* 'Magnoliifolia', whose glossy dark green blades may achieve a foot in length; it is, too, a very large grower and suitable for semi-woodland even on limy soil. But those of us who garden on lime-free soil in sheltered conditions are not likely to plant it, since we have a range of great-leafed rhododendrons to choose from.

In addition to large leaves, the species I am about to mention have a poise and dignity of tree-like growth that make them objects of veneration when achieving some 20 to 30 feet. Of all shrubs and shrub-like trees they merit planting early in one's life, if such be possible. I know of few plants, apart from the noblest of trees, which give so much satisfaction through the years, while culminating in that supreme moment when one can actually look up into the canopy of dark leaves contrasted with their undersides, brown or greyish with indumentum or down.

Standing away from the huge mounds at flowering time, one is especially struck by the crowns of flowers poised over the rosettes of great leaves, their delicate tints enhanced by the crisped bell-like individual blooms, often with a dark eye. So one might stop fussing with the delicate ones and worship even the hardiest and most wind-resistant, two species of the Falconeri Series, *R. rex* with grey indumentum and its subspecies *R. fictolacteum* with brown. I have seen these thriving in Northumberland, in a position completely exposed to the north.

Their relative *R. falconeri* has a majesty all its own; often wider than high it thrives in woodland conditions even in drier areas. Its rich dusky appearance, large leaves and great trusses of light or dark parchment-tinted bells provide a highlight in the year's round, utterly shaming our little efforts in our flower borders. But the thought immediately returns, that few of us have room to play with a shrub which may soon exceed 30 feet in height and width. And even this may be excelled by the magnificence of the best yellow forms of *R. macabeanum*. Then, in the same botanical grouping, there is *R. sinogrande* itself, which in the best of conditions may have leaves 3 feet long. For us dwellers in the drier, colder parts of England, these giants of the tribe must remain a holiday experience, as we stand agasp in silent awe.

Regarding these tender rhododendrons in Cornwall, Sir Joseph Hooker, director of the Royal Botanic Gardens at Kew, 1841–1911, is reputed to have claimed that "they flourish better here than in Sikkim".

Cutting Twenty-Five —

The Maximum Display
in the Least Space

There come many times during the year when loved plants cease their display, the petals drop and the space occupied is empty. We can lessen this sense of loss by choosing plants which flower for a long time. Take for instance roses, shrubby potentillas, *Hypericum × moserianum*, hydrangeas of the Hortensis section, and hardy fuchsias; their display extends into many weeks, even months. But a garden composed of so few genera would begin to pall by late summer, and there would be no flowers for winter, spring and early summer.

I should like to review in the next few paragraphs how we can get over this difficulty in gardens where space prevents the growing of a vast variety of plants. Of course, there are plants with "coloured" leaves to help us, variegated and tinted other than with green — but there again, too much variation from green can also pall, and even be upsetting. Plants, shrubs and trees which repeat their flowering are hard to find. Certain tall Bearded Iris cultivars are being bred which flower again in early autumn, and if well-nurtured lupins and delphiniums are cut down after flowering, well watered and given a fertiliser, they will often throw up good secondary spikes. The short-growing day lilies, *Hemerocallis* 'Stella d'Oro' and 'Happy Returns', will seldom be out of flower from July until autumn. The small-flowered creamy yellow *Rhododendron* 'Yellow Hammer'

Hypericum × moserianum

regularly flowers in November as
well as in April, and *Syringa micro-
phylla* 'Superba', if pruned and fed
after its initial flowering, will usually produce good secondary spikes
of its small pink, scented blooms
through later summer. But these are rare,
isolated examples.

What we should look for in our smaller gardens
of today are trees, shrubs and plants with at least two seasons of beauty,
of flower, foliage and berry (fruit). As a start we might cite the Crab
Apples, small trees which produce a smother of scented blossom in spring
and then give us another equally good display of colourful fruits in early
autumn. The best are those with green leaves and white or pink blooms;
'Dartmouth' and 'John Downie' delight us with bright red fruits, 'Golden
Hornet' with bright yellow. Unfortunately, those with the richest coloured
flowers and fruits have rather dirty coppery foliage in summer. The
Japanese cherries, colourful though they are in bloom, seldom produce
fruits, but on the other hand the leaves of most give autumn colour,
especially *Prunus sargentii*. Some other reliable double-performers are
Prunus 'Jonioi' and 'Shimidsuzakura', both white — the first single and

well scented, the latter double and highly elegant. And with these go the apples I mention in Cutting 58. The amelanchiers (loosely called Snowy Mespilus, though this term really only applies to *A. ovalis*) are small trees with not only prettily tinted young foliage and white flowers, but splendid autumn leaf-colour as well; *A. lamarckii* is a worthy species. It is worth noting here that *Wisteria sinensis*, which can be an overpowering climber or can be pruned to quite a small-sized bush or little tree, frequently gives a second display of flowers in late summer or early autumn. This is well scented, too, a reminder that fragrance is another character which adds a lot to the scales when assessing the garden value of plants.

There is no lack of good shrubs which give us beauty at two or three seasons of the year, and when they have good foliage they should be prime favourites for our gardens. Pyracanthas are much appreciated for their brilliant berries throughout the gardening world, though I must admit that the depredations of birds lessen their value. My own choice would be *P. rogersiana* or its yellow-fruited variety, *flava*, for its flowers are a clean creamy white, very prolific and sweetly scented, whereas many others are of a less clear white and their fragrance is not so refreshing. The values of *Cotoneaster conspicuus* are equally good, though different: the flowers make a snow-white canopy and the prolific berries seldom attract birds, frequently remaining on the branches through the winter.

If you can accommodate and withstand the fierce orange colour of the flowers of *Berberis darwinii* in spring (they blend well with daffodils, wallflowers and the coppery foliage of certain shrubs), you will be gratified with the unusual blue colouring of its berries in August. Another *Berberis* comes to mind, also of unusual colour: *B. dictyophylla* has pale yellow flowers, followed by pink berries in autumn coupled with brilliant autumn leaf-colour, after which the stems reveal that they are covered, apparently, with whitewash. A good contrast in the winter garden.

For lime-free soil are *Pernettya*, *Fothergilla*, *Eucryphia glutinosa* and *Rhododendron*. We have already briefly looked at *R.* 'Yellow Hammer', and while the following usually have only one season of flowering, they can be added

to our tally because of their tinted foliage. In winter the foliage of
R. saluenense subspecies *chameunum* turns to a shining beetroot purple; its
flowers look at you like pansies in rich purple-crimson. Closely related,
the cherry-red form of *R. calostrotum*, 'Harry White' ('Gigha'), is made the
more appealing by its glaucous leaves. These are both low, dwarf shrubs.
Rather larger is *R. lepidostylum*, with remarkable pale jade green leaves,
fringed with white hairs, and small flowers of Chinese yellow. The leaves
last in beauty even in winter. Considerably larger are some species of the
Cinnabarinum Series, notably *R. cinnabarinum* itself and varieties and
forms of *R. concatenans*. These have tubular flowers of varying tones of
orange, salmon and wine-colour, but long after these exquisite blooms
have dropped the young foliage retains a glaucous colouring, almost
turquoise-blue. Azaleas, all botanically rhododendrons, are noted for
their brilliant flowers, particularly the large-flowered groups called
Ghent, Exbury and Knap Hill; the Japanese semi-dwarfs also become
prettily tinted, though they are mainly evergreen. And of course, if you
can secure a seedling of *R. luteum* (*Azalea pontica*) with good autumn colour
your cup will be filled to overflowing, after its glorious scented display
of yellow flowers.

The pernettyas are headed by *P. mucronata*, a freely suckering bush not
suited to small gardens, but of considerable visual significance in its red
stems and tiny glittering evergreen leaves. The males are the most free-
flowering; multitudes of tiny white bells in early summer are followed in
autumn (on the females) by long-lasting berries of good size from white
through pink to crimson and purplish tones. The 'Davis Hybrids' are
supposedly self-fertile. The fothergillas also sucker, but in a more compact way. They are substantial shrubs excelling in their tufts of white
scented flowers in spring before the leaves open, which themselves assume
the richest of autumn colour. One of the last and longest lasting of shrubs
with notable autumn leaf-colour is *Eucryphia glutinosa*. Their colour lingers
into November, a reminder of the superb, white, cup-shaped flowers
each with a brush of tinted stamens in August. Of the pierises, I grow the

dainty and elegant 'Forest Flame' whose tiny white bells — like Lily-of-the-valley — in early spring are followed, if the frosts allow, by the bright scarlet tint of the unfolding leaves. This is a shrub to treasure on lime-free soils.

We have wandered rather far from shrubs whose berries are the second attraction. In this respect few can equal the rose species. The common Sweet Briar, *Rosa eglanteria*, and *R. rugosa*, the Japanese Ramanas Rose, are much to the fore, the former with single pink flowers in June and glittering oval heps in quantity in autumn. The latter has such a long flowering period that the later magenta flowers coincide with the large scarlet heps — not a happy combination. But we can avoid this by choosing either *R. rugosa* 'Alba' with large single white blooms, or 'Fru Dagmar Hastrup' in clear light pink with *crimson* heps. There are many good fruiting roses, and I want especially to mention *R. glauca* (*R. rubrifolia*) with single pink flowers and red heps in autumn: if it is grown in shade the leaves are grey; if in sun, they develop a rich purplish tone the whole summer. The most conspicuous heps come from the great group of Chinese species headed by *R. moyesii*. If you choose its offspring 'Geranium', raised at the Royal Horticultural Society's Garden at Wisley, you will get the most compact grower, with good fresh green leaves, and blazing scarlet single flowers followed in late summer by large bottle-shaped heps, also of scarlet. In either season it takes some beating.

There are a few very large shrubs to be considered: *Cornus mas, C. kousa, Acer palmatum* 'Senkaki' ('Sangokaku') and *Cotinus cogyggria* (*Rhus cotinus*). I should choose *Cornus mas* 'Variegata'; the white-variegated leaves make an excellent contrast with the red cherry-like fruits in summer, a legacy from the tiny yellow flowers which appear in February. *Cornus kousa* is a noble flowering shrub or small tree of elegant tabular growth with handsome large white bracts, turning to pink in summer, followed in autumn not only by strawberry-like fruits but by gorgeous leaf-colour. *Cornus alba* 'Sibirica' has vivid early autumn colour coinciding with white berries, after which the red stems are with us through the winter. The 'Senkaki'

Maple delights us with coral-red stems and twigs as soon as the leaves have turned to their salmon and yellow tints and dropped. As for the Sumach or *Cotinus coggygria*, we have first the fluffy heads of pinkish blossom — or purplish, in the forms with dark leaves — which turn to snuff-brown, what time the leaves become scarlet.

Now for a few smaller shrubs. A much neglected Flowering Currant is *Ribes odoratum*, which has long been known in gardens as *R. aureum*. Both names refer to the yellow, scented flowers in spring, but do not call attention to its brilliant autumn leaf-colour. Of similar attraction is *Spiraea prunifolia* 'Plena', with arching wands of small double white flowers and equally brilliant in autumn. Another spiraea is *S. japonica fortunei* 'Macrophylla', in the same group as 'Anthony Waterer' but not so good in flower. Its large bullate leaves yield a rich assembly of tints in October.

Lastly there is *Hypericum inodorum*, whose 'Elstead' form cheers with its bright yellow flowers with brightest scarlet fruits through late summer. It is unfortunately subject to rust disease in dry, hot conditions.

There are a few climbers for our purpose. The Passion Flower, *Passiflora caerulea*, is hardy on warm walls in Britain and contrasts its delicately coloured flowers with large orange fruits through late summer and autumn. Several species of *Clematis* excel in their silvery seedheads after the flowers are over, and none is better in this respect than *C. tangutica*, whose yellow bell-flowers excite us in late summer. And the lovely *Schisandra grandiflora*, for a shady wall in cool soil, has red dangling flowers followed by fruits like red currants.

There are even some herbaceous plants for inclusion in our list. Who can resist the lovely marbled leaves of *Arum italicum*, in the form known as 'Pictum' in gardens, which appear in autumn? They last through to late spring, accompanied by large pale green spathes with spikes of scarlet seeds in summer.

This long list has only touched on my subject; I have scarcely mentioned variegation, or summer leaf colour, which alone could at least double it. The brilliant foliage colours of conifers and ericas can make a winter garden as brilliant as any summer effort. However, when all is said and done, green is the garden's main colour and one cannot beat the old stalwarts of *Viburnum davidii*, hollies, bergenias and mahonias. It is such as these that restore our equilibrium.

Jasminum nudiflorum

Cutting Twenty-Six —

Jasmines

Who that hath reason and his smell
Would not among roses and jasmine dwell,
Rather than all his spirits choak
With exhalations of dirt and smoak,
And all th' uncleanness which does drown
In pestilential clouds a populous town?

—Abraham Cowley (1618–1667)

In choosing plants for my 'desert island' (Cutting 3), I left out one I regard with great affection, the Winter Jasmine, *Jasminum nudiflorum*. This would cheer me for several months, providing the island were not all sand and palm trees,and I should have to forget that its flowers have no scent.

A point that all kinds of jasmines have in common is their green stems; this they share with the brooms (*Cytisus* and *Spartium*) and with *Leycesteria*. Though all are deciduous, their green bark adds quite a rich tone to the winter landscape. Coupled with its bark the Winter Jasmine has dark green shining leaves, an asset in summer.

Yellow jasmine, delicate on stiff branches . . .
In spare December's patient nakedness

is a vision of Laurence Binyon's that rings very true. For the whole of my life I have been able to pick its blossoms in winter, and have been known to suggest that it is one of the first six plants to put in every garden.

It is a rather extraordinary plant. Apart from a form with yellow blotched leaves, it has not varied in our gardens since it was brought from China by Robert Fortune in 1844. Moreover, so far as I am aware, no fresh stock has been introduced since then, and little variation is known. In our gardens it sets no seeds, and I have a suspicion that it may be a sterile form or hybrid. At all events, it would pay botanists to do a little research in the neighbourhood of China whence it came, to discover, if possible, a fertile form.

The other well known jasmine is the sweet-scented white *Jasminum officinale,* which has been far longer in cultivation; for so long, indeed, that nobody is certain to which parts of Asia it is truly native. It has been a favourite in British gardens for more than 400 years, treasured because of its delicious fragrance. It used to be coupled with the Musk Rose (*Rosa moschata*) as the most fragrant of plants, and I can well believe it. Unlike the Winter Jasmine it is a true climber, and will twine up wires or other supports on a warm sunny wall: it is not reliably hardy in cold districts. The variety or form *affine* ('Grandiflorum') is larger in flower and touched with pink, but is not more free with its flowers or scent than the type species, which has white- and yellow-variegated forms. Crossed with *J. beesianum,* which has crimson flowers, it has given rise to a pleasing pink-flowered hybrid named *J.* × *stephanense.* This also has yellow-tinted leaves and, though raised deliberately in France, has also been found in the wild, in Yunnan.

Closely related to *J. officinale* is *J. polyanthum.* In Britain this is hardy in warmer gardens but is usually seen in conservatories, which it floods with fragrance from its white flowers touched with pink. It is a frequent delight in florists' shops at Christmas, but does not take kindly to central heating in our rooms. Also for mild districts is *J. mesnyi* (*J. primulinum*). This, like the Winter Jasmine, is probably an old Chinese garden plant, for it has semi-double flowers, of bright yellow in spring.

We might leave out *J. fruticans,* which is another yellow-flowered species, of more shrubby growth than the above; its flowers are small and it is seldom grown. On the other hand, I consider *J. humile,* another Asiatic species which has somehow acquired the name of Italian Jasmine, to be a neglected garden treasure, especially in its lovely form 'Revolutum'. Here is a beautiful semi-evergreen shrub spangled with clear yellow flowers in clusters for several weeks in summer. Moreover, they are sweetly fragrant.

And lastly, for small gardens there is little *J. parkeri.* Usually seen on rock gardens, for it is a dense, dwarf, spreading shrub, it can weep down the face of rocks to several feet. Tiny leaves and tiny flowers add up to a small shrub of character, not often seen.

There is little doubt, though, that the White Jasmine and the Winter Jasmine hold our affections most, the first because of its scent, the second because of the blessing it brings with its flowers appearing in latest autumn. When the last roses have gone, the last chrysanthemums and nerines are a mush, then does this stalwart cheer us with its ever-fresh, clear yellow flowers, regularly every winter, without stint except during hard frosty spells. And cutting it for the house does it good; it flowers best on the side-shoots which grow out of the extra strong shoots of the previous year.

Cutting Twenty-Seven —

The Perennial Peas

It is strange how we have all taken to heart the Sweet Pea (*Lathyrus odoratus,* a native of Sicily) and love it tenderly, taking great pains with spring cosseting and sticks or strings or other support in order to produce long straight stalks bearing four or five blooms. Apart from the delectable range of clear colours brought forth by the breeders and fanciers, frilled and goffered and delicately scented, there are some ancient types still available, of redoubled fragrance though of smaller size and more sober colourings. These are being sought by discerning gardeners who prize fragrance more than mere size. And there is, in all, that pure intriguing shape of the true pea-flower, with its stigma and stamens enclosed in the unique projecting envelope of petals, with the great guard-petal behind. This shape is found in all pea-flowers and runs through the varied assembly we are about to appraise.

It would perhaps be best to look first at the next best known, the Perennial Pea, *Lathyrus latifolius,* often erroneously called the Everlasting Pea. It was so-called, I think, to differentiate it from the annual Sweet Pea in days gone by, for it is an indestructible perennial in well drained sunny positions. In Britain one even sees it naturalised on railway embankments, sprawling amongst the grass or climbing up a bush. Like the Sweet, the culinary and all other peas, it climbs by means of spring-like tendrils which grow from the ends of the leaf stalks. The usual colour of the Perennial Pea is a rather strong pink, verging on magenta, but for those who find this colour difficult to place, there are very pure whites and some with the faintest blush of pink. They all breed more or less true to

Lathyrus nervosus

type. But, alas, they have no scent. Gertrude Jekyll, having more staff at hand than most of us, used to drape the white one over spent *Delphinium* stems for its three weeks or so of bloom, and then bring forward a Clematis to prolong the display still further.

The real Everlasting Pea, a sound, even invasive perennial, has long graced the Old Garden at Hidcote Manor in Gloucestershire, bringing just those tints of warm magenta-pink on guard or standard petals coupled with keel of richest murrey-red. It is a flower of size and great quality and rewards the intimate gazer with its quality and tints. It needs the support of brushwood or a neighbouring bush.

In an old garden I once came across the flamboyant Persian Everlasting Pea, *L. rotundifolius,* another somewhat invasive plant and not scented, but which intrigues all who see it. The smallish flowers are borne for several weeks amid fresh green leaves, and I think are best described as coppery pink with a more-red-toned keel; as they age they turn to a curious slate-blue tint and so are just right for associating with *Clematis × durandii,* whose large flowers of subdued blue-violet are likewise produced on annual herbaceous stems. I let them ramble together. At Sissinghurst Castle is a different form of the pea, of richer colouring and less invasive root. Close relatives of this species are *L. tuberosus* in pink and *L. undulatus* in red-purple. They all hail from southern Europe or the Middle East, are not fragrant, and need support.

There is no doubt that even in June, when so much beauty crowds our senses, these peas and my next two can well hold their own, and it is strange that they are so seldom seen. It was in Ireland that I was introduced to *L. pubescens* and given seeds. I was disconcerted to read that it was tender: however, it seems perfectly hardy, a semi-woody plant providing a beautiful display annually in my garden. With the aid of pea-sticks it ascends to some 4 feet and makes a real smother of lavender-blue flowers nestling amongst hairy growths. Moreover, it is sweetly scented. Its provenance is given as Chile and Uruguay, and no doubt some of its geographical forms would prove tender.

While the above species are all sound perennials, I cannot say the same for *L. magellanicus* and *L. nervosus.* They are both of a bluish colour and hail from South America, like *L. pubescens,* but *L. nervosus* is a native of Patagonia and *L. magellanicus* (as its name suggests) comes mainly from the far south of the great continent. They have both been in fitful cultivation since the eighteenth century but, though semi-woody perennials, do not seem to be able to cope with the British climate, at least in Surrey. However, they set seeds which germinate readily. *Lathyrus magellanicus* is described in the reference books as Lord Anson's Blue Pea, but I gather that this title is really attributable to the even more beautiful *L. nervosus* which blends its lavender-blue flowers, borne in small sprays, with extremely glaucous blue leaves and stems. It is a real joy to see it in flower and to savour the penetrating sweet odour of its blooms. It is not to these virtues, however, that it owes its introduction to our gardens. When Admiral Lord Anson was circumnavigating the world in the 1740s his sailors developed scurvy from a lack of fresh vegetables and fruits, as was usual; and the ship's surgeon, on going ashore on the south-eastern coast of Argentina, found this blue pea and included it in the diet, with good results. He also brought back seeds to the Anson estate at Shugborough in Staffordshire. This all came to light when the National Trust was refurbishing the garden at Shugborough Hall, in the 1960s, and it is good to feel that this blue pea is now growing there again. It is a noteworthy plant of unique colouring and well worth the trouble of annual raising to guard against losses. It seems to be able to survive the winter but becomes vitiated, and is unable to make a good plant in the second year. At least, that is my experience, and it appears to hold good for *L. magellanicus* as well, which is not of so distinct colouring.

There are yet some other species of note in this genus, strangely neglected by gardeners; they lack the tendrils which enable them to climb, being short-growing perennials. Both *L. aureus* and *L. vernus,* natives of Europe, may be seen at Hidcote Manor; the former adds to the yellow colouring of Mrs Winthrop's Garden, though "yellow" is perhaps a poor description of the flower colour, which is best described, I think, as a brownish amber. They are produced abundantly in early summer over the leafy clumps. *Lathyrus vernus,* likewise about a foot high, is an equally stalwart perennial, with sprays of small flowers of richest violet marked with crimson, fading to nearly blue in the normal form, which seeds itself freely in any sunny spot. There are enchanting dwarfer variants, which may be slowly increased by division, in pale blue-and-white, pink-and-white, and also true albinos.

Perhaps these few paragraphs may result in keen gardeners taking a closer look at a delightful genus.

Cutting Twenty-Eight —

Nancy Lindsay

My association with and enthusiasm for shrub roses goes back principally to 1937, when I paid my first visit to Ireland and found at Glasnevin in Dublin and at Daisy Hill Nursery, Newry, in Northern Ireland, several varieties which were not then grown in England. I was manager on a large wholesale nursery — T. Hilling & Co., Chobham, Woking, Surrey — and it so happened that before the Second World War had really started, three large collections of roses came on the market. One, principally of species, assembled by George Beckwith of Hoddesdon, Hertfordshire, we purchased; another, containing many old-fashioned roses, from Daisy Hill Nursery, was taken in lieu of cash. Yet another was purchased in part by the Royal Horticultural Society. This was that of George Bunyard & Son of Maidstone, Kent, which nursery had the leading collection of old and obscure roses at the time. In due course this collection also found its way into the hands of T. Hilling & Co. The roses mostly remained untended in a weedy patch until after the war, when I started searching for more from gardens and nurseries around the world.

One obvious source was the Royal Botanic Gardens, Kew. Prior to the war Nancy Lindsay had been on a plant collecting expedition to Iran (Persia), concentrating mainly on the Caspian province to the north of the Elburz Mountains. She brought back a number of plants to Kew, new to cultivation: *Prunus cerasifera* 'Lindsayae', a pink flowered, green-leafed Myrobalan or Cherry Plum, an arum of the *A. italicum* group with extra large pale green spathes (N.L. 1234), and several roses. These were numbered and named by her: N.L. 292 'Ispahan'; N.L. 465 'Sharas-tanek', which I have lost and should like to acquire again; N.L. 849, 'Rose de Resht', which is probably an Autumn Damask or even perhaps the 'Rose du Roi' — at all events, James Russell tells me it was growing at Castle Howard, Yorkshire, before the Second World War and also in France; N.L. 1001 'Gloire de Guilan', a silvery pink Damask used for the extraction of attar in the Caspian provinces of Iran; and, among others, N.L. 1409 'Rose d'Hivers', a possible *R. alba* hybrid whose dainty white or palest blush flowers remain in bud formation for some days and are picked and dried for winter decoration.

The Curator at Kew very kindly let me have budding eyes of these and other roses for my growing collection. A few years later I met Miss Lindsay and we exchanged visits. It was then that I was told that her roses and other plants had been lodged at Kew for safe keeping, as she had no garden to accommodate them, and that they should not have been given to anyone without her permission. I received a tirade by post a day or two later, of which I give the gist:

> I was *stunned* when I saw my precious 'Rose d'Hivers', N.L. 1409, in your nursery! I risked my life in the wilds of the Guilan Mountains to get that rose! I only got home one or two bits of root which I gave to Kew to look after for me, strictly on the understanding that *no one* was to have it ... Every time I've been to Kew I've asked after it and could never track it down ... could never find the darling of my heart! If you and I were not old friends I'd be *speechless with fury* at Kew having given you bits of my *own pet particular precious roseling* whose habitat has particular memories for me. It's almost more than even my placid nature can stand to find someone else has plants of my pet before I even have stock of it! I don't know how Kew *could* have made such a mistake!
>
> You see, when I went to Persia I was not paid by Kew. I went on my own, as a free agent, on my own money with only a grant of £100 in addition from the Natural History Museum (and equipment, presses,

etc.) lent by the N.H.M. to collect Herbarium material and insects. I brought the best of my living plants and seeds to Kew on the agreement that they would look after them for me and return me half later on ... and that none would be passed on until they had been named, shown and recorded and I'd given my permission. As it's you I shan't kick-up an unholy row and take it up with my old friends Sir Arthur Salisbury [sic] and Harry Aberconway. But I really am *stunned!* ... *I ought to have had stock of it first,* and had it named and shown it *myself.* What I'll propose to you as we are old friends and you of course are quite innocent; of course I don't blame *you* ... I can't agree to your putting it into your catalogue ... until I also, its Mama, so to speak, have equally stocks with you to also offer my *own special* rose from the wild tribal area of Guilan where probably no other European will be able to go for lifetimes, I propose you splitting your stock with me, old and young. I want it shown next year, and I'll give you permission to show it *for me.* I want Kew to name it for me ... I'd always hoped that my rose would be named after me, whatever else wasn't. I never worried very much about the "garden" roses such as 'Gloire de Guilan', etc., which I found in relatively civilized parts of Persia, but this *very distinct little* rose from the unexplored wilds was always the pet and darling which I mourned for. *I know you will understand. ...* It's not a question of N.L. 1409 being an old rose rediscovered: *it's my very own new 'new' rose!*

This little rose grows at Mottisfont, together with 'Gloire de Guilan' and 'Rose de Resht', but has never been shown or officially named. Miss Lindsay also found *Iris unguicularis* 'Nancy Lindsay' above Toulon in 1939. It was the most spectacular dark purple of the *speciosa* forms that I have ever seen. The rich purple falls were pale grey at the back and made a great contrast. It was not particularly free of increase and regretfully I have lost stock; I should like to get it again.

James Russell and I paid our first visit to Miss Lindsay's garden on 30th June 1946. The address was Manor Cottage, Sutton Courtenay,

Abingdon, Berkshire, and in those days the journey involved both rail and cycle. It was a small garden but exceedingly well stocked, mainly with alpine and herbaceous plants, and shrubs and climbers, mostly trained on old walls. She had amassed a great quantity of special forms of plants from the numerous gardens she had visited; few people had a better "eye" for a good plant, or guarded it more tenaciously when they had acquired it. Three of her main hunting grounds were Hidcote Manor (she was a friend of Lawrence Johnston) and Abbotswood, in Gloucestershire, and the Botanic Garden at Oxford. All three, particularly the last, were rich in plants. It so happened that Mr G. W. Robinson, Curator at Oxford, was an expert plantsman and had given to her and to me cuttings of a special *Erodium*, of *macradenum* persuasion with an extra large black eye. In spite of knowing whence our stock originated, she persisted that "yours is the same as mine but mine's better". Delusion and approbation could scarcely go further than that.

But it was Nancy Lindsay's roses that we particularly went to see. We had had lists of her roses with lengthy descriptions, and were enthralled by her enthusiasm. The thought-provoking names poured from her. For some years I was frustrated by these names because I could not find them in any of the old French books in my possession, nor in the Lindley Library. At length the reason dawned on me. Finding an unknown rose in an old garden without a name she let her fancy run free and coined a name for it. Thus did the following names appear in commerce (in her own catalogue):

'*Souvenir de la Princesse de Lamballe*' which proved to be 'Bourbon Queen'.

'*Souvenir de l'Impératrice Joséphine*' was the same as one I acquired from The Honourable Bobbie James, known as Miss Willmott's Rose, reputedly brought from France by the *émigrés* and now known (without foundation) as 'Empress Josephine'.

'*Rose des Maures*', another name without foundation, a rose now known as 'Sissinghurst Castle', commemorating the garden where it has so long been grown.

'Souvenir de la Bataille de Marengo' which turned out to be 'Russeliana' or 'Scarlet Grevillea', a *R. multiflora* hybrid.

'La Tour d'Auvergne' which proved to be the Damask 'Oeillet Parfait'.

There were many others, all since resolved.

Miss Lindsay's catalogue was a masterpiece of embroidery and exaggeration coupled with spelling mistakes and a more unbridled use of adjectives and adverbs than it has ever been my fortune to find excelled. Here are a few examples:

'Madame de la Roche-Lambert'. A fascinating Autumn Damask moss, whose folatre buds are fantastically beplumed and befeathered magenta-tinted mignonette, and whose exotic quilled flowers are made of shimmering fuchsia-red Chinese silk deepening to Tyrhian hearts and languishing a romantic heliotrope.

'Souvenir de Pierre Vibert'. A gala Autumn Damask moss-bush bedizoned with plushy cupidon buds diademed with plumes of tropically verdant moss and royal sprays of sumptuous blooms of lurid dragon's-blood velvet, splendid as Ceasar's mantle.

'La Belle Gitara'. Exquisite almond-green bushes, spangled with glittering camelias of amaranthine-fuchsia ripening to a lucullian cardinal-purple.

'Amelia'. An elegy from the battlefield of Minden, near on two centuries ago, the lovely mist-green foliage and silken rose-madder petals still grace the ancient owl-green stones of Winchester's cathedral precincts.

'Rose de Resht'. N.L. 849. A curious rose of a similitude to the 19th century European breed of Hybrid Perpetuals but happened on in an old Persian garden in ancient Resht and owning its origin to the tea-caravans plodding Persia-wards over the Central Asian Steppes. Sturdy yard-high bushes of a glazed lizard-green, perpetually emblazoned with full camelia-flowers of pigeons-blood ruby irised with royal purple haloed with dragon-sepals like the painted blooms on oriental faience.

No fulsome praise was too much for her beloved roses. Nobody could excel her lavish imagination and great sense of history; only a few could also see the differences between closely similar plants. She had a unique whole-hearted enthusiasm and was moreover a skilled and green-fingered gardener. If one could put up with the lengthy embroideries one was always in for an interesting time. Differences of opinion were often greeted with a deep intake of cigarette smoke (she chain-smoked a Turkish brand in a well-yellowed short holder) to be expelled all over one with an explosive "No!" She invariably wore an old pair of once-coloured plimsolls and wrote all her letters in a neat hand, sloping regularly backwards; no margins were left and there were few paragraphs to divide the pithy comments.

Nancy Lindsay died in 1979 or 1980. I often think how enthralled she would have been to see The National Trust garden of Old Roses at Mottisfont. It is most appropriate that her plants should also be there, since before the south front of the mansion is a planted parterre designed by her mother, Norah (Mrs Lindsay also did admirable work at Blickling Hall, Cliveden, Nawton Towers and Newby Hall).

Nancy Lindsay. Courtesy Ethne Clark

Rosa moschata
and double form

Cutting Twenty-Nine —

The Tea-Noisette Roses

Oh, how much more doth beauty beauteous seem
By that sweet ornament which truth doth give!
The rose looks fair, but fairer it we deem
For that sweet odour which doth in it live.

—Shakespeare, Sonnet LIV

To no group of roses do Shakespeare's thoughts apply more aptly than those which are the subject of this Cutting, for at the spring of all the pedigrees of the varieties chosen is found *Rosa gigantea,* the tea-scented species from China, whose palest yellow colouring had such a marked effect on hybridisation in the nineteenth century.

Although the earliest intercrossing of roses in the Western world has not been fully established, since there is no record of much before the beginning of that century, it is fairly well traced through the experiments and writings of Dr C.C. Hurst reproduced in my book *The Graham Stuart Thomas Rose Book.* He relates how certain roses native of southern Europe and the Middle East, namely *R. gallica, R. phoenicea, R. moschata* and *R. canina,* formed groups of hybrids through long centuries and were preserved as garden plants and for medicine and preserves until the end of the century, when a remarkable series of events occurred. All unknown to the Western world, the Chinese had likewise been treasuring certain hybrid roses, probably equally old, or older. The first of these hybrids reached Britain about 1793 and was immediately valued for its recurrent flowering habit, though it was not markedly vigorous or fragrant. We called it Parsons's

Pink China Rose, Common China or Old Blush China ('Yue Yue Fen', in Chinese). The second, Hume's Blush Tea-scented China, arrived in 1809, and the third, Parks's Yellow Tea-scented China ('Danhuang Xianshui'), in 1824. These are all believed to be hybrids between *R. chinensis* var. *spontanea*, a vigorous climber from Hupeh, flowering once at midsummer, and *R. gigantea*, another vigorous climber from farther south. It is a strange fact that many dwarf growing hybrid roses are recurrent flowering, and hence we received bush roses of the first two, not climbers. But before them, in 1792, a short-growing sport or hybrid of *R. chinensis* had arrived over here which came to be known as Slater's Crimson China, ('Yue Yue Hong'). This or something very like it still grows in Bermuda; in Britain its colouring is found in close types known as 'Willmott's Crimson China' ('Chi Long Han Zhou') and the vigorous 'Bengal Crimson'.

Thus within about a quarter-century were gathered into Europe this historic group of Far Eastern roses. As the century proceeded they had a profound effect on the multitudes of seedlings and hybrids raised in France and England, combining the unique merits of the roses from both sides of the Old World. To the whites, pinks, mauves and murreys of the European, very hardy, mostly once-flowering Gallicas, Damasks, Albas, Centifolias and Mosses — all richly and sweetly scented — were added recurrent-flowering roses of delicate petallage, delicate tea-scent, many of weak growth but with tints verging towards soft yellow, peachy and apricot tones hitherto not seen. This new tinting, coupled with true crimson and the recurrent habit, were the outstanding results of this merging of the Eastern and Western races. Deliberate hybridising was not understood until the later years of the nineteenth century, but bees did wonders in uniting the two races. Although the results often lacked stamina, growers gradually picked out the most vigorous seedlings and before long a new group had grown up — the Bourbons, leading to the Hybrid Perpetuals.

Apart from the advent of real rich crimson, it was Parks's Yellow that created the biggest stir. This delicate yet vigorous light yellow, semi-double, tea-scented hybrid became merged with the Musk Rose, *R. mos-chata*, resulting eventually in the first climbing yellow-flowered hybrid ever seen. In South Carolina, John Champneys crossed the Musk Rose with Parsons's Pink China. From this union sprang 'Champneys' Pink Cluster': this flowered once only, but a seedling from it raised by Philippe Noisette of Charleston was a tall, climbing, blush-pink double rose which he sent to his brother Louis, who was a nurseryman in Paris. It quickly became popular and was named 'Blush Noisette'.

In the early nineteenth century there were, among rambling roses, only white and blush varieties, flowering only at midsummer. But the rose growers got to work to hybridise 'Blush Noisette' with Parks's Yellow and as early as 1830 two seedlings had been named, 'Lamarque' and 'Desprez à fleur jaune' ('Jaune Desprez'). From them, ever crossing with the larger and more yellow seedlings, a new race of yellowish coloured repeat-flowered climbing roses gradually appeared — perhaps the greatest triumph in bringing together East and West. They were in advance of climbing roses of other colours. In fact, until the end of the century, or more, they had no rivals in size; moreover, even today they hold their place, mainly on account of their fragrance and warm, soft colouring.

It was inevitable that rose breeders should use again and again Parks's rose and its hybrids, in spite of their tenderness. Although Parks's rose grows in Britain and occasionally produces those exquisite, few-petalled, tea-scented blooms, it suffers in cold winters and springs. Nevertheless, descended from it are some irreplaceable favourites. Nearly white but large-flowered and double is 'Lamarque', raised in France and thriving best in Britain on a warm sunny wall. Also needing similar conditions and also raised in France is 'Desprez à fleur jaune'. This has comparatively small double flowers in clusters and is a vigorous rambler. My first sight of this rose was on a house wall, every hanging shoot ending in a cluster of flowers of warm peachy apricot and with an unforgettable fruity scent. There is no rose like it, none more fragrant nor so persistently giving fresh crops of blooms until the autumn.

Raised in Devon by one Foster and launched into commerce by the famous nurserymen Lucombe, Pince & Co. in 1841, 'Devoniensis' produced a climbing sport in 1858. It is through this variant that it exists today, a fine strong-growing, recurrent-flowering rose worthy of any garden. The large, well filled, regular, double blooms are creamy white, tinged with crimson in the bud. They frequently show a flush of apricot around the button-eye on opening. It is richly tea-scented.

'Céline Forestier', a French variety of 1862, grows to perfection on the south front of the mansion at Mount Stewart, Northern Ireland. It is trained up to some 15 feet and then hangs down, bringing its deliciously scented flowers to the nose. They are well filled with petals — often with a button-eye — are soft sulphur-yellow on opening, tipped with crimson, and fading to creamy tints, offset by light green leaves. In my own garden, in comparatively cold Surrey, it has achieved about 8 feet and would grow taller if my bungalow walls were higher. It flowers repeatedly from summer until autumn. Two seedlings from 'Lamarque' ('Chromatella' or 'Cloth of Gold', and 'Solfaterre') appeared a year later than 'Céline Forestier', also in France, but it has not been my good fortune to grow them. They no doubt lurk in gardens in warmer climates.

We enter into rather a different chapter when considering some later roses. They are the results of using Parks's Yellow again and again, giving rise to Climbing Tea roses, or Tea-Noisettes. Who has not heard of 'Gloire de Dijon' of 1853 — one of the most famous, successful and desirable of yellow climbing roses? It is a large-flowered, fully double climbing rose, possibly descended in part from the equally famous 'Souvenir de la Malmaison'. No rose is more full of scent, its deep buff-yellow flowers being flushed with pink and offset by notably good broad foliage, coppery when young. It ushers in the rose season early on a sunny wall — though quite hardy — and also introduces us to the warm yellow colouring which has always been the rarest tint in the hundreds — even thousands — of roses which have come and gone during the last 150 years or so. People are apt to say that it has lost its vigour, but that has not been my experience.

'Rêve d'Or' of 1860 takes after 'Gloire de Dijon' in rich colour, freedom and hardiness, but is not so fragrant. For about a hundred years, 'William Allen Richardson', a sport from 'Rêve d'Or', was the brightest rose, almost orange or yolk-yellow. It has a comparatively small flower, fading to cream in hot sunny weather, but is an abundant flowerer, and vigorous. Today it is rather outclassed, but remains a landmark.

The king of all the Tea roses of this warm colouring is undoubtedly 'Maréchal Niel' of 1864. Its flowers are large, loose-petalled and nodding, and it is vigorous; on a warm sheltered wall it can be trained to 12 feet or more, flowering well in dry warm weather on shed or wall, but it gets rapidly spoiled in wet weather. Warm days and nights bring out its best and ensure plenty of its rich tea-scent. It would be my choice for a large, cool conservatory.

Two near-white Noisettes may be mentioned here; in spite of our predilection for bright colours today, they are not entirely out of favour, and approximate the Tea-Noisettes in many characters. They are 'Madame Alfred Carrière' of 1879 and 'Mrs Herbert Stevens', a rose raised in 1910 which produced a climbing sport in 1922. The former has a slight pinkish tint on opening and is seldom out of flower, doing well on the cottage wall at Sissinghurst Castle; the latter is a nodding Tea rose of lemon-white. Its nodding flowers are at no disadvantage on the climbing sport, and in this form I should always grow it.

Of the same date (1910) is 'Lady Hillingdon', again a nodding rose, whose climbing sport originated in 1917. This is a very vigorous plant and has achieved some 30 feet on the south wall of the mansion at Mottisfont Abbey. I have seldom been there when there have not been flowers showing. They are perhaps the richest and warmest apricot-yellow of all roses, loose and gracious, and full of rich fragrance; to me it is redolent of apricots in the morning and tea in the evening. The foliage is glossy and leathery, deeply tinted with red-brown when young, in satisfying contrast. Gardeners with high sunny walls should treasure this rose.

We are left with two comparatively small-flowered Noisettes. One is 'Alister Stella Gray', introduced by George Paul in 1894, which is *never* out of bloom from June to November. First the short, small shoots produce two or three blooms, and later in the season are succeeded by great shoots from the base bearing large branching heads in the manner of 'Blush Noisette' and the Hybrid Musk 'Vanity'. Each flower expands from a perfectly formed bud of warm yolk-yellow, opening to flat blooms often with a button-eye. The scent enriches the exquisite buds in the button-hole. It is a big, bushy, semi-climber. (A much smaller but very similar Polyantha called 'Perle d'Or', of 1884, descended from the yellow Tea rose 'Madam Falcot', is more suitable for smaller gardens.) The other rose, 'Claire Jaquier', is close indeed to 'Alister Stella Gray', with almost indistinguishable buds, flowers and leaves, but is a climber, with unfortunately only one season of flowering. It is a much more vigorous plant, dating from 1888, and was for many decades the only yellow rambler; there are still extremely few. At the other end of the scale is the showy 'Crépuscule' of 1904, a splendid shrubby plant with plenteous flowers of loose shape and deep buff-orange colouring.

The roses in this little recital, raised over a span of a hundred years, are remarkable in two ways. First, they represented yellowish colouring in so few varieties, while many hundreds of varieties of whites, pinks and crimson appeared (of which the majority have been lost). Second, why were greater efforts were not made to increase their numbers? Theirs is the rarest colour in roses. The latter part of their story is of their eclipse by the shrill lemon and canary yellows which resulted from the bringing into the already mixed hybrid strain the strident colours derived from *Rosa foetida*, around 1900, and its forms 'Persian Yellow' and 'Austrian Copper'. These are the ancestors of all the fierce colours of today, further strengthened by the spontaneous occurrence of the dazzling pigment, pelargonidin, in 'Gloria Mundi' (1929).

The climbing Tea-Noisettes represent a unique chapter in the history of roses and neither their lovable characters nor their potentiality for breeding should be neglected.

Cutting Thirty —

In the Front Line

Paths rest the eye from the fullness of borders and beds, but they can be very severe unless plants are allowed to grow forward and soften the lines. With gravel or paved paths this is a simple matter; it just depends on the amount of softening you wish to achieve, or will tolerate. Grass paths are not so easily managed; it is a nuisance, when mowing, to have plants flopping over the edges; more- over, they destroy the grass and ren- ovation of the greensward is some- times necessary. In my opinion there is nothing so satisfactory as a strip of paving between grass and border. This allows plants to flop forward pleasantly without getting in the way of the mower.

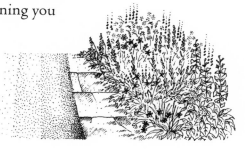

In gardens where there is little traffic the flagstones should be laid about two inches lower than the grass. This enables the edging shears to be used effectively, but where feet will trample down the grass edge I believe it is best to lay the flags level with the grass. Edging shears can still be used if a narrow slit is kept vacant between grass and stone; alternatively, trimming can be done with a sharpened half-moon cutter, or, in quite small plots, with sheep-shears.

There is no finish to a garden to equal trim lawns and paths. In fact, I often think that if it comes to the pinch in regard to time available, trim edges to the grass are more important than cutting the lawn. Whatever the state of the trimming, we should always remember that this and the front line or so of plants are what make a garden most appealing. Wherever possible, therefore, choose plants of a long duration of beauty for the front line; their flowering period brings charm but it is the foliage, long-lasting, which is most valuable. Such plants should not of course be in a line along the front, but should be disposed in different sized groups and even run back into the border here and there.

The plants chosen should also bring solidity and substance to the whole border, so evergreens are best, such as the invaluable bergenias. Among them are some coarse growers, but if we keep to more compact types such as 'Sunningdale' we shall achieve our purpose. Totally distinct is *Euphorbia myrsinites*, a sprawling plant with vivid grey-blue leaves, which erupts into heads of yellow-green stars in spring. There is another euphorbia for our quest, *E. polychroma* (*E. epithymoides*), a most brilliant yellow-green flower of spring, the foliage persisting in beauty till the autumn, a foot to eighteen inches high. I have particularly admired a broad edging, flowing onto the paving, of *Arabis caucasica* (*A. albida*) 'Variegata' — it is beautiful through the year, in sun or shade. Likewise the handsome lobed leaves of varied green tones of the little known, slowly increasing *Pachysandra procumbens*.

Alchemilla mollis is a candidate too, although it is not evergreen and is apt to spread freely from seed—unless the feathery heads are picked off as soon as they begin to turn brown—but its late summer leaves are very good and solid. While the many larger plants and shrubs in the depths of the border are in flower from July onwards, we need firmness at the front from good leaves such as those of *Geranium* 'Johnson's Blue'. If the flowering stems are removed from the base after the flowers have fallen it will produce a most handsome clump of dark green, fingered leaves until the onset of frost. *Pulmonaria saccharata* (*P. picta*) is, on the whole, the best of the lungworts, for it begins to open its flowers very early in winter ... and continues till Easter, after which come the fresh dappled leaves, wellnigh as ornamental as the blossom. They make a good clump for the rest of the season, and a strong contrast against A. T. Johnson's *Geranium.*

There are several dwarf shrubs which blend well with other front-liners, such as the Winter Savory, whose little flowers do not appear until very late summer, and the various types of grey-leafed Cotton Lavender or *Santolina.* It is not generally realised that one can get away from the strident yellow of the usual *S. chamaecyparissus* and nearly as harsh *S. pinnata neapolitana* by choosing *S. pinnata* 'Edward Bowles' or 'Sulphurea', with flowers of a pale creamy yellow. But of course all these plants should be clipped over hard in spring to produce their masses of grey foliage, in which case the flowers will not appear, since they are only produced on the previous year's growths. Lavenders, apart from 'Hidcote' and 'Twickel Purple', may be rather large, except for really big borders, and should likewise be clipped over in spring. 'Jackman's Blue' Rue (*Ruta graveolens*) also benefits from a spring clipping so that its flowers will be scarce and the plants dominated by their filigree of leaden-blue leaves. And the sages, *Salvia officinalis*, are valuable for augmenting colour schemes — purples, yellows and variegated — but can be somewhat frustrating: any pruning should be left until May, with the consequence that it is July before they look respectable again. The same applies to the delightful free-flowering, narrow-leafed *Salvia lavandulifolia*, a hardy treasure from Spain.

All the above are sun-lovers. Turning now to shady borders, we have again the bergenias and *Pachysandra procumbens*, also the invaluable hostas in a variety of sizes and variegation, and that splendid plant, the Hart's-tongue fern (*Asplenium scolopendrium*) in rich green, lasting in beauty (unlike the hostas) well into winter. The stronger-growing *Epimedium* species and hybrids, *E. perralderianum* and *E.* × *perralchicum* and *E. colchicum* itself, are imperturbable evergreens, completely weed-proof, which delight us in spring with flights of citron stars. In my own rather frosty garden I am never quite sure how it is best to treat these. If one wants the flowers, it is best to cut down the foliage to ground-level in February, though the young flower stems then run the risk of being frozen. If, however, the leaves are left, the flower stems have to exert their whole strength to get above them. I always cut down the old fronds of the common polypody fern likewise, but not till April or early May, to make way for the new fronds in June: in this almost full summertime it is very pleasant to find fresh spring-like green leaves arising.

There is one dwarf shrub that gives me the greatest pleasure from its bright verdant green, year in year out, and this is *Hebe rakaiensis,* which used to be called *H. subalpina.* The little spikes of white flowers in summer are an added attraction, it is true, but I prefer to clip mine over in spring, and the dense tump of green that accrues I find most satisfying. It is as bright as the lawn in summer, out-greens everything else for the rest of the year, and will make a handsome full stop a yard across and a foot high.

Cutting Thirty-One —

The Use of Glaucous Leaves

On taking over a new garden it is wise to assess not only the possibilities of the site and whatever features may be present, but also their colour — the colour of the walls and shrubs.

My own bungalow is built of warm-coloured bricks of varying tones from yellowish brown and "red" to the dark tones of cinders. Furthermore, at the back, helping to screen the neighbouring house, was a very large *Elaeagnus pungens* 'Maculata Aurea'. This links well with the brickwork, there at least, whereas I wanted to keep the border by the shady front walls for mauve winter-flowering rhododendrons, such as *R.* 'Praecox' and *R. dauricum.* I resolved this aesthetic problem by covering the walls with white-variegated ivies and *Euonymus fortunei* varieties.

The question was, how to cope with the brickwork and the *Elaeagnus* on the sunny side of the house, namely the back garden, to be devoted mainly to summer-flowering plants. I also like soft mauves and pinks with their appropriate companions among the grey-woolly leaves of *Stachys*, sages and *Santolina.* Clearly I should have to be very careful about their placing. I hit upon a compromise: to keep these soft colours well away from the walls, which would in any case be more or less covered with greenery, and to plant the main borders with bulbs, perennials and shrubs which would give flowers of white and yellow, blue and purple. To keep this area totally distinct from the other, the complementary planting was to be plants with glaucous foliage and a few with that indefinable tint which we gardeners call coppery purple, principally *Ajuga*, and *Heuchera* 'Palace Purple'.

161

These would both augment the blue flower colours; there is never a shortage of white and yellow. Glaucous foliage is a soft and retiring tone, at its most blue in 'Jackman's Blue' Rue, whose dense hummocks of filigree foliage are at their best after midsummer — that is, if you prune them over in late spring, which as a rule does away with most of the greeny yellow insignificant flowers. Other ideal frontal plants are the sprawling *Euphorbia myrsinites* whose crisp leaves bedeck with regularity stems which erupt into heads of yellow-green stars in spring, gradually turning to parchment and even pink in summer. These plants are allowed to grow forward onto the paved edges of my borders, along with *Othonnopsis cheirifolia.* In this the leaves are held upright; the plants are decorated with yellow daisies in summer.

There is no doubt that the common Seakale has the grandest of all low glaucous foliage, twisted and curled and lobed into fantastic shapes; it is seldom seen away from the kitchen garden, much to the disadvantage of the flower borders. The flower heads in the bud stage can be cooked and savoured, without forcing, but you may rather enjoy the heads of ivory flowers. The other two frontal plants which I should not like to be without are old clove carnations, whose foliage is of a special bluish glaucous tint, and the old *Iris pallida* var. *dalmatica.* Apart from the beauty of the lavender-blue scented flowers in early summer, it has leaves of a pale grey-blue colouring which, unlike those of other irises, last in beauty until late September, and the erect, sword-like blades give a good relief to clumps of other foliage. As to the carnations, I chose 'Lord Chatham' in rich salmon, a plant dating from 1780 or thereabouts.

Here and there one can introduce dwarf shrubs to sprawl over the verge, and I know nothing better, where suitable, than certain hebes, the wide-spreading *H. pinguifolia* 'Pagei' in bright, pale glaucous tone, and the even more prostrate and glaucous 'Sussex Carpet'. This is a form of *H. albicans,* itself a good grey, which originated at Wakehurst Place, the Sussex outpost of Kew.

There are three taller perennials which will carry on the same blue-grey effect. In spite of its height in flower (4 to 5 feet) *Rudbeckia maxima* should be near the front of the border because its leaves, which are mainly basal, are so effective — large, broad, erect, glaucous blades, over which tower the tall stems bearing bright yellow daisies with striking black central cones in late summer — "a very striking herb, which, as a native of Texas, should be given a place in full sunshine and plenty of moisture". Much earlier is the sulphur-yellow *Thalictrum speciosissimum.* The flowers can be removed after they are over, leaving the stems about 4 feet high bearing their elegantly lobed grey-blue foliage. It is thus they are used in Mrs Winthrop's Garden at Hidcote Manor. There is also that symphony in leaden grey, *Lysimachia ephemerum,* whose spikes of grey-white tone in so well with the leaves.

Of the many shrubs available I think I should choose *Elaeagnus commutatus;* there is no question about its aesthetic suitability, but it unfortunately has wandering roots. The offending portions can, however, be removed easily by a sharp spade. It has no particular beauty of flower, whereas that other wanderer (with a vengeance), *Romneya,* can be a weed when established — but when it produces throughout summer those great white poppies, all is forgiven.

The plants listed above — in fact most glaucous and grey-leafed plants — are at their best in full sun. The glaucous tint, a waxy covering, like the silky or woolly coverings of other leaves, is there expressly to minimise the burning effect of the sun's rays. Some parts of my borders, devoted to the same colour scheme, extend into the shade. Here we can draw upon the great race of *Hosta,* giving pride of place, presumably, to *H. sieboldiana elegans,* though I have a particular penchant for *H. fortunei hyacinthina* because it has almost as glaucous leaves and much more beautiful lilac-blue flowers. The much smaller, extra grey 'Halcyon' is quite striking in its glaucous tint, and highly elegant in flower.

It will be seen from the above little catalogue that we have added a good lot of grey-blue foliage, plus yellow, white and lavender-blue flow-ers. These all blend well with early and late lemon-yellow day lilies (*Hemerocallis*), darker yellow *Hypericum kouytchense,* Rose 'Golden Wings' and self sown clumps of 'Allgold' Lemon Balm and Golden Marjoram, whose leaves keep up their colour display until early autumn. There are lavender-blue and white campanulas. Good lavender-blue comes from *Geranium* 'Johnson's Blue' and *G. himalayense*, irises of all three colours, and the lavender blue of *I. missouriensis,* with striking erect grey leaves.

True blue is never easy. I rely on *Veronica* 'True Blue' and *Cynoglossum nervosum* for sun, with late colour in the shade from *Gentiana asclepiadea* and the dark, almost navy-blue of certain aconitums. In September a pleasant combination occurs with *Aconitum japonicum,* whose luminous lavender-blue lights a cool corner with the apricot tint of *Crocosmia* 'Lady Hamilton'. Turning from this assortment of colours it is but a short step to the other colour scheme of pinks and mauves with grey woolly or silky foliage, though this is screened from view by various shrubs.

There is no doubt that, given preconceived colour schemes such as the above, it becomes a real battle sometimes to know where to place a kind gift, or a plant that one simply couldn't resist in a garden centre! But gardening, though often a salve for jaded nerves, is almost always a battle as well. Just think of the snails, slugs and weeds!

Cutting Thirty-Two —

The Portland Roses

Roses are very old plants in the sense that they have been in cultivation since before history began. I am sure that they owe their earliest popularity as much to their fragrance as to their medicinal properties: not only is it delicious, but it is lasting, even from dried petals. *Rosa gallica* has this price-less attribute, and it is a principal ingredient of pot-pourri for this very reason. The Damask Rose, on the other hand, is the main source from which rose-water and attar are distilled throughout the Middle East and beyond.

The Damask Rose, correctly *Rosa damascena,* is thought to be a hybrid of *R. gallica,* and today we have three distinct historic kinds in cultivation. Nobody knows when the hybrids occurred; the best known is thought to be a hybrid with *R. phoenicea,* a single white species of pronounced fragrance of the Synstylae or Rambling rose group. Like its parents it flowers once only during the summer. Similar to it and possibly a sport of it is the York and Lancaster Rose, which has white or pink or parti-coloured blooms — not striped, as in the *R. gallica* 'Versicolor' or Rosa Mundi. The third is quite different: it is a more sturdy, erect bush bearing double pink blooms repeatedly from the summer flush until the autumn, and is called *R. damascena* var. *semperflorens* (or *bifera*); it has long been known as the Autumn Damask or 'Quatre Saisons'. It is believed that this unique rose inherits its recurrent flowering habit from *R. moschata,* a close relative of *R. phoenicea.* This was pointed out by Dr C.C. Hurst some seventy years ago, but in spite of his close work on hybridity and genetics there is no

Rosa damascena var. *semperflorens*

proof that he remade those putative hybrids; nor did he self-pollinate the plants in order to prove his theories. There is still work to be done here, to check his conclusions. Be that as it may, it is difficult to surmise how else the Damask rose could have occurred, knowing as we do what species grow around the area which we call the cradle of our civilisation. *Rosa moschata* itself is a somewhat doubtfully wild species: it is uniform wherever it grows around the Mediterranean and is known to sport to double flowers from the normal single creamy white. It has an incredibly sweet fragrance, and was treasured for this beyond most flowers.

These are the kinds of conundrum we encounter when looking into the origins of ancient garden plants. Nothing is definite. What I suppose may be looked upon as the original Autumn Damask was probably that used nearly 2000 years ago for Nero's autumn and winter feasts. Quantities of blooms were imported from warmer Alexandria. Even so, although the early European herbalists refer to the Autumn Damask rose, we cannot be sure that the one we grow is identical to that grown for Roman feasts, though it is more than likely. A rose with such a priceless attribute would have been greatly treasured and preserved: to have a rose flowering throughout the growing months is what we still desire. Through the kindness of Mrs Gwen Fagan in South Africa I have recently acquired the white sport of the pink 'Quatre Saisons' — another link with the past.

We next hear of this Autumn Damask rose from another hybrid, thought to be a back-cross with *R. gallica*. Probably it was a hybrid with the semi-double *R. gallica* var. *officinalis*, which was richer in colour and larger-flowered than the ordinary single pink *R. gallica*, and is said to have been brought from the Middle East by the Crusaders in the thirteenth century. (It is this form which has been used through the centuries for dried petals and conserves.) We do not know when this comparatively new hybrid originated, nor where, but it is supposed to have been grown by the second Duchess of Portland about 1775. It bears a close resemblance to *R. gallica* var. *officinalis* in growth and flower shape, but has a brighter colour than the light crimson of var. *officinalis*, so bright indeed that it became known as the Scarlet Four Seasons, also the Portland Rose or 'Portlandica'. Though by no means scarlet, it was the nearest to bright red at the time and has the bushy, vigorous, suckering growth of var. *officinalis*, as opposed to the rather lanky Autumn Damask, which will ascend to six feet.

I found this Portland Rose, without a name, in several old gardens in England when I was originally looking for such things some forty years ago. It is a thoroughly reliable, vigorous rose producing three or more crops of blooms, from the earliest days of roses until autumn, if pruned suitably. The secret is to thin out part of the first crop while still in tight bud, and to remove all dead flowers as soon as they fade. No doubt this recipe would apply to all Portland varieties.

Sometime during the nineteenth century the French nurserymen must have neglected to dead-head their plants, because a series of seedlings was raised with the same admirable character of flowering, if not repeatedly, at least recurrently. A marked trait that most of them have is the sort of collar of leaves just under the flowers, which I always call the "high-shoul-dered" effect. This character is also found in some of the early Hybrid Perpetuals, inherited from the Portlands.

Several of these Portland heirlooms have come down to us, though their nomenclature is a little uncertain. In fact, looking through French books of the nineteenth century, it is apparent that there is considerable confusion between the roses listed as Portlands or Portland Damasks, and early Hybrid Perpetuals. One that has reached me from the Roseraie de l'Haÿ is 'Arthur de Sansal', a small dark reddish purple variety with the date 1855. However, as it is recorded that this is a hybrid of 'Géant des Batailles', which was a Hybrid Perpetual, our 'Arthur de Sansal' may be a Portland of some other name. 'Blanc de Vibert' is a double white, lemon-tinted in the centre when freshly open. But the most splendid I know is one we call 'Comte de Chambord', which it is possible is in reality 'Mme Boll'. It has light green foliage and a copious and prolonged display of superb, fragrant, clear pink flowers, fully double and with rolled petals. Another good, strong plant is 'Jacques Cartier', with stout upright stems;

each flower or bunch of flowers sits on a ring of light green elongated leaves, and the flowers open flat with a mass of short petals of clear pink, quartered and with button-eyes. There are enthusiasts today who wish to call it 'Marquise Bocella', but this was a small grower with flesh-pink flowers.

One which has recently come my way is 'Indigo', raised by Mons. Laffay in France; it is perhaps the richest of the murrey-purples, flushed with crimson, often showing a few stamens and occasionally a white streak; it is much richer in colour than 'Marbrée' and with a strong, sweet scent. Fresh green leaves and few prickles on a good bush, and flowers well filled, of deep lilac-pink, fading paler, are the characters of 'Delambre'. It has a very sweet scent and short hep.

A rose about which we know little is one brought from Iran by Nancy Lindsay and called by her 'Rose de Resht', after the town where she found it; it was, however, in cultivation in this country under some other name before she imported it. When we have managed to sort out all these obscure roses, it may prove to be the long-lost 'Rose du Roi'. It is a neat, upright bush with abundant crops of comparatively small, fully double, cerise-crimson blooms. The proof would be to obtain 'Panachée de Lyon', which had pink stripes; it is recorded as a sport from 'Rose du Roi'. 'Pergolèse' is another of the purplish varieties, a colour in which the Portland roses were prolific, and which can be traced back to the Gallicas. 'Sultane Favorite' is a light pink rose with small flowers, round and densely packed with petals, prettily quartered, on a tall arching shrub flowering rather late in the season. 'Rembrandt' is a light crimson speckled with pale pink, with long pointed leaves, narrow heps covered with glandular hairs, and a true scent of attar; its name, however, is in doubt.

It is extremely unlikely that we shall ever get all these names verified. There are such brief descriptions in old French books and unfortunately, in the two largest historic collections on the Continent, the Roseraie de l'Haÿ near Paris and Sangerhausen in Germany, the nomenclature is muddled and unchecked. On the other hand, is it not better to preserve and enjoy these valuable old roses, regardless of their names? They represent a very special phase in rose hybridising, bringing in the recurrent-flowering habit before the influence of the China rose was used, to the same end but with very different effect.

As a footnote it may be worth mentioning here that this 'Quatre Saisons' rose gave a sport with mossy foot-stalk, buds and leaf surfaces which was known as 'Quatre Saisons Blanc Mousseux'; only the white occurred. It has reverted several times since, thus proving its identity. The "moss" is harsh to the touch, unlike that of the better known sport of *R. centifolia.* Due to the fact that the Damask form is recurrent-flowering, like its parent, it was much used to produce recurrent Moss roses, so that once again we are indebted to this noteworthy landmark among rose hybrids.

Crataegus × *lavallei* 'Carrierei' and
Iris foetidissima 'Citrina'

HARVEST

Now thin mists temper the slow-ripening leaves
Of the September sun: his golden gleams
On gaudy flowers shine, that prank the rows
Of high-grown hollyhocks, and all tall shows
That Autumn flaunteth in his bushy bowers;
Where tomtits, hanging from the drooping heads
Of giant sunflowers, peck the nutty seeds;
And in the feathery aster bees on wing
Seize and set free the honied flowers,
Till thousand stars leap with their visiting.

Robert Bridges, *Shorter Poems*

Cutting Thirty-Three —

After the Phloxes

There comes a day in the summer progression of flowers when the first phlox opens, usually at the end of June, in early seasons, or a week or two into July. It comes as rather a shock, for it is a warning that the apogee of summer is past and we only have the run-down of the season to anticipate. In gardens where phloxes are a great feature it is manifest at once that no other hardy perennial makes such a satisfying mass of colour and scent. Moreover their colours, though mainly on the blue side of the spectrum, nevertheless also contain varieties of great clarity of crimson, red and pink, suitable for the brightest of schemes. And here a word should be added in regard to white varieties; some, such as the renowned, short 'Mia Ruys' and the very tall 'Fujiyama' ('Mt Fuji') have creamy yellow eyes, which makes them invaluable for the blending of brighter tones. Phloxes are therefore valued components for summer colour-scheming of all kinds, and the warm light tends to go out of borders when they have finished. It is sad that 'September Schnee' never seems to have become popular; it is a good pinky-white which follows the main assembly, just as 'Fujiyama' does. The latter is a noteworthy plant since although its five-foot stems may bow over after a heavy rain, they right themselves the next day without assistance.

The two white phloxes mentioned above are keen enough in colour to act as a blend between the bright scarlets and the multi-hued and multi-named varieties of *Hemerocallis,* usually called day lilies from the short life of each flower. There is a whole new range of colours here, from yellow through orange and red to maroon and from thence to mauve and pink — truly a difficult lot to place; much care is needed. I find they are rather heavy in tone except for the pale yellows, which incidentally are usually the best scented. Their leaves are good both before and after flowering but, except for a few late kinds, the blooms tend to go over with the phloxes.

And so the phloxes have gone. What can take their place in late August and September? The most important groups of self-reliant perennials for this period are undoubtedly the crocosmias, in orange, flame and yellow, and the Japanese anemones. Both groups have the great merit of looking respectable and leafy as soon as they are a foot or so high, and they remain in good form long after they have faded. The anemones are all white or of varying tones of old-rose pink. There are times when, on contemplating the common white 'Honorine Jobert', I find myself thinking that no flower of the year surpasses it. Surely it has everything we could want, except fragrance: good foliage, superb stance, weather resistance, and tidy seed heads. Few flowers can compete. Its roots wander about, but who can grudge it the ground it takes up? And the original single pink (of which 'Honorine Jobert' is a sport) is nearly as good. The selection does not end there; there are semi-doubles in white and varying shades of soft pink.

As to the crocosmias, the common *C. × crocosmiiflora* is a freely-increasing weedy though pleasing plant, but the many hybrids raised in the early years of this century are slowly being rediscovered and there are gems among them. They blend well with, but are rather overpowered by, the day lilies. Of late years we have been helped by the botanists, who have caused us to reappraise the old *Curtonus* genus and call it *Crocosmia.* Its strong branching, stems coupled with the vivid forward-pointing glowing flowers of *Crocosmia masonorum,* have been drawn together by Alan Bloom of Bressingham Gardens, Norfolk with astonishing results, witness his 'Firebird' and 'Lucifer' of dazzling colours.

In many gardens where tender plants are grown, such as penstemons, osteospermums and the like, summer certainly does not begin to fade with the phloxes. There is no lack of colour to be had from these and other plants, together with those of annual duration. A wonderful display can be kept going until frosts stop them, if you are prepared to put up with the trouble of replacement in spring. I prefer not to have this bother, and like my plants and shrubs to go on year after year, without trouble. So I should add to my post-phlox assortment some further good perennials, never forgetting *Aster* × *frikartii* 'Mönch' and 'Wunder von Stäfa', and that little 'Nanus' form of *Aster thomsonii*, one of their parents. *Aster thomsonii* itself seems to have died out from our gardens, but nobody could be disappointed with the hybrid × *frikartii*, made with an *Aster amellus* variety. They last in flower until October is running out.

Very self-reliant are some of the monkshoods. Those which flower late, in September and October, are of a bright lilac-blue; *Aconitum carmichaelii* and the hybrid *A.* × *arendsii* are very stalwart, stiff and upstanding with dark filigree foliage. Of recent years a more charming species has come to us from Japan, *Aconitum japonicum*, with the same bright colouring but with much lighter green foliage and a graceful habit. All are ideal companions for those other plants of Ranunculaceae, species of Bugbane or *Cimicifuga*. Anyone with a group of *C. racemosa* at the back of the border will surely be captivated by the lofty tapering spires of tiny creamy white flowers in July and August, followed by the shorter growing *C. simplex* in September and October. And a form of *C. simplex* has cropped up in Germany called 'Brunette' ('Atropurpurea'), in which the leaves are of beetroot colouring — a magnificent contrast to the white flowers. These all have most elegantly divided foliage and like a cool position.

But these are tall plants. If we look around for something shorter, late August and September are the days for the colchicums, often called autumn crocuses, although they belong to the Lily family. Many people hold up their hands in horror at the thought of the colchicums' overweening aspidistra-like foliage in the spring. It is true it is overweening, and moreover dies off a dirty yellow at midsummer — but in the spring, apart from the leaves of hardy arums and certain day lilies, there is no such rich

Aconitum carmichaelii
var. *wilsonii* 'Barker's Variety'

and magnificent greenery about, the daffodils and tulips being grey-green. So I forgive the colchicums, and if anyone is not yet convinced let him purchase a few of that superlative white, *Colchicum speciosum* 'Album'; I shall be surprised if its great goblets do not enthrall him, especially when growing through some *Ajuga reptans* 'Atropurpurea'.

There are certain good perennials which wait for the cooling airs of early autumn to bring forth their flowers, as fresh and surprising as those of spring. I give a specially good mark to the way that *Crocus goulimyi* has settled down, increases and flowers freely, its blooms so like those of *C. tomasinianus* in February and March. In fact, it will be surprising if *C. goulimyi* does not become, over the years, as prolific a bulb as Tommasin's. The only thing against this is that at its flowering time the borders are rather full of other growth and leaves. Those South Africans, the forms of *Schizostylis coccinea*, in crimson, pinks and white, are so like miniature gladioluses that it is obvious they are closely related. They need a sunny spot, but must have moisture for the roots. *Nerine bowdenii*, also from South Africa, grows best against a hot sunny wall, producing its exquisite pink lily-like flowers with crimped petals as soon as the September sun begins to lose its power. A fine form is known as 'Fenwick's Variety'. As a complete contrast, try the bright yellow crocus-like flowers of *Sternbergia lutea* 'Angustifolia'. If you can plant the black leaves of *Ophiopogon planiscapus nigrescens* close by, the contrast will greatly please.

Certain red hot pokers are useful and astonishing plants from South Africa, too, and they also delight in reasonably moist ground. Apart from the common one, *Kniphofia rooperi* ('C. M. Prichard') has rather large ovoid heads of orange and yellow, very late in the season. But it is rather of the refined small species that I would write, achieving as they do seldom more than 3 feet and needing no staking. Their tidy grassy leaves are no disadvantage and their slender spires of blossom are all that could be desired. *Kniphofia triangularis* stands at the head of the group, in the garden clones known as 'Galpinii' (apricot-orange), and 'Nelsonii' and 'Macowanii' (coral-scarlet). There are several others of varying tints, and the very late

'Brimstone' is vivid sulphur-yellow. Rather larger and later than 'Galpinii' is a hybrid of it called 'Underway'. This is a warm apricot-orange, ascending to 4 feet with foliage to match.

One of the most surprising hardy flowers of late September and early October is *Begonia grandis* (*B. evansiana*), from the Far East. It has lived and increased by bulbils, occasionally scattered, for many years here in Surrey, and seems quite hardy. There is no doubt it brings a new note, with its broad, lopsided leaves, in sallow green but crimson-lit beneath, and its airy flights of clear light pink, glistening flowers. This likes a cool, shaded position, and it is well to encourage in the same conditions the violet-purple *Crocus byzantinus*. This is also known as *C. iridiflorus*, on account of its iris-like flowers, accompanied by orange stigmata. Most autumn-flowering crocuses do best in sunny positions, but this is an exception.

Lastly among these smaller plants there is the flaming magenta of *Senecio pulcher*, a dark leathery-leafed plant with heads of wide-open daisies, decorated with a tuft of lemon-yellow stamens; it is a very 'shocking' magenta and perhaps needs white as a companion, though I think I should like it near to *Kniphofia* 'Brimstone'.

Of course, one of the joys of autumn is the smell of chrysanthemums; no whiff conjures up the season in quite the same way, unless it is the pungent tang of fallen poplar leaves and that marvellous aroma of strawberry jam given off by the strewn leaves of *Cercidiphyllum*. A disaster appears over the horizon: the botanists have ordained that what we know as chrysanthemums shall henceforth be labelled *Dendranthema!* But they will smell as sweet. I love all the smaller flowered types for the October border, leaving the big ones for the show bench. There is my own pro-tégé, 'Emperor of China', which has been growing in our gardens since before 1890, and of which I have of recent years been distributing roots; it is a pleasing pink with Chinese-type quilled petals. But there are many good varieties now available in all colours, rather taller than little 'Dr Tom Parr' and 'Anastasia', to say nothing of Ingwersen's 'Mei-Kiyo' and its sports.

A plant which is rather difficult to place is *Hosta plantaginea.* Most hostas like cool conditions, but this species flowers very late and needs warm sunshine to hasten it. Perhaps a position near the garden tap would be best, in full sun, so that they are hastened along to regale your nose with the delicious scent from the white trumpet-flowers. I have been given a small division of the double white 'Aphrodite' which I am nursing with every care, though I am not sure that the doubling of a *Hosta* flower will be a great advantage, unless it has also doubled its scent.

Cutting Thirty-Four —

True Blue

Although pure orange may be considered the rarest colour in gardens, I think that true blue is the most sought-after. There is unfortunately much misconception over blue as a colour. To many people, any sort of bluish tint is accepted as such, but if we limit ourselves to the true blue of the spectrum the choice is greatly narrowed. Not long ago I heard of someone who had a blue Lily-of-the-valley: I found it was the rather subdued pink form known as *Convallaria majalis* 'Rosea'. In some lights and when fading it might be said to be lilac, but never blue. The Hybrid Tea Rose 'Blue Moon' is another exaggeration: it is merely another pale and rather dirty pink. In any case, though 'Blue Moon' was named in 1964, it should be remembered that 'Reine des Violettes' (raised in 1860) remains the nearest to blue in roses.

True blue, like the other primary colours red and yellow, is not always easy to place in the garden; it needs white and pale yellow as accomplices. On the other hand, the terms lilac-blue, violet-blue, lavender-blue and heliotrope denote tints which marry in with other colours easily. And if the three primary colours are thought difficult to manage in any sort of sequence, the rainbow teaches us all we need to know about the merging of colours. Our paint-boxes give us ultramarine, cobalt and permanent blue as true tints from the centre of the spectrum, whereas Prussian blue is towards the greenish side. We only have to look at plants of the bedding *Lobelia erinus, Gentiana verna, G. cruciata* or *Salvia patens,* or a true-blue Delphinium, to realise that while these may all be termed true blue, there is a lot of variation between them. I have considered blue in another Cutting, but it is so important a colour and so much misunderstood that I feel impelled to write of it again.

Among shrubs, blue is very rare. The genus *Ceanothus* helps us considerably, and fortunately there are kinds which flower in spring, such as those found under the old garden names of 'Veitchianus', 'Dentatus' and the like, through the summer-flowering *C.* × *delilianus* hybrids to the late flowering 'Autumnal Blue' and 'Burkwoodii', the last being very true blue. This colour is more often seen among herbaceous perennials and annuals. The Borage family is particularly rich in true blues: witness *Anchusa italica* and *A. sempervirens*, *Brunnera macrophylla*, *Borago laxiflora*, and of course the much-loved ordinary Forget-me-not. In the strain most often seen in gardens this is of a pure, pale, limpid tint, enhanced by a tiny yellow star in the centre which turns to white after pollination. With these go *Pulmonaria azurea*, *Mertensia* and *Lindelofia*, with *Lithospermum prostratum* and *L. oleifolium* for the rock garden; but there are more. Of these essentially spring flowers, none can hold a candle to *Omphalodes cappadocica.* A gentle surface spreader, this refutes the epithet that might be levelled at other members of the Borage family — that of being rather coarse and hairy: this *Omphalodes* has comparatively smooth, tongue-like leaves which make a good ground-cover for semi-shady spots, and regales us for weeks with a display of large Forget-me-not flowers in rich, intense deep blue. This is one of the best blues of the whole year, but seldom exceeds 9 inches in height.

The first real splashes of blue in the spring come at daffodil time. There is *Scilla bifolia* and its hybrid *Chionoscilla* × *allenii*, with *Chionodoxa sardensis* by far the richest colour. Eclipsing them all is *Scilla sibirica*, of which the form 'Spring Beauty' should be sought. This grows well and increases by division and seed to make a spectacular clump. A series of mild winters in the British Isles has led to an increase in molluscs, and last year they ate all the blue segments, returning a few nights later to polish off the incipient seed pods. But this does not usually happen. Almost before these are over, *Muscari armeniacum* 'Heavenly Blue' will open and give us another good patch of colour. *Anemone blanda* and *A. apennina* are a long-lasting pair, thriving even on excessively limy soils.

By June, forms of *Veronica teucrium* will be in flower; this is really a garden name for *V. austriaca*, and 'True Blue' is a noted selection; there is also 'Shirley Blue', rather shorter. A taller species is *V. spicata*, which also has good blue forms. But one must beware of the invasive creeping little weed, *V. filiformis*, however captivating its flowers may be. While thinking of these lowly plants we must bear in mind two very blue small onions, *Allium cyaneum*, only a few inches high, and the taller *A. beesianum*.

Returning for a moment to Boraginaceae, there is a rather coarse, tall plant called *Symphytum* × *uplandicum* whose leafy stems produce nodding heads of tubular flowers of a pronounced clear blue, though sometimes from pink buds. It usually needs staking. Rather shorter and thus more manageable is *S. caucasicum* in a lighter blue. *Aquilegia caerulea* has both blue and white petals and can be obtained from seedsmen under such names as 'Blue Star'.

Somewhere between late spring and summer, those of us who live in cooler districts may be captivated by the silky blooms of the Himalayan *Meconopsis*. It is only in conditions of coolth and moisture that these will reveal their clearest colouring, otherwise being tinted with mauve. 'Slieve Donard' is one of the most reliable, also 'Sherriff 600', but if you are looking for pure colour, avoid 'Branklyn', its vigour notwithstanding.

There is no doubt that the *Delphinium* provides us with the most stately of summer flowers and, despite the delectable creams, whites, pinks, mauves and rich purples that are available, when one is confronted with a true blue all the other colours go out of one's head: there is nothing to touch it, whether with black or white centre. July border flowers also include good blue *Eryngium tripartitum*, and *Echinops ritro* and *E. ruthenicus*. These will reach to 3 or 4 feet or taller, and thrive in hot sunny positions in well drained soils.

We need not be without good blues for late August and September; we have already glanced at *Ceanothus* hybrids in this respect, and that rather tender plant of astonishing blue, *Commelina coelestis,* will put to shame all the asters of violet-blue tint. Meanwhile annuals like *Nemophila, Nigella* and *Phacelia campanularia* have come and gone, and *Penstemon ovatus* has regaled us with good spikes of small flowers of a clear tint.

We are still left with three gems for early autumn. There are two plumbagos of note. The clear cobalt flowers of *Ceratostigma willmottianum,* produced as soon as the days really shorten, have been known to attract humming-bird hawkmoths; it is a shrubby plant which in Surrey usually dies to ground-level in winter. Its close relative *C. plumbaginoides* is a lowly, invasive plant whose dark blue flowers usually coincide with a crimson colouring of its leaves in autumn, completing a very fine picture. But I must give the final accolade to *Salvia azurea.* This is a tall, willowy perennial that usually needs supporting, for it will reach 6 feet, setting its topmost shoots with plumes of the clearest azure. Few summer flowers can compete.

From this rather cursory list it will be seen that true blue is available throughout the growing season; even so, I have missed out several treasures such as *Convolvulus* and *Ipomaea.* The next thing to do is to site them in the garden. I venture to suggest that white and pale yellow are the necessary companions; while pinks and reds tend to clarify the blues, they also detract from their purity. And of course, plants with silvery foliage are always desirable foils.

It is a somewhat pregnant thought that very few genera among our hardy plants have all three primary colours (red, blue, yellow) in their various species. I can only think of *Lobelia, Lathyrus, Gentiana* and *Delphinium,* at the moment, and even of these the various species would not necessarily flower together. It is as if Dame Nature sensed the hard contrasts that would occur, and is inclined to leave it to the muted colours to achieve harmony.

> . . . Soft stillness and the night
> Become the touches of sweet harmony.
> Look, how the floor of heaven
> Is thick inlaid with patines of bright gold.
> —Shakespeare, *The Merchant of Venice*

Gardens of One Colour

Green being the predominant colour in most gardens, it is manifest that it must be present, whatever may be the flower colour we choose to accompany it. There are a few green flowers — *Bupleurum*, for example, has several species which are occasionally seen — but they are not really necessary in a scheme entirely of green because we have an infinite variety of leaves with which to achieve plantings of great and satisfying quality. I know of a Silver Birch wood where a green picture was made with graceful bamboos, tropical-looking *Fatsia*, soothing hostas and graceful ferns, with a ground-work of *Luzula maxima* varied with areas of fallen brown leaves. It was of the utmost simplicity, but wholly satisfying. Of course, something quite different might accrue in tropical countries, where glaucous leaves and others of distinct tones might predominate.

Given that many of us are saddled with green as one colour, we might perhaps look through various flower colours to see how they can be used in contrast. I saw a garden some years ago in Scotland where one of green's nearest relatives, yellow, had been used as the second dominant tint. To me it did not seem to "come off" — yellow being insufficiently distinct from some of the greens. I thought it needed a third clear colour, either cooling the scheme down with white or toning it up with orange.

In the 1930s and later the blue borders at Hurstmonceux Castle in Sussex were much lauded, and they were undoubtedly a great success as far as they went; but, not surprisingly, the blue was adulterated with many lavender-blues and mauves: there are not enough flowers of true blue to make any but small schemes. In any case, with or without the lavender-blue tones, I felt that the borders would have been more satisfying with some white and palest yellow flowers and silvery foliage added.

Pink might be selected as another possible second colour, but it would not be good with all the greenery unless some silvery foliage and some very pale pink flowers were added. This would make things more gentle, while a heavier effect would be achieved by the addition of coppery purple foliage.

There is red to be considered, and by red I mean the colour at the centre of the spectrum with the crimsons and plum colours on one side and the scarlets, flames and even oranges on the other. I have written elsewhere of the dangers of mixing these separate tones. The second, brighter group is very successfully handled at Hidcote Manor in Gloucestershire with the admixture of dark purple delphiniums and coppery purple foliage. The first group I have used, enriched again with coppery-purple foliage, and with plants having glaucous leaves.

This brings us to white, which while not really considered as a colour has a special value in gardens; and so often we find that a white variety of a strain is stronger growing and of better quality in flower than the darker variants. But what is white? We seldom see it in gardens. It is usually muted towards grey, cream or blush, and in consequence these are wonderful colours for blending. Pure white flowers are rare; some that come to mind are *Exochorda* 'The Bride', 'Morello' cherry, *Campanula latiloba* 'Alba', and *Phlox paniculata* 'Fujiyama', which has a creamy eye whereas some others have pinkish eyes. This little difference can be delicately balanced in different schemes. The first all-white garden I ever saw was at Hidcote Manor, where the whites are of a surprising number of tints, but all accentuated by the dark green of clipped evergreens and the scarlet threads of *Tropaeolum speciosum* swarming up them. Much larger is the white garden at Sissinghurst Castle in Kent where again, because of the need for enough varieties to fill the numerous beds, the whites are surprisingly and successfully varied. (This garden was made expressly for viewing at night.) Once again darkest green is favoured, but also some silvery foliage. I remember James Russell and I found, when putting up our large exhibits at Chelsea Show, that in spite of the kaleidoscopic array of colours round the exhibit — mainly of rhododendrons and azaleas — there was nothing so effective in showing up big blocks of white as big blocks of darkest green.

The fact that all these colour contrivances need a dark green background presumes that they are part of a large garden. Small gardens are not suitable for such specialised schemes; they are not fit for small areas, nor would there be sufficient interest if the whole area of the garden were given to one such scheme.

The surroundings have also to be considered. There is the colour of the gravel or paving or walls of garden or house to be assessed, as to what colours would go best with them. Staring "red" bricks may upset soft colour schemes, and I have seen a white garden arranged in a walled enclosure, which should have been successful but was marred by the choice of plants; many of them were blue-white or grey-white, but the walls were of yellow stone. Had the whites been kept to creamy whites and greenish whites, all would have been well. It proved once again what a variable tone white is; it has as many variations as red itself.

Forgetting true blue, much can be done with purple in its many variations, witness the purple border at Sissinghurst Castle. It owes most of its long-lasting *éclat* to the several varieties of large-flowered *Clematis*, which make such a superb backcloth. Without a rich retentive soil and adequate watering, it would not be worth attempting. The colours flow forward to the front of the wide border but are offset by the daring inclusion of several *Rosa moyesii*. The vivid tomato-red flowers of *moyesii* appear before the border has reached its zenith, but the occurrence in August and September of the large orange-red heps gives a jolt — and only goes to show that a fundamental difference in colour can be effective, if only one is bold enough.

These separate examples are all taken from gardens of considerable size. Such schemes are successful and intriguing when we can pass from one colour to another in anticipation. Miss Jekyll first showed the way, and it is worth studying the sequences she chose. In small gardens, however, I believe a different approach can be just as enthralling; rather than including a whole range of colours to achieve a sequence, try omitting one decisive colour from each part of a small garden. The result, I believe, is wholly satisfying and comparatively easy. The two big borders of perennials at Cliveden in Buckinghamshire were designed with just these thoughts in mind. One has blues, mauves and pinks omitted, and in the other there are no reds, oranges or yellows.

As a general rule, light colours are the most telling and restful in a garden, but a few dark colours within the range are required for contrast, to bolster the values of the pale tints. In this way I believe the general tones can be realised successfully, and will give repose and quiet results, whereas a labouring after definite colour sequences can become too contrived.

In the spring one welcomes all flowers; every fresh one that opens is a new joy. While the daffodils are with us there is a superabundance of yellow. A little planting I once saw in Sussex brought home the fact that one can achieve relief from yellow quite easily by a planting of white narcissi under a pink cherry. By the time the rhododendrons and azaleas arrive our notebooks should be busy with jottings about colour combinations amongst these too-frequently warring genera: it is fortunate that they can be so easily swapped around when young, even when still in flower. It is full summer, when the free joys of spring are past, before we get down to colour schemes in our borders, and realise to the full what riches are to hand.

The Japanese Garden

The laws of direction, of harmony, of five elements, and the principles of cause and effect, of active and passive, of light and shadow, of male and female, or of the nine spirits of the Buddhist pantheon, are still strongly insisted on by some in determining the general plan of the garden or in grouping stones, etc.

— Jiro Harada, *The Gardens of Japan* (1928)

My first real introduction to this mystical subject was the delightful book *The Flowers and Gardens of Japan* (1908), by Florence and Ella DuCane, containing many exquisite watercolours painted on the spot by the latter. I must confess that in after-years much of delight in the colourful sketches of azaleas and other shrubs has been clouded over by subsequently learning that floral colour was not sought by the makers of Japanese gardens. Rather they looked for form and contrast of greenery — mostly evergreen, from diminutive moss to leaning pines — contrasted again by rocks, water, stepping stones, sand, and garden ornaments such as bridges, fences and stone lanterns.

Many gardens have been made in western countries by Japanese artist-gardeners, and also by western "experts". I remember such at exhibitions at Chelsea and at other flower shows. All was perfection and much was authentic. The idea was to follow and interpret nature in miniature, much as would be done by an artist on a small canvas. It was so different from an English garden that it had a considerable, though transient, vogue.

As to examples in the western world, their strangeness and appeal have been such that, unless kept private and attended by Japanese artist-gardeners, their charms have been eroded by hordes of visitors and neglect of the delicacy of preservation and constant care necessary to interpret the continual growth of plants.

What, then, can be the excuse for the inclusion of this Cutting? It is to call attention to certain ideals which are continually being used as extras to our own garden schemes. There is first, perhaps, the use of rock in gardens. Our own use of it in the making of rock gardens for the growing of alpine plants and the simulation of alpine scenery is governed by geological rules. Not so in the Japanese garden: here each rock is considered for its aesthetic value, regardless of its geological origin, and its shape will determine entirely its placing. The imagination overrides all else.

Whereas the pine tree to us spells lofty height, dark shadow and woodland, to the Japanese it is more often a weatherbeaten and even decaying old piece leaning over a lake or cascade. The bamboo, more often than not the Japanese species *Pseudosasa japonica* (*Bambusa metake*), and some of the dwarf species, is present everywhere, giving an inimitable touch to any scenery. Hardy palms add majesty, and full use is made of *Fatsia japonica*, *Mahonia japonica* and, in milder parts, *Aspidistra lurida*, also *Acorus* species. These shrubs and plants are popular in the West today simply because our garden designers have  learnt from the Japanese concept of contrast and shape. From early spring when the Japanese Apricot (*Prunus mume*) flowers, advertising its presence by exhaling a subtle, delicious aroma, through to the cherries in early May, admirers will walk the ways in Japan almost worshipping the beauty spread around. The spirit of Spring pervades all, but with that, apart from the *Wisteria* and water irises, most flowers are left to the working part of the

garden. Here are grown in containers the tree peonies, the lilies, chrysanthemums and other highly bred flowers which simply could not be contained
within the delicate structure of a landscape. And how right they are! I mention elsewhere ("The Pergola") how readily *Wisteria* lends itself to pruning,
and thus the Japanese *W. floribunda* can be controlled to fit a garden of any
size. There is no other hardy climber with so many assets. Reginald
Farrer was deeply impressed with its beauty, "trailing down those violet
garlands ... while the still green water, swelling lazily against the rocks,
sent back in shifting catches of colour the image of that riotous loveliness."

There are several azaleas native to Japan; each has great floral beauty, but
when they are used in gardens constant pinching-out of the shoots prevents
them from flowering; thus they conform to the size and shape dictated by
the artistic overtones of the garden. On the other hand, some excel in
autumn colour, and this is enjoyed. While every tree and bush must be
made to conform to the overall picture by the Japanese artist-gardener, as
likely as not this artistic sense is not sufficiently developed in the western
gardener who takes control, and the delicate shaping of every branch is lost,
the result being an effect of clipping each bush into a rounded shape. When
an authentic Japanese garden is created outside Japan I believe it can only
be maintained and *developed* (which is most important) by Japanese artist-
gardeners. I have used the last two words repeatedly because they sum up
for me the whole spirit of the enterprise — it is horticultural skill allied to
sentiment, art, history and all that can be read into such ideologies. We do
not have the gift, assembled over the centuries. It is said that the first book
on landscape gardening in Japan appeared in the fourteenth century, when
we were still growing roots and herbs simply for the pot. On the other
hand, if an authentic Japanese garden is commissioned, its very perfection
and unique qualities will excite curiosity and cause visitors to come and
stare, and ruin the whole thing with too much traffic and too many people.
A Japanese garden cannot take more than a very few visitors at a time.

Looking through some of the many books about Japanese gardens
which have been published in the West since Josiah Conder's seminal

work, *Landscape Gardening in Japan,* one wonders whether gales ever wreaked havoc in the many notable old historic designs. I expect there were disasters, but no books that I have seen give evidence of them.

It may be asked again, what is the value of this negative essay? It is to make us realise that another country's unique contribution to the art of gardening cannot be reproduced elsewhere with the certain knowledge that the skills for its development are forthcoming. Though the Japanese style is certainly the most advanced exposition of garden art, it is not necessarily *better* than a western garden. So much depends on your point of view. At the entrance to a garden of any great size in Japan a native pine will be placed on either side of the gate: *Pinus thunbergii* of rugged appearance on one side, to represent the male element, and the more graceful *P. densiflora* on the other side, representing the female. Can we imagine this importance being given to a pair of trees in the western world? There is no doubt that the Japanese have made us look afresh at the artistic side of planting.

True to their predilection for imitation, the Japanese horticulturists are turning themselves afresh into plant fanciers. One hears of exhibitions of all sorts of plants which we might vaguely group under the embrace of "alpines" — such as *Adonis* and *Hepatica nobilis.* Their thoroughness in everything they do has caused certain Japaneese enthusiasts to start breeding roses along western lines, despite the hundred and more years' start which we have gained. The spirit of endeavour and also patience will both have their fling in that string of notable islands, and there is no doubt that they start with the advantage of a rich native flora containing flowers of surpassing beauty. But this brings to the matter a western view; I began these notes with a tribute to what the Japanese have brought to garden design:

> Give me a land of boughs in leaf,
> A land of trees that stand;
> Where trees are fallen, there is grief;
> I love no leafless land.
>
> — A. E. Housman (1860–1936)

Lady Moore

Whether anybody told me to go west when I was a young man, I cannot say, but Ireland, its people, its gardens and its countryside have always beckoned me. I have been paying visits since the late 1930s, due originally to my friendship with Tom Blythe who was a fellow student with me at the University Botanic Garden, Cambridge. He was a nephew of G. N. Smith of Daisy Hill Nursery, County Down. Shortly after the war I spent a fortnight or so in Ireland — only experiencing one wet afternoon — in June; it was then I made my first visit to Willbrook House at Rathfarnham, the home of Sir Frederick and Lady Moore.

Sir Frederick Moore died soon after I met him; he had almost entirely lost his memory ("Some people, Graham, live too long", Lady Moore had said to me), but his work in horticulture, like that of his father, lives on. Between them they directed the National Botanic Gardens in Dublin for 84 years.

I had, I felt, known Lady Moore through being acquainted with *Chaenomeles* — or *Cydonia*, as it was then — 'Phylis Moore', a rather sprawling plant, admirable on a wall, with fully double flowers of clear bright pink darkening with age to a vivid vermilion pink.

In those days there were no speed restrictions in Dublin. I had hired a car, and on receiving it from the garage was rapidly carried to the outskirts of the city, before daring to turn right or left. I was on my way to Mount Usher, which I must be sure to visit, Lady Moore had told me in a letter (I did not regret the instruction, and Mr E. H. Walpole and I became

Lady Moore and friends at Cooldrinagh

good friends). Eventually I arrived at Willbrook. I have not forgotten the pleasure of my welcome, and the delight at meeting so renowned a gardener and plantswoman. Theirs was a garden of about three acres, with a pleasant curving drive lined with good shrubs and trees. Only the beeches were of great age, because everything else had been planted by the Moores. There were *Nothofagus dombeyi* and *N. antarctica; Abies magnifica, Picea breweriana* and *P. omorika*, and *Magnolia × watsonii*, that elusive and lovely hybrid whose powerful scent wafts across any garden. When seeds set — as they not infrequently do — the resulting progeny are always *M. hypoleuca* and not *M. sieboldii*, which is thought to be the other parent. Both are specially fragrant. One plant that stays particularly in my memory was what Lady Moore said was the erect form of *Pyrus salicifolia*. The weeping form is well known, but I have never seen the erect form anywhere else. It seemed to be a true *P. salicifolia* — moreover, the Moores were not likely to make a mistake about it—as silvery as the weeper, which rules out related plants like *P. elaeagrifolia, P. nivalis* and others. I wonder whether anyone else remembers this tree, and indeed whether it still lives, or was propagated.

Salix fargesii was there, and the coral-bark maple, *Acer palmatum* 'Senkaki', or as it was then known, 'Sango-kaku'. *Hamamelis mollis* had reached a great size, and *Viburnum grandiflorum* was 13 feet across.

Willbrook House was stone-built, a good solid building, sitting well in its garden. And everywhere were plants gathered by those two keen spirits, though I felt that, knowing Sir Frederick's predilection for orchids and other greenhouse plants, most had probably been selected by Lady Moore. There was no doubt she not only had an eye for a plant, but knew how to place them in the garden. A great beech tree stood not far from the house, its side and roots fully exposed to the sun, resulting in very dry ground. "I always choose silvery-leafed plants for that sort of position," she said, and how right she was. There were *Cineraria maritima, Artemisia stelleriana, Centaurea clementei, Convolvulus cneorum, Phlomis* of several species, and the great silver leaves of *Senecio doronicum*. This produces large orange-yellow flowers and also used to grow well in Ireland, but it would never grow for me in Surrey. Not far from the house was a plant of *Jasminum parkeri* 3 feet high and 4 feet across, flowering freely. Along the sunny wall was the gooseberry-leafed rose, *Rosa stellata mirifica*, from the Sacramento Mountains, New Mexico; the flowers are like those of a *Cistus* in magenta-pink. The species seems to have died out, but this form is in fairly general cultivation and quite hardy. *Carpenteria californica* was there, too, an especially large-flowered form obtained from Edward Woodall's garden at Nice; I suspect the good form grown today as 'Ladhams' Variety' is the same, for Ernest Ladhams had a way of appropriating to himself epecially good forms of plants which he found in gardens, such as *Phlox decussata* 'Elstead Variety' and *Cimicifuga simplex* 'Elstead Variety' commemorating his interesting nursery, full of good plants. *Dendromecon rigida* had romped up to 15 feet or so, and the rare *Hippeastrum* × *acramanii* was at its foot. That uniquely apricot-tinted yellow rose 'Lady Hillingdon', with its contrasting dark coppery foliage, enchanted me; it was the climbing form. "She is no good in a bed," said Lady Moore; "best against a wall."

I was at that time collecting the old roses, and it gave me much delight to see *R. rugosa* 'Fimbriata' (sometimes called 'Dianthiflora' or 'Phoebe's Frilled Pink'); it is of pale pink with prettily fringed petals, and a good grower. It thrives at Rowallane, Co. Down. Several other rare old roses were treasured at Willbrook: a huge bush of *R.* × *hibernica*, found in 1795 near Belfast, believed to be a hybrid between *R. canina* and *R. pimpinellifolia*; *R.* × *pruhoniciana* 'Hillieri', very tall, and *R. farreri*, carefully placed in part shade, which should always be given it if the foliage is to remain green. And then there was the heirloom which Lady Moore has handed down to us and which she named 'Souvenir de St Anne's'. This is a nearly single sport of the original bush 'Souvenir de la Malmaison'; it originated at the Guinness family home, St Anne's near Dublin, which is now a public park with a large new rose garden. I was delighted to find, during my last visit, that a large bed was filled with 'Souvenir de St Anne's'. The bush forms of this rose are constant in production until the autumn, and I rank 'St Anne's' above the original (named by the Grand Duke of Russia in honour of the Empress Josephine's garden, after her death) and its lemon-white sport, 'Kronprinzessin Viktoria'. Lady Moore was a regular exhibitor at the Royal Horticultural Society of Ireland's Rose Group Show, usually taking first prize for a vase of mixed old roses.

The old yellow Scots Briar was just going over, likewise several others of the same family, including the grey-backed purple 'Mary Queen of Scots'. I remember, too, on one visit being greeted by the sumptuous blooms of some tree peonies, including 'L'Espérance' and 'Souvenir de Maxime Cornu'.

On another occasion I stayed a couple of nights at Willbrook, a most comfortable home, though a bit old-fashioned. Nellie, the housemaid, and Norah, the cook, looked after the whole of the house for Lady Moore. I was awakened soon after 7 a.m. with a large jug of hot water which Nellie brought up to me; she pulled back the curtains and let in the sunlight. On rising, what was my surprise but to look down into the garden and see Lady Moore out there picking raspberries for breakfast! She did not waste time, nor was she tolerant of time-wasters. As far as I remember she kept one gardener, and the whole garden was in good order. At the side of the kitchen garden was a broad gravel path and a broad herbaceous border, backed by a wall on which were climbing plants. She did not waste space or opportunities, either! Her love of plants embraced tiny ones like *Veronica teucrium* 'Trehane', whose yellow leaves make so bright a contrast to the vivid blue flowers, *Geranium psilostemon*, bergenias, species of *Eremurus*, and *Aster forrestii* whose orange eyes vie so strongly with the lavender-blue daisies. *Clematis macropetala* was on the wall, and also *Ribes laurifolium*. And in the shade was my first sight of that most beautiful small funkia (as they were then known), *Hosta tokudama* 'Variegata', its blue-green leaves striped with yellowish green. This had been a gift from Lady Burnett of Leys, at Crathes Castle, Kincardineshire, where it originated.

In 1955 Lady Moore took me to Miss Freeman's garden at Cooldrinagh, Leixlip (Laois) — a garden well stocked with herbaceous plants, including a light blue form of *Geranium* × *himalayense* (*G. grandiflorum*) which I have never seen elsewhere. (I was glad to take a plant over with me on my last visit, to re-stock Irish gardens.) There were other lovely visits to Irish gardens, and they prompted me to start collecting the more unusual herbaceous plants, as well as roses. Irish gardens were full of them, to say nothing of Glasnevin.

Lady Moore came to see my garden with Mrs Ruby Fleischmann, an old friend of both of us. Ruby asked for a plant of some interest which I had growing — I forget what it was — and Lady Moore said in a winsome way, "Do you think, Graham, that plant might have a little brother?" This was Lady Moore: keen, kindly and with a good sense of humour. She had a great influence on Irish horticulture, and I bless her memory.

Cutting Thirty-Eight —

The Pergola

This is a term used fairly freely of a garden feature, but one not always fully understood. Strictly speaking a pergola is a pathway more or less enshrouded with pillars connected by trellis work. More often, in practice, it is a series of arches along a walk with connecting members of wood or rope. Sometimes, but rarely, it is a series of metal arches connected in some way overhead. However it is made, it produces a partially shady walk, displaying greenery and flowers.

The pergola has a long history. Old engravings show it surrounding a sunken garden in which would be a parterre. Passing gently along, in the shade, one would get views of the garden between the uprights. It seems that shade was more sought in gardens centuries ago than it is now, when sunshine is almost worshipped and tanned skin is a summer's desire. "Aleys in gardens and covered with Vines and railed up wythe stakis vau[l]t wyse do great pleasure with the shadowe in parchynge heat" is a phrase from William Hormon's *Vulgaris* of 1519. The same pleasure can be detected in the "whole galleries of shady verdure trained on a foundation of wooden treillage". They were commonly planted with Hornbeam or Wych Elm. Shade is not of paramount importance today, except in hot climates, or to make the desirable contrast between light and shadow.

We can visualise the grander sort of pergola, with stone, brick or plaster uprights, being used in Italian gardens, often with a covering of vines. So into the last century or so, and the pergola became a great feature when at last the landscape garden had run its course and a return to formality was allowed.

I remember seeing in a Scottish garden a wooden pergola some fifty feet long, stuck in the middle of a lawn as a feature, not connected with anything and leading to nothing. It is best for a pergola to have a reason, to lead somewhere, or to something such as an arbour or bower or garden ornament. With its covered pathway it can act as a dividing factor between two parts of a garden, or lead from one to another. In short, deep thought should be given to the project, answering several questions which are relevant. What is its reason or, in more ways than one, its direction? Then there comes the question whether it will be, to be effective, too large a feature for the garden concerned. Next comes a practical point: who will ascend steps and ladders to do the pruning and tying annually? Lastly, if the expense of providing masonry uprights is too great or if the garden is too small to allow of so great a feature, can the owner tolerate the thought of having to replace flimsy woodwork in sections every few years, with all the work entailed in unravelling the climbers? In short, look before you leap and weigh up the practical and aesthetic points

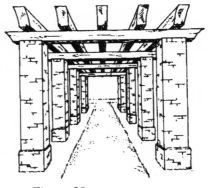

carefully — but these are considerations that should be given to all gardening.

Let us take for granted that a pergola is needed, leads somewhere or to something, and that the garden is big enough to accommodate this large erection. One of the most important points to be settled is the construction

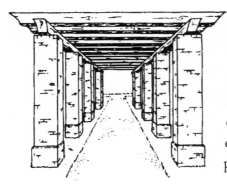

of the overhead members. Sometimes — as for instance at Kew Gardens, in the walk through the Order Beds — the mass of heavy timber overhead is like a railroad reversed, with the sleepers dominant and oppressive. I favour substantial cross-members linking the opposite uprights, and connecting them with lighter members running lengthwise. This gives a much lighter effect.

The most splendid pergolas for large gardens are made of local stone, rough or smooth, or of brick, tiles or a mixture of all three, the section being square or rounded. Sometimes rough stone or flints are covered with plaster. It is usual for the main cross-members to be bevelled and to project clear of the line of uprights, as at Mount Stewart in Northern Ireland. Whatever the materials used for the uprights, it is an aesthetic gain if the crossing members have a slight upward camber; this is a reason for not using straight larch. Sweet Chestnut or Ash, with bark removed and treated with preservative, will be found not only almost everlasting but easier to the eye, and the camber will give added strength. On the other hand, some may prefer the level straightness of a pergola made entirely of larch or sawn timber. Metal is sometimes employed, but is not to be recommended except in very mild districts because metal takes the cold severely and may damage plant growth in bitter weather.

The portion of the pergola below ground is very important. To start with, it is essential that all uprights shall be completely vertical and in line both ways. This may seem an unnecessary proviso, but it is surprising how often attention to this vital point is neglected: the uprights perhaps do not follow an exact line, or timber posts give way and tend to lean. Adequate foundations will obviate masonry failings and adequate depth of insertion will minimise the lean of timber. Removal of bark and either charring — a difficult job with posts of great size — or treating with preservative is recommended. Complete preservative treatment of the whole of the woodwork is to be preferred.

However a pergola is made, it provides more homes for plants and thus pleases the ardent plantsman. But first must be considered the matter of levels. Is the pergola to be seen principally from above — that is, from higher ground — or is it to be enjoyed as a covered walk? Different kinds of plants are appropriate to either construction. If they are to be seen principally from above, the flowers of the climbing plants or shrubs should be produced vertically, whereas the tunnel effect is enhanced by flowers hanging down. The two styles can be seen at Bodnant Gardens in North Wales: the wonderful laburnum tunnel, and the elegant trellis-pillars and connections which one can look onto as well as from the sides or underneath. Here roses are much used, and this brings me to another important point: that of rambler roses, one of the most popular coverings for garden arches of any kind. It is easy enough to train ramblers on the supports, but it should be remembered that when they are in flower, the weight of the flowering shoots will cause the trails to twist from any single rope, pole or beam so that all flowers hang downwards and no longer furnish the members. They behave properly at Bodnant, because each horizontal is a weaving of trellis; an alternative is two ropes or rails kept apart by struts.

Laburnum — of which the best is a hybrid, 'Vossii'— needs uprights of at least 8 feet in height (which will influence the width of the pergola) in order that the racemes shall hang clear of one's head. The same applies to that even more wonderful plant *Wisteria sinensis,* which echoes the yellow grace of the Laburnum in lilac-blue. "Mr Gerald Loder has secured a charming effect at Wakehurst Place, Sussex, by planting wistaria to grow with laburnum, the flower racemes being similar in size and shape, but respectively of the complementary colours, yellow and violet." While Laburnum is a mighty grower and will make high shoots during the summer after pruning, the old short spurs will produce plenty of flower regularly. *Wisteria* behaves in the same way, and it might be thought too rampageous for even a large archway; it makes a mass of trailing shoots of 12 feet or more every season, but by pruning can be kept to any size; witness the fact that plants are often grown as short standards. The pruning on an arch or pergola, wall or fence consists of the removal of all the long trailing shoots when once the plants have been encouraged to cover the space allotted to them, leaving spurs about 3 inches long, which will gradually branch with annual pruning (in September) and build into projecting short shoots covered with flower buds. This all applies to *W. sinensis* and its colour forms — which often produce a second smaller crop in late summer— and *W. venusta*. *Wisteria floribunda macrobotrys,* which used to be called *W. multijuga,* is not so suitable; its racemes are often 3 feet in length and would hang down too low. Besides, though so elegant and long, the racemes are usually past their best nearer to the stem while flowers are yet opening at the end of the trail.

This spur-pruning applies to so many climbers. It certainly applies to vines, which were a traditional pergola plant in Italy. One can savour in thought a sun-drenched archway hung with luscious bunches of grapes at mouth level! Pruning should be done before the sap starts to rise in spring, or bleeding will ensue. For a sizeable, substantial construction vines are almost essential; their large leaves, or those of the Dutchman's Pipe, *Aristolochia macrophylla* (*A. durior, A. sipho*), alone can give a suitably majestic canopy to balance the masonry pillars. Of the ornamental vines, *Vitis vinifera* 'Purpurea', whose leaves turn nearly to the colour of its small black grapes before becoming crimson, makes a good contrast to the fruiting variety 'Black Cluster', whose young shoots are clothed in white down. Both kinds fruit after a warm summer, though they are not really palatable. They and the *Aristolochia* will provide much shade if that is what is required, and are as good to look down upon as to walk under. The counterpart in evergreens to these plants with large leaves is surely the ivy *Hedera colchica* with dark, lemon-scented leaves, and its magnificent variegated form *H. c.* 'Dentata Variegata'.

To return to roses, what are known as "pillar" roses are of no use, and the climbing sports of Hybrid Teas and others tend to display their flowers upright or else, as I have intimated about ramblers, they are apt to slew round awkwardly. The most graceful roses are among the 'Albéric Barbier' class of ramblers, and they do not require the same selective pruning as the ordinary Wichuraiana and Multiflora classes. The stronger Hybrid Musks such as 'Moonlight', 'Pax' and 'Buff Beauty', if on good soil, are highly suitable, and again do not depend for display on excessive pruning.

Species and varieties of *Clematis* are prominent among garden climbers. Fortunately for our purpose there are those that nod their flowers downwards, such as the spring blooming *C. macropetala* and *C. alpina* in a variety of tints, while the large-flowered late summer hybrids mostly look up to heaven unless they are trained on a wall. In between comes the prolific race of *C. montana.* There are times when at the height of its flowering it could be considered the most beautiful (and fragrant) of climbing plants. There is the early white *C. montana* itself, followed by var. *rubens* and other pinks and the late white *C. m. wilsonii.* Their pruning consists only of thinning out the trails *immediately* after flowering; this can be, after some years of neglect, an awesome job, yet never a thankless task: " . . . as a wall plant or a rambler over growing trees or tree stumps it is hard to beat." Another first-class kind in the same genre is *C.* × *vedrariensis* and its pink form. And although they are best cut down almost to the ground every February, I should find a place for those quick, vigorous growers in the Viticella class, 'Abundance' in heather-crimson and the white 'Alba Luxurians'.

An evening walk at the time when the scented honeysuckles are in full flower is a delight. Their fragrance is mostly reserved for the evenings, when moths with a long proboscis can get at the nectar. But most of their flowers are held aloft. The evergreen Japanese Honeysuckle, *Lonicera japonica* 'Halliana', is a "must" on account of the long display into autumn of its lavishly scented cream flowers. In very mild districts fuchsias of the stronger hardy sorts such as 'Riccartonii' would survive the winter and would make a fascinating drooping display.

If your aim is a shady covered way, some vine-relatives cannot be surpassed, including *Parthenocissus henryana* with velvety dark leaves and gorgeous autumn colour. *Ampelopsis chaffanjonii* with bold-fingered leaves and its unique relative *A. megalophylla* with doubly pinnate handsome foliage both also have good autumn colour.

Two evergreens which strike an unusual note are attractive brambles: the large-leafed *Rubus flagelliflorus*, whose leaves are covered with creamy fur beneath, and *R. henryi*, deeply lobed and dark green. They are scarcely prickly.

Hanging its crimson flowers and berries, like red currants, the vigorous twining *Schisandra rubriflora* is a very desirable plant, in display in mid and late summer, likewise the notable and neglected *Schizophragma integrifolia*. This is a climber related to the hydrangeas and the choice is usually given to *Hydrangea petiolaris*, a rampageous grower with a comparatively short flowering period. The *Schizophragma* displays its beautiful cream flowers for nearly three months, and makes a wonderful contrast in September with the trumpet creepers, *Campsis* × *tagliabuana* 'Mme Galen' and the even more resplendant *C. grandiflora*. As these thrust their blooms aloft, they are best appreciated from above; both need to have their spent flowering shoots cut away in the spring. Since the *Campsis* species are usually devoid of lower foliage, it is a good plan to plant on the same pillar *Clematis macropetala* or *C. alpina*. In the same way, clematises of the kinds which need to be cut down every spring are just the things to add later flowers to gaunt spring-flowering shrubs and climbers.

There are many more climbing plants suitable for our purpose, and a number of shrubs as well which can be suitably trained over arches: *Exochorda* 'The Bride', for instance, to produce a shower of snowy white in spring; the graceful pink *Escallonia* × *edinensis* for June; *Cotoneaster* 'Gnom' ('Gnome') for autumn berry; blue shrubby *Ceanothus* hybrids such as 'Delight' and 'Autumnal Blue', which can be successfully trained to conform in warm districts. In fact, most shrubs of short annual growth are adaptable, by pruning early flowerers immediately after flowering, and leaving the late-flowering ones for attention in spring.

The actual method of training all the above plants depends on their mode of growth. Those which twine will need vertical wires (*Wisteria, Schisandra, Aristolochia, Lonicera*), others will need horizontal wires, in order to ascend the uprights.

There is usually something rather unsatisfactory about the base of these uprights: intent upon growing aloft, most climbers tend to become bare below. To add a bit of furnishing at the base in the shape of dwarf shrubs will help the appearance of the whole thing. It may be best to use only one kind of plant in every little bed — presuming that surrounding the beds there will be gravel or paving or grass. Alternatively, it would be possible to have an assortment. Dwarf ground-covering plants would be best, such as, for the sunny side, Catmint, *Helianthemum*, *Liriope muscari*, *Iberis sempervirens*, *Hebe pinguifolia* 'Pagei', *H. rakaiensis*, *Santolina*, *Lavandula angustifolia* ('Hidcote'), and *Salvia officinalis* varieties. For the shady side we might choose *Omphalodes cappadocica*, *Saxifraga* ✕ *urbium* and *S. geum*, *Fuchsia* 'Tom Thumb' and 'Lady Thumb', *Tiarella cordifolia* and *Tellima grandiflora*, *Waldsteinia ternata*, the same two hebes, dwarf varieties of *Euonymus fortunei*, also *Asplenium scolopendrium* and *Polypodium vulgare* (ferns). But these all need careful consideration.

Cutting Thirty-Nine —

Water in the Garden

This is something we all yearn for but which seldom comes with the property. Perhaps it is just as well: running water provided by nature can be at times tempestuous, in spate even ungovernable, and can wash away banks and plants. In any case, a natural stream or pond promotes extra lush growth and weeds of great proportion, doubling the work expended on keeping a normal garden in order. This is looking on the black side of things, and I know of no joy so complete as the sound of a trickling stream threading its way down a slope where calthas, primulas, astilbes, lythrums and other moisture-lovers grow. Beautiful anywhere in the garden, where natural water abounds it provides the perfect setting and brings all into harmony. I have longed for such an asset all my life, but have had to be content with comparatively dry soil and without even an artificial and formal pool. Even so, it is amazing what can be achieved if one takes full advantage of the bit of shade provided by odd trees or shrubs or north-facing bank or wall.

As to the artificial pool, our desires are controlled by the supply of water. The little electric pumps available today can be suited to the volume of water to be recycled, and turned off and on at will. There is one cardinal point to be observed and obeyed, and this is that the siting of an informal pool *must* be in the lowest position in the garden. Anywhere else, the pool must be of formal shape, as it will obviously be an artificial feature, and as such can only be an adjunct to a design which owes its composition to set-square and compasses. In exceptional circumstances and given great skill, an artificial rill can be created, so long as it flows in low ground.

There are many ways, obtrusive or unobtrusive, of introducing water to a scheme. Often employed is the direct approach of a mask set in a wall above the pool, the water descending with a good splash from a jutting pipe. Or a jutting pipe can be employed without the mask; or again the mask can be an animal's head. There are many ready-made examples on the market. If water is provided in the garden, the owner will usually hanker after water-lilies, but it is worth noting that these plants do not benefit from being splashed all day: keep them well away from the falling and rebounding water. Since the dimensions of the pool will need to be considered at the outset of scheming, it is well to stress that any depth less than 2 feet will result in mud being stirred up by the falling water, or by any small fish such as golden carp which feed in the mud. And muddied water is not pleasant to contemplate.

Consideration of a formal pool of any size will involve its surrounds. A stone-paved edge will do away with the risk of heavy rains splashing soil into the water, as, of course, will an edging of dense growing carpeting plants such as *Gunnera magellanica*, saxifrages of the Mossy or London Pride type, very dwarf willows, or *Waldsteinia ternata*; for a larger pool there are good dwarf cotoneasters, but I should not consider junipers or other conifers; they surely demand a drier-seeming place. It is indeed in the best interests of our purpose to keep to the semblance at least of waterside vegetation and to remember this when choosing plants. Plants with narrow rush-like leaves — *Acorus*, grasses and sedges, irises and the like — and nearby shrubs of pretty drooping growth and small leaves, all help. John Keats captured the essence of the desired picture in his lines:

> Then in a wailful choir the small gnats mourn
> Among the river sallows, borne aloft
> Or sinking as the light wind lives or dies.

For it must be remembered, in our choice of plants, that the soil around a formal pool will not be made moist by the presence of the water; only will it be cool immediately *behind* and below the structure.

There is also the question of levels to be considered. Even quite a small pool, when excavated, will result in a considerable bulk of surplus soil. This should be spread away unobtrusively; on no account, near a formal pool, should it be upgraded into a mound, complete with rocks and a Japanese maple or a gnome.

Perhaps the most compelling position for a mask or spout, being the entry of the water, is that often used by Sir Edwin Lutyens, where the pools recede in a half-circle into the walls at the back of the feature and thus allow the mask to be poised over the centre of the pool; the reflections of the watery circles move constantly over the stone apse. This is real artistry and holds the eye for a long spell. It needs the full light of day shining in it — and this brings me to one of the most important points in siting any water entry, apart from a central fountain: for what time of the day is the picture composed? This opens up all sorts of thoughts which will cause much deliberation.

A pool can be the final point in a vista, or it can be the local set-piece of a paved area for chairs. The water should make a sound, whether it be merely one little strand from a spout, a fountain with a spray of several strands, or, the boldest of the lot, a perpendicular jet making a pronounced "plop" as it falls. There are so many possibilities to be considered that in the space of these few paragraphs I can but offer suggestions and avenues of thought. As with all gardening matters and design, proportion is at the foundation of everything; proportion not only in size and style of design, but also of association and planting.

Some of us would use a pool of any type as a heaven-sent opportunity to indulge our yearning to grow a great variety of water-loving plants, not only semi-submerged aquatics like water-lilies and the important lesser plants that keep the water clear and oxygenated, but also "marginal" plants to be grouped round the fringes of the pool, either supported in containers or planted in special recesses made at the time of building. But to whatever the enthusiasms run in plants, it is my belief that *two-thirds* of the water surface should be devoid of plants. We must, in times of temptation by yet another plant, ask ourselves what the water is for. Surely, as a rest and change for the eyes after a garden filled with plants or lawn? To allow the calm water to be over-invaded with leaves of one kind or another seems to me to defeat the whole object.

While writing these notes I have had at the back of my mind the terrible thought that some readers may rush off at once and buy a ready-made plastic pool. As likely as not it will be insufficiently deep for the water to keep clear. Moreover, it will tend to let the water become warm in hot weather — for nobody would site a pool in the shade — with consequent rank overgrowth of water weeds.

In spite of the work involved, in spite of the mess which will occur all round the site, the labour entailed and the time taken, I am sure that a properly constructed concrete pool is the best. Then shall we have that coolness at the base, those shelves and compartments for our marginal plants and varying depths to suit diverse plants, even when considering a formal pool. The strict, architectural pool should, of course, contain only water and a few oxygenating aquatics to keep the water clean — but there are many learned articles and books to be read before spade is placed in the soil for excavation.

Wherever most of the land is comparatively flat, the temptation is to make a formal pool. Don't make it surrounded by lawn grass: on the day when you mow the lawn before visitors arrive, a breeze will be sure to scatter the mowings over the water! Where rocks abound and the ground is hilly, opportunities of all kinds present themselves, but watch your step and study long and hard the probabilities of flood water after storms.

Cutting Forty —

Knots and Parterres

In these days of competition in our gardens we strive hard to have something different from our friends and neighbours. With the welter of forms and varieties and even hybrids among our plants, the actual planting can always be widely different, but in the generally restricted area of our gardens today it is not always easy to hit upon a unique design. After all, there has to be a path to the front door and to the back — perhaps combined with a drive to the garage. Various beds and borders follow.

I have noticed of late years a tendency, coupled with more adventurous cooking, to return to sixteenth- and seventeenth-century plants and ideas, culminating in the growing of herbs for their use, ornamental value and general historic interest, and arranging them in a formal design. For want of a better label these designs are called knots or parterres, however far they may be 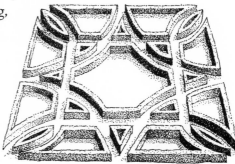 removed from such original historic schemes. Very broadly speaking, these knots may have an intricate design of beds and be filled with spaced shrubs — not with groups of plants, but each one growing isolated and singly. This is because we are harking back to the period when plants were looked upon as interesting individuals, grown for their medicinal, culinary or botanical properties and characters; their use as garden furnishing, except for the outlining of beds and borders or the covering of arbours and bowers, had not yet been embraced. Sometimes these beds and borders, often of intricate design, were edged with stones, timber, tiles, bones or other materials, but as likely as not with neat dwarf plants. It is these that have come into their own again in our search for novelty in design.

Let it be said at once that a dwarf evergreen is the best choice, not only to provide a pattern of enjoyment even in winter, but also as a contrast to the formless planting within the beds, lending coherence to the design. I think no plants can surpass the claim of Dwarf Box for this purpose. To give it its full title, it is *Buxus sempervirens* (which is the common native Box) 'Suffruticosa', and it was known and grown by about 1750 and probably much earlier. In spite of having been vegetatively propagated for all these years, it remains a healthy plant and fulfils our requirements admirably, only needing one clipping per year. This is best done in late May, or immediately the Box has achieved its maximum annual growth.

Other old evergreen garden plants which have been used in the past are Common Thrift (*Armeria maritima*), Common Thyme (*Thymus vulgaris*), Winter Savory (*Satureia montana*) and Shrubby Germander (*Teucrium chamaedrys*). Of these, the Thyme and Savory have great value in the kitchen, the former for mixing with stuffing, the latter excellent for adding piquancy to a green salad. Apart from the Thrift, which is a dwarf clump-forming plant and needs dividing and replanting every year or two, they all benefit from clipping to keep them compact, neat and perhaps 6 to 9 inches high. Other clump-formers of neat array are the blue-grey grass *Festuca glauca* and *Potentilla alba*, but neither of these is evergreen.

As a permanent dwarf hedge to contain all the beds something rather larger is required, and thoughts at once go to a dwarf Lavender, such as that known as 'Munstead' or 'Hidcote', Blue Rue, and *Santolina*, or Lavender Cotton as it is confusingly known, for it has no connection with Lavender. All three should be clipped over severely in spring to keep them compact, and during the summer may reach 1½ feet in height, or rather more. This applies to *Ruta graveolens* 'Jackman's Blue' and *Santolina chamaecy-*

parissus; S. pinnata is taller. It is not generally known that there are two dwarf variants, *Lavandula* 'Nana Alba', a bare 9 inches in flower, and *Santolina chamaecyparissus* 'Nana', only a little taller.

But I have opened the gates to innumerable other dwarf plants in leading you away from the Dwarf Box. The question arises whether the Elizabethans would have used many and varied plants if they had had access to them, and I think there is no doubt that they would. They were avid for variety, splendour, colour and texture in their tapestries, embroideries and vestments. Unless we want to make a period piece of our knots and parterres, I see no reason why we should not draw upon the garden riches available to us for outlining beds and borders. For instance, if we allow the use of Rowland Jackman's selected blue-leafed Rue, we should also consider the undoubted value of certain hebes. I find that they stand clipping well in the spring, thus avoiding the production of the unwanted flowers, which are usually white among hardy kinds. A fairly strong grower, *Hebe rakaiensis*, which used to be known as *H. subalpina*, can be kept to about a foot high and wide and presents throughout the year a most brilliant green, as good as a well-fed lawn in winter. Of a similar size but of cool grey-green is *H. topiaria*, while one extra-bushy, and with rich green small leaves is 'Green Globe'.

Also fairly vigorous, but suitable for little hedges a foot high and wide, are two strongly contrasting plants which are used effectively at Mount Stewart, Northern Ireland, in the great parterre; they are the rich dark coppery purple *Berberis thunbergii* 'Atropurpurea Nana' and *Thuja occidentalis* 'Rheingold'. A more striking contrast could hardly be devised; the *Thuja* is a yellowish green turning to almost orange as the season advances. Still further contrasting is the old original white-variegated form of *Euonymus fortunei*, 'Variegata'. Much more compact than the more modern varieties, this stands clipping well, and is a great success in the Long Garden at Cliveden in Buckinghamshire. For all of these, clip in spring.

If the beds have brick, stone or wood edgings, some of the smaller ivies are useful. Trails can be economically planted alongside edgings and subsequent branches nipped out as they appear. I have seen the small, narrow leafed *Hedera helix* 'Caenwoodiana' successfully used, not exceeding 6 inches in height and width. Small-growing, white-variegated 'Adam' would be equally adaptable, while for a striking bit of dark winter colour there is 'Atropurpurea': dark green for the whole of the summer, with the approach of cold weather the leaves turn to darkest maroon and remain so until the spring. In knot gardens in which the patterns of the edgings interweave and appear to overlap,  some careful thought with some of these contrasts would be very rewarding.

For those gardening on neutral or lime-free soils there is a choice of heathers. The most compact types are those headed by *Erica carnea* (flowers in winter or earliest spring) and *E. cinerea.* The latter will not thrive in limy soil and flowers in August. The pink flowers of *Erica carnea* 'King George' (winter) and 'Vivellii' (dark pink, late spring) are two of the most compact.

A good plant seldom seen is the pretty white-flowered × *Gaulnettya* 'Wisley Pearl'; the flowers are followed by maroon berries. Also for lime-free soil is *Vaccinium vitis-idaea* 'Koralle', a neat little evergreen whose red berries follow the pinky white flowers; clipping over in autumn, after the berries have had their say, would be best.

With this wide choice of little plants before you it is possible for the edgings to provide a lot of interest during the winter period as well as in summer. It is a case of suiting the choice to the season when the plants in the beds are least colourful — which is from autumn to spring, if you are going to fill the beds with old traditional plants. There is no doubt that we are very lucky these days to have an almost limitless choice of plants to turn to, flowering at different times throughout the year. In days of yore the flowering plants finished their display by about the end of June and there was nothing to look forward to until the aconites and snowdrops appeared, except a few berries and fruits.

As to the clipping, it is a chore that can be made easy. Where the paths are of brick or stone it is a simple matter to sweep up the clippings. On the other hand, paths of gravel or grass can make the clearance difficult and a bore, but a sheet of some material laid alongside will collect all the snippings and make disposal easier. And of course, if you don't mind the noise, small power-clippers have revolutionised the initial work; for a large parterre or knot they are essential, but for a miniature knot I should prefer to use ordinary shears — though the finished product is perhaps not quite so smart. Most of the little plants I have mentioned above are easy to strike from cuttings, and thus from an initial expenditure on a dozen or so plants, stock can fairly quickly be multiplied.

To gain the greatest joy from these formal designs they should be viewed from a terrace or upper window. "Knot" stems from the inter-weaving of the little hedges; "parterre" indicates something being laid out on the ground. Now for a parting shot from Sir Francis Bacon: "Knots . . . they be but toys; you may see as good sights many times in tarts."

Cutting Forty-One —

Trees in the Garden

It is a great responsibility to plant a tree, anywhere. A tree will in all probability outlive the planter, who may own the soil where it grows but can scarcely be said to own the tree, a product of the soil and of greater nature. The responsibility is dependent upon what the tree does to the soil, the air and the environment. In my book *Trees in the Landscape*, I endeavoured to assess the value in the countryside of the many British trees, together with a few exotics which we may be said to have "adopted" as natives — sycamore, cedars and some poplars, for instance. From this detailed study emerged the fact that among natives there are very few that are small enough in height and bulk to warrant inclusion in a list of trees that might be used in our gardens, where there is seldom room for a Beech, Elm or Lime. We are thus thrown back onto what are called flowering trees — though all trees flower, of course. These embrace such as the Rowan, Whitebeam and Service trees (all *Sorbus* species) and the Crab Apple (*Malus*).

In the earlier part of this century the popular garden trees were the Almond (*Prunus dulcis* or *P. communis*), the coppery-purplish-leafed *Prunus cerasifera* 'Pissardii', the variously tinted Thorns (*Crataegus laevigata* or *oxyacantha*) and Laburnum. Rather later, in the 1930s and after, the foreign crab apples and Japanese cherries took the British gardening world by storm. Today, partly owing to the depredations of birds, coupled with the coarse suckering roots of the wild cherry upon which the Japanese kinds are grafted, the latter have decreased in popularity. The modern enthusiasm for comparatively small trees has fallen upon species of Rowan and maples from the Far East.

This recital has, of course, not included that first favourite of gardens through the centuries, the Apple. When allowed to grow into a gracious tree, thinned but not pruned, it takes a high place in our affections. "Of all the floral displays of British springtide, there is none more exquisite than an old crab in full flower, standing in a sea of blue hyacinths ... none of us seem to think that the crab-tree is worth anything except as a stock for grafting orchard apples on." Nor have I included that very old favourite in gardens, the Common Holly in its many varieties — but this would open the selection to other evergreens, which I consider elsewhere.

Even these smaller trees, of which there is a bewildering variety available, need the most careful thought in their selection and placing. The district in which I live has good evidence of its wealth of nurseries in the huge selection of shrubs and conifers found in its gardens — a breadth of choice not so apparent in its municipal planting of trees, where the London Plane, in spite of its vast size, gets chosen again and again to grace small shopping precincts and other limited areas. Municipal plantings offer suburban dwellers a wonderful opportunity of seeing what they might choose or avoid in selecting trees for their gardens.

A tree must be considered from several points of view. There are its roots, which are going to affect the soil and possibly invade drains. There are its leaves, which though they may cast desirable shade, may also clog the gutters. There are the branches, which will nearly always develop a greater spread than is envisaged. These are all practical points to be considered; to be balanced against them is the magic of the tree in its youth or old age, and the passage of shadow across the lawn or the benefit of coolth from its powers of breaking the hot sunshine and making suitable spots for shade-loving plants. And it is worth reiterating that there are just as many beautiful plants that thrive in shade as there are those demanding full sun.

Some books and catalogues provide diagrammatic outlines of the mature shapes of trees. There is, to put it mildly, a huge variety in these ultimate shapes, making it a hard, even difficult choice when it comes to selection. There is the height, width and density to be considered, apart from more easily obtainable details of leaf and flower colour, and again autumn colour and fruits. There is also the soil itself to be taken into account, and  every plot is different. Apart from extremes of shapes, such as bolt upright or weeping, there is infinite variety available, to complement or war with your shrubs and plants and house.

Having selected the right sort of tree, one takes on a responsibility towards the tree itself, seeing that it has adequate preparation for its root-run, for instance, and is held firmly by a stake — for no tree will catch hold of the soil if its head is constantly moved by the wind, resulting in the roots moving also. If you have the patience, always plant a youngster of, say, 3 to 5 feet in height: what is known as a "whip" or "feathered" tree. Except in windy sites, such trees will seldom need a stake, whereas a full "standard" tree with a six-foot stem and a developed head above that certainly needs one. Having taken out an adequate hole, perhaps 3 feet wide and half as deep, hammer in your stake, and then place the tree. Material such as old tyres should be used to prevent the bark from rubbing against the stake, and indeed to prevent the ties from cutting into it. But there are good broad ties available which can be adjusted as the tree grows. After the first year or two the girth rapidly expands and the ties will need frequent examination; the same is true of encircling plastic labels, which do not expand but throttle.

The next responsibility is to see that the young branches are not going to be too low when weighed down by the foliage. To avoid big scars from large branches that have to be removed later, it is best to decide early what should come away, so that the scars heal over quickly. If it is a tree that is to be of a formal, erect shape, keep an eye aloft so that unwanted subsidiary leaders can be removed early. For the average garden of today a stem of 7 or 8 feet is usually required. A point often overlooked is that, while any cut should be made quite close to the stem, it is important that the little fold of the bark (between stem and branch) should be left intact: from this the healing bark will most quickly grow.

Trees grown specifically for the beauty of their bark need a fresh paragraph. It is my opinion that they should seldom be trimmed to one stem. Usually, in maturity, the colourful bark for which the tree is chosen will become corky and dark at the base of the trunk. This is particularly noticeable with birch trees. Provided there is room for them, I prefer to leave most erect side shoots on the stem, so that at eye-level there is plenty of colourful bark. The skill in trimming off unwanted shoots is restricted to pruning or even rubbing off small twigs when quite young. If removed at pencil thickness the resulting scar will usually heal over quickly, and this work can be done yearly, in summer, as the tree grows. It is a very satisfying job.

There has always been an unsatisfied demand in nurseries for specimen trees with three or four stems, to grace important positions. There is only one satisfactory way of achieving this, and that is to cut down to ground level an established tree, and then to train up the required number of shoots. If it is a grafted tree, of course, the cutting-down must be to well above the rootstock and an eagle eye kept for suckers coming from below the graft. It is well nigh impossible to plant three or four trees together in order to achieve the same effect; the tree whose roots are lowest will always win, and if the trio is planted wider apart to avoid this disaster, the effect will be lost.

Cutting Forty-Two —

Little Trees

My title begs two questions. The first is "What is a tree?", and the second is "What is meant by 'little'"? A tree is a woody plant or shrub which is capable of making a single stem over 6 feet in height; its eventual height overall may achieve or even exceed a hundred feet. Very few can be described as "little". But there is a need today in our smaller gardens for little trees, and I want to think about how we can find them. In the transience of today, many people are happy to plant a tree or trees which will grow reasonably quickly to achieve this desire — whether it be for height in relation to the garden and shade for coolness in sitting out, or for the purely aesthetic pleasure of watching shadows moving across the garden, or as a practical way of providing cover for shade-loving plants. And although there are few trees that can be called "little" — they all get to the size of an apple tree or more in time — we should not be deterred from planting one even in a very small garden. There is nothing that gives at once such a touch of maturity and scale.

One way out of the difficulty is to select a strong-growing shrub, then train it up with the aid of a stake, removing gradually all lower branches and encouraging it to make a "head" of its own. Suitable species are found among the hybrid cotoneasters of the *C.* × *watereri* breed, such as 'John Waterer' (red berries) or 'Exburiensis' (yellow berries). Even *Pyracantha atalantioides*, the strongest growing species, will thrive on one stem and give good berry amongst its glossy dark leaves. Another possibility is *Berberis valdiviana* and its notable new hybrid 'Goldilocks'. They are both magnificent evergreens with orange-yellow flowers. An alternative with pink berries turning nearly to white is the pretty, feathery *Sorbus vilmoriniana*, but far choicer is *Styrax japonica* in its white- or pink-flowered forms. Some of the pink-flowered species of *Robinia* or False Acacia are of small stature, but the branches are so brittle that they are only suitable for the most wind-protected gardens; my choice would be *R. hispida* 'Macrophylla', which has the most conspicuous flowers. Among the Japanese maples there are many grown for their resplendent autumn colouring; they too can be trained up on one stem, tree-like, but are more often seen as bushes. Some favourites are *Acer palmatum* 'Ozaka Zuki', *A. japonicum* 'Aconitifolium' ('Filicifolium'), and indeed any seedling *Acer palmatum* of vigour and good autumn colour. Other possibilities are *Photinia beauverdiana* and *Poliothyrsis sinensis*, the first for its long-lasting autumn colour and the second for its white flowers in late summer.

There are just a few real trees that are small of stature, or at the least very slow-growing. If you garden on limy, gravelly soil, you might try that most beautiful of flowering crab apples, *Malus ioensis* 'Plena' with blush-pink, violet-scented, double flowers which appear after most other crabs are over. I would put in a special plea for the inclusion of a miniature Linden or Lime tree; it is *Tilia miqueliana*, which has deeply cut leaves and a display of scented cream flowers in late summer. Not only is the leafage delicate, but these flowers cause delighted surprise.

There are also an Ash and a Horse Chestnut which are eligible. The first is *Fraxinus mariesii*, one of the so-called "flowering" species (but of course all trees flower) with feathery white flowers in early summer; the second is *Aesculus chinensis* with tapering spires of white flowers. Both are natives of China and need no special cultivation. Then there is one Thorn, *Crataegus orientalis*, and several species of *Sorbus*. The Thorn has white flowers and noticeable fruits of orange-red, both of good size, nestling amongst pretty, deeply divided greyish leaves.

The flowers of most species of *Sorbus* are creamy white, often with rather an offensive odour, but *S. cashmiriana* has heads of sweetly scented pink flowers followed by marble-sized white fruits in late summer and early autumn, at which time (and especially later, when the leaves have fallen) they make a distinguished display. It is one of the rowans or Mountain Ash group, with pinnate leaves. The other pink-flowered kind of small stature is a hybrid in the other great group of species, the Aria group of Whitebeams, with entire leaves. The hybrid *S.* × *bostii* is a bit variable and the best compact form should be sought. *Sorbus alnifolia* is another Whitebeam of small growth, white flowers and red berries.

There is no doubt that most people looking for a little tree would expect to find it among the conventional groups of *Malus* (crab apples) or even apples themselves, *Prunus* (Flowering Cherry or Plum), *Laburnum* and *Crataegus*. But almost all will in time reach 18 feet or more in height, and many as much in width. I cannot therefore indicate them as "little" trees; though they may be enjoyed as such for 10 or 12 years, the time comes when they have to be reduced, and a reduced or lopped tree never looks the same again. There are two alternatives: to plant a narrow-growing (fastigiate) tree, or to prune to the required dimensions. Though they have their uses in confined spaces, fastigiate trees lack all the points that go to make a tree, grace and arching branches in particular.

There are two kinds of pruning that can be employed to keep a tree in relative scale to a small garden. The first is to prune out very long branches from the inside of the "head" of branches every year. This seldom destroys the lightness of the tree, at least for some years. Eventually the head will get too bushy, but a lot of this depends on how the tree has been treated in the nursery, in infancy. It is a practice in nurseries to shorten the shoots to make them branch into a "good bushy head": sometimes I think this is a mistake, and one should allow the head to develop in a more wayward shape. In these days of plant centres one can never be sure which side of the sapling was to the north or south, but some cultivators assert that it makes a lot of differ-ence after planting in the garden; I have never noticed the matter myself.

If your garden is of a formal nature there is no reason why your crab apples, apples or thorns should not be treated like topiary, and formed by pruning into formal rounded, square or beehive shape — or pyramids, Noah's Ark fashion. I know several gardens where this has been done with great success, particularly with *Malus floribunda* and related kinds. Having achieved a good stem, the secret is to spur-prune in late summer. This removes all the long summer shoots and reveals the display of crab apples. So they remain for the winter, and in spring become a dense mass of blossom. *Malus floribunda* is naturally freely branched and is highly suitable for this treatment, but while the flowers are prolific and charming the fruits are yellow and rather small. A close relative is *M.* × *atrosanguinea* in a richer flower-colour. 'Lemoinei' and 'Profusion', though richly dark-coloured in flower and young foliage, are dull in summer with dark, slightly purplish leaves. I would rather have green-leafed kinds such as 'John Downie', enjoying its white flowers and conspicuous, pointed, scarlet fruits, or darker 'Dartmouth' or bright yellow 'Golden Hornet' There are many others; the most suitable for our purposes are those with thin twigs.

Among the red and pink single-flowered forms of the thorns or May, *Crataegus oxyacantha* (*C. laevigata*) are best for this pruning treatment because they bear usually a heavy crop of berries, thus making them ornamental trees for two seasons. A variegated form, 'Gireoudii', has young foliage of pink turning to white; it responds excellently to close pruning and is usually an object of great interest to those who like variegated trees.

It seems to me a little odd that this creating of formal trees has not become a common practice. After all, it is only bringing to another shape the skill of the fruit tree grower with his summer pruning of pyramids, cordons and espaliers. Crab apples are only descended from wild species of apples, and thorns are only a step removed. In France, in small as well as large gardens, much thought and care is given to tree pruning.

Cherries are not good for close pruning, one reason being that they are propagated by grafting onto the strong-growing Wild Gean. It is an unsatisfactory stock in any case, given to suckers and to heaving up paving or lawn. Most crab apples are grown on vigorous seedling crab; the nurseryman prefers this because he can thereby produce a tree more quickly than if he used a dwarfing understock, as for cordon apples. I have not mentioned the plum tribe because they are also not so responsive to hard pruning, while their summer foliage is not attractive and is subject to aphides.

From what I have written it will be seen that there is a lot to be thought about when choosing "little" trees. I only hope I have not made the whole subject sound too difficult.

Cutting Forty-Three —

Ornamental Herbs

The Bay leaves . . . serve both for pleasure and profit, both for
ornament and use . . . and for physick, yea both for the sicke and
for the sound, both for the living and for the dead; . . . from the
cradle to the grave we have still use for it, we have still need of it.

—John Parkinson, *Paradisi in Sole Paradisus Terrestris* (1629)

In an endeavour to have a garden different from those of the neighbours,
people today are resorting to parterres and herb gardens. There is no doubt
that there is a lot to be said for herbs. They are mostly good perennials
and easy to manage on any well drained soil in a sunny position; they have
a long association with gardens, and an intriguing assembly of scents,
flowers and uses, mainly for the kitchen. But except for a few, they cannot
be said to give an abundance of floral colour, though in general they are
attractive in a subdued way.

I propose to concern myself in these few paragraphs with herbs
which are useful in the kitchen. Not all of us have a garden large enough
to devote a portion of it to a grouping of herbs, however useful, which
do not add very much to the garden display. Fortunately there are several
good cultivars with distinctive foliage and flowers showy enough to warrant their inclusion in the general mixed borders where shrubs, perennials
and bulbs find a home. Take for instance the humble Chives (*Allium
schoenoprasum*); its flowers are normally a dull rosy mauve, but a few years
ago a clone occurred in Holland with heads of clear pink flowers. It is
named 'Forescate', after the town where it originated. For their few weeks

of floral display in June, often repeated in late summer to a certain extent, especially when frequently cut down, they make a pretty patch or edging to any border, achieving about a foot, with abundant bright green tubular leaves. They increase freely at the root but are not invasive and the foliage, cut into tiny pieces, adds piquancy to salads, soups and sandwiches.

I suppose the most common of culinary herbs in gardens is Mint, popular for flavouring new potatoes and salads; its roots, however, are very invasive and difficult to eradicate, invading every plant and taking command of the border. The best way of preventing Mint from becoming a nuisance is to plant it in a reasonably stout polythene bag, having cut off the bottom at about a foot, which results in the Mint forming a non-invasive clump. But there is no need to grow the common mint, which is not overendowed with floral or leafy beauty. There is the grey-green *Mentha longifolia*, which has good flower spikes of cool mauve, though I should not accord it a high place for flavour. Perhaps the most useful *and* ornamental is *M. × rotundifolia* 'Variegata', elegantly marked or particoloured in creamy white. It is well flavoured and a strong grower, though this form does not normally exceed a foot in height. With dark green leaves marked with yellow is *M. × gentilis* 'Variegata'. So here are several mints which with due regard to curtailing their spreading roots can be grown with satisfaction in the mixed border.

There are likewise the variegated thymes and marjorams which are just as useful and flavoursome as the usual green types. I do not find the yellow variegated Thyme quite so reliable a garden plant as the green, but in well drained soil in sun it usually comes through British winters unscathed. The special yellow variegated form, named after its finder 'Bertram Anderson', is not so resistant to wet and cold. As to the lemon-scented hybrids, they are equally susceptible to wintry weather and are best kept on the rock garden. In recent years a very fine Marjoram (*Origanum vulgare*) has been selected, called 'Hopley's' after the originating nursery. It is a fine upstanding plant with good branching flower heads of rosy mauve which protrude from dark bracts. Prior to this cultivar I only grew the yellow-foliage variant ('Aureum'), which is a compact dwarf plant with all the flavour desired.

One of the most useful yellow-leafed plants is 'Allgold' Balm — a form of *Melissa officinalis.* It is a good perennial, able to spread itself true to colour by seed, and delicious for imparting a lemon flavouring to whatever it is brought into contact with. In the fullness of a hot, burning summer its foliage turns pale and often gets scorched, which indicates for it a position where in the hottest part of the day some shade is afforded by a neighboring shrub.

The various forms of Sage, *Salvia officinalis,* are invaluable for mixed border planting. While I would give a sunny spot to the common culinary form, 'English Broad-leaf', I would not raise it from seeds because there is so much variation in leaf and growth. This selected type has good leaves of soft grey-green and does not usually flower. On the other hand, *S. o.* 'Purpurascens' is really showy in its violet flowers over a long summer period. I remember a spectacular display made by a huge mound of this at Graigue Conna, near Bray, County Wicklow in Eire, which had been invaded by the lovely form of *Vinca major* 'Elegantissima' whose foliage is so strikingly marked with cream. The two together provided a long-lasting display of foliage augmented by the flowers of each.

Both these two strong-growing sages are well flavoured, as are the next variants, but these are more suitable for smaller gardens, being much more compact in growth. First there is 'Icterina', whose foliage is prettily marked with pale yellow; it is fairly vigorous, as is 'Aurea', in which the leaves are a uniform yellowish green. I suspect it may be a sport of 'Icterina'. Much slower and more compact is 'Tricolor'; it is a striking little plant whose young foliage is purplish while in later life some leaves are creamy variegated and also reveal pink splashes. It is not an easy plant to place in the garden, being a bit "spotty" in effect, but all three are of good flavour and to be recommended for hot sunny positions — like all the forms. There is a white-flowered form of the common type, but it has not much garden value.

I always give pride of place to *Crambe maritima* — the common Seakale of Britain's sandy shores — when considering glaucous foliage; so did Miss Jekyll. This plant is an ornament in its own right and has no variegated form; on the other hand, some forms which should be sought are those which in spring have young foliage of rich purplish colour; others are pale green. The only trouble about growing this plant in the ornamental garden is that one cannot very well force its delicious stalks, as is customary in a vegetable garden. Even so, I enjoy the big heads of flower buds cooked — unless one is preserving them for floral display, for which they take a high place before the majority of perennials are in flower. They turn into pea-sized pods later, which are not without beauty. There is no doubt that the foliage of Seakale is the most magnificent of all glaucous greens, folded and twisted into a great variety of curves and lobes. Nothing surpasses it, though I know of one keen gardener who threw it all out — calling it a vulgar old cabbage!

In the winter one does not wish to traverse wet lawns and paths, and so I keep a Bay tree by the back door and Rosemary by the side door. Neither is particularly hardy in my garden; a really severe winter will cut them to the ground, but as a rule they will sprout again, especially the Bay; they also appreciate what shelter is available from the house walls. They both creep into these paragraphs by proxy, so to speak: the Bay because it has a yellow-leafed variant, *Laurus nobilis* var. 'Aurea' — and a very handsome thing it is, too, though the ordinary green is a shrub of great quality. Of the Rosemary there is a variegated form, but it is not a plant of much value; I prefer to grow 'Sissinghurst', which I find reasonably hardy and a fairly good blue in flower. The richer blues are usually even less reliably hardy. And so I have Rosemary handy for whenever I am cooking lamb (for which I deem it essential), and Bay for chicken, in winter; I prefer Tarragon with it in summer, but Tarragon is an invasive plant and not to be trusted in the mixed borders; nor can it be called ornamental.

My last two plants are here in their own original forms. So far as I know there are no "grandiflora", variegated, or otherwise extra-ornamental forms of Winter Savory (*Satureia montana*) and Sweet Cicely (*Myrrhis odorata*). While the latter is a good ornamental plant of the Cow Parsley persuasion, producing its flat heads of tiny cream flowers soon after the daffodils fade, its feathery elegant leaves making a fine tump for many weeks afterwards, when they come in nicely for giving a mellow flavour to stewed rhubarb, it is not until the end of the summer, sometimes as late as the end of September, that the Winter Savory produces its small pale lilac-white, thyme-like flowers over the twiggy little bushes. Through the winter its evergreen leaves are invaluable, specially with fish and mixed salads.

Nearly all these plants have to be cut or bruised to give out their odour or flavour, though on a hot day Rosemary will be detectable. But nothing compares in this way with the Sweet Briar (*Rosa eglanteria*) on a warm day after a shower. None of the hybrids and forms of this lovely species is as good as the wild species, which with its display of flowers and later glittering heps takes a high place among dual purpose shrubs for ornament, though not for culinary purposes as a rule.

Cutting Forty-Four —

Weeping Trees

If any kind of tree has a special association with one kind of gardening, it is surely the Weeping Willow beside water. There is the echo in our minds of "by the waters of Babylon we sat down", coupled with the fact that the best-known Weeping Willow used to be called *Salix babylonica* 'Ramulis Aureis'. The mind is also at work in achieving the utmost contrast between the flat expanse of water and the vertically falling twigs and branches. It is no wonder, then, that the making of even a small pool seems to engender a yearning for a small weeping willow to grace it. But there is not a *small*-growing weeping willow. *Salix* ✕ *chrysocoma* ('Ramulis Aureis') is an immense tree and cannot be kept to a small size by pruning. The only substitutes among willows are *S. purpurea* 'Pendula', which makes an untidy and scarcely weeping head of interlacing branches, and *S. caprea*, which has given us a definitely weeping form of elegant drooping habit when grafted onto a tall stem, but has rather coarse dark green leaves all summer and no autumn colour. It *is* a comparatively small-growing Weeping Willow, but be sure you get the male cultivar 'Kilmarnock', which has large bright yellow catkins before the leaves appear in spring; the less attractive female variant is known as *S. c.* 'Pendula'. The matter is fraught with confusion because both selections have at some time been known as the Kilmarnock Willow.

It might be worthwhile to consider in turn some of the largest of weeping trees; nothing can compete with the Beech, *Fagus sylvatica* 'Pendula'. There are some immense specimens about, which are all of the green kind; the Copper Beech has also produced a weeping sport but it is a much smaller tree.

This is the place, I think, to call attention to the different methods of propagation which nurserymen adopt. Layering, which may well be practised with the green form, results in a natural shape when the layer is trained more or less erect as a young tree; grafting on top of a tall straight stem results in an umbrella-like head artificially balanced on a pole. Because the copper variety of Beech is much less vigorous than the green, it is usually top-grafted, and so also are most other weeping trees. We have to put up with this incongruousness in nearly every purchase. One only has to go to Stourhead in Wiltshire to see revealed the extra grace achieved by a Weeping Ash grafted lower down, about three feet above the ground. The Ash, *Fraxinus excelsior* 'Pendula', is a tree of great character, particularly in winter when its thick, stiff branches create a bold silhouette. It was a favourite tree in Victorian and Edwardian gardens, frequently used to make a bower, out of the sun. So also was the weeping form of the Wych Elm, *Ulmus glabra* 'Horizontalis' ('Pendula'), whose branches grow up and outwards with great verve and majesty. Owing to the Dutch Elm disease we never see them in British gardens today, though the more drooping 'Camperdownii' is still occasionally to be seen in city parks where the disease was not so prevalent.

We have, however, two noted trees to consider before the more popular flowering and fruiting trees, namely the weeping forms of the Japanese Pagoda Tree and the White Mulberry. The former, *Sophora japonica* 'Pendula', will make quite a large tree in time but is slow growing, and noted for its decisive line, dark green twigs and pretty pinnate leaves. I have never seen it in flower, like the species, which is sad. The *Sophora* fortunately lifts itself up by means of occasional more erect shoots and so avoids the "umbrella" outline, but as a rule the Mulberry, *Morus alba* 'Pendula', needs some help, as do others of this fraternity. It is, after all, rather boring to have a formal, umbrella-like shape in a tree planted in what is usually an informal scheme. The weakness can be easily adjusted by tying a cane to the stem, projecting upwards, and securing to it a pliable central twig. This will usually result in an extra flow of sap and the making of a new, more lofty "umbrella", and may be repeated again and again. It will help in achieving the objective if a few lower branches are pruned away, out of the immediate head — the lesser spokes, so to speak, of the umbrella. A tree whose natural bent is to grow downwards will benefit from these attentions. And, I may add, this underpruning and thinning of branches is in no tree more desirable than in *Pyrus salicifolia* 'Pendula', the popular so-called Weeping Silver Pear. An unattended tree will soon form an untidy mass of branches growing in every direction, but making on the whole a drooping outline. Contrast this with one that has been thinned from underneath the crown and it will soon be evident what is needed. The pruning is a sort of spur, making the tree grow upwards as well as downwards. A half-day annually spent in thinning is well worthwhile, and the result is a thing of great beauty from spring, in its white dress, until autumn.

There is a Laburnum of drooping growth, accentuated by its hanging yellow racemes — *Laburnum alpinum* 'Pendulum'. It can be very characterful leaning out over water, perhaps next to a standard *Wisteria*. This brings me to another point: all these weeping trees should have a level standing-ground, whether of water, lawn or paving. If there are other shrubs and plants beneath them they lose much of their inherent beauty, except perhaps that strange Apple 'Eva Rathke', whose stout branches project stiffly and almost horizontally and bear good apple-flowers, foliage and fruit.

We now come to several popular members of the Rose family, *Malus* and *Prunus*. I think there is nothing that speaks to us so delicately of spring as the dainty, gracefully weeping branched head of *Prunus subhirtella* 'Pendula', every twig set with many small single pink flowers, almost scintillating in the gentle sunshine, for it flowers early before the leaves appear. A form 'Rubra' has darker flowers, but it is no more attractive.

There is a notable weeping form of *Prunus* × *yedoensis* 'Shidare Yoshino', with stiffly pendent branches; here is a tree that needs a helping hand with secateurs and ties. The single pearly pink flowers have a delicious scent.

One of the most spectacular and luxurious of weeping cherries is 'Cheal's Weeping', often labelled 'Kiku Shidare Sakura'. It is a graceful tree with wide-arching branches, strung with bunches of large double pink flowers, and later some autumn colour. In common with others of these weeping trees it is grafted high upon a stem, but does not develop a uniform umbrella-head. It is one on which the stem may suddenly throw a vertical branch of the single, common Gean; these should be removed immediately. While many of the big double Japanese cherries droop with age, there is one that is especially what we are looking for, weeping under the weight of its white, pink-tinted, frothy blossom with so much abandon that its branches soon begin to touch the ground. It used to be called 'Oku Miyako', now 'Shimidzuzakura', and is of great beauty though not so definitely a weeper as the others I have mentioned.

When cherries take the lead, can crab apples be far behind? I am going to single out just two of great excellence. Both have green leaves and pretty pinky-white scented blossom. *Malus* 'Excellenz Thiel' is a small grower suitable for confined spaces and is possibly the smallest weeper we have so far noticed. The dark twigs make a good contrast to the blossom. The much larger, wide and graceful 'Red Jade' supplements its spring display with a wonderful autumn array of scarlet fruits, a-dangle all over the tree until winter comes, and even then lasting a while.

Lastly there are two quite small weepers, *Caragana arborescens* 'Pendula' and its close relative 'Walker'; they have small dainty foliage — particularly laciniate in the second variety. I have seen both, grafted on short stems, making dainty little trees — which brings us back to our first paragraph: here is the prettiest small weeper for that small pool. I have not included *Cotoneaster* 'Hybridus Pendulus'. It is a true weeping plant which is evergreen and berries well, but the berries turn black with early frosts and unfortunately stay on the plants in their disfigurement.

In our thirst for colour from flower and fruit we must not forget that in this instance it is the line of the falling twigs that is of the greatest importance in our gardens, regardless of seasonal bonuses.

There are good weeping evergreens among hollies and conifers, including the Weeping Blue Cedar, but they must wait for another Cutting, as also must the great weeping Larch, which has been known for more than 150 years but is seldom seen.

Cutting Forty-Five —
The Exclamation Mark

The vertical line is an indispensable extra when it comes to calling attention to something, in gardening or in writing, but in either occupation it should be used only sparingly. We can call to mind that gentle placid scene of water and partly submerged bridge at Blenheim Palace in Oxfordshire, so dramatically contrasted by a group of Lombardy poplars; or the no less placid lake at Bowood in Wiltshire, which also has its poplars. These are of course majestic conceptions, comparable to some of our greatest gardens where the columnar Redwood (*Sequoia sempervirens*) provides the vertical line. I should make it clear at the outset that I am only intending to write  about plants of columnar, not conical, outline; the former are the more rare when one calls to mind the shapes of most conifers.

In Britain in the period between the two world wars, an organisation known as the Roads Beautifying Association advised the Ministry of Transport on roadside planting. Their exotic notions did not please everyone, but they did hit upon one excellent idea, which was to mark side-turnings off the new bypasses with a pair of Lombardy poplars to catch the eye and prepare the driver for a turning long before a signpost came into view. Unfortunately, owing to road-widening and other alterations, frequently only one Poplar remains today. It is worth mentioning here that there are several different types of fastigiate poplars which are usually called Lombardy. On heavy clay or chalky land unhealthy root-action may result in fungal attacks which cause them to grow thin and unattractive. They thrive on most normal soils, but where there is a chance of their not thriving it would be better to plant the fastigiate Oak, *Quercus robur* var. 'Fastigiata'. Here again, one needs to be sure of the genuine article, for when they are raised from seed, some variation is often apparent. An excellent narrow specimen can be seen at the Royal Horticultural Society's Garden at Wisley in Surrey, by the small pond; it is easily mistaken for a Lombardy Poplar. The fastigiate Oak is much slower in growth than the Poplar, but also much longer-lived. They are both immense trees, and only suitable for consideration in the greater landscapes.

There are several other large deciduous trees which have fastigiate cultivars. Foremost is the Dawyck Beech, *Fagus sylvatica* 'Dawyck', a splendid slender tree whose shoots grow aloft sinuously, like smoke from a bonfire or a tree from the brush of Van Gogh. For those wanting a colour other than green there are 'Dawyck Gold' and 'Dawyck Purple', but these are very slow growing.

Turning now to rather smaller trees, there is the *Robinia* 'Fastigiata'; I am not recommending it wholeheartedly because it has to be grafted upon seedlings of its type species, *Robinia pseudacacia,* and these have a horrid habit of suckering. Even so, it is a very appealing, feathery, narrow tree. There are two excellent maples, *Acer platanoides* 'Columnare' and *A. rubrum* 'Scanlon', both of which excel in autumn colour and are thoroughly attractive.

In this sort of size one would call to mind that little known, seldom planted Poplar, *Populus simonii* 'Fastigiata'. This is a most pleasing tree of moderate growth with attractive feathery outline and shining obovate leaves. The type species is said to be subject to canker, but this is less likely to be a trouble on well drained normal soils. There is no doubt that the fastigiate form of the Tulip Tree, *Liriodendron tulipifera* 'Fastigiata', can make a good columnar tree, but in my mind's eye I can see so many superb specimens of normal growth — it can be one of the most glorious of all trees hardy in the British Isles — that I do not think I could find room for its narrow form, in which the great leaves are squashed together instead of being displayed.

In our smaller gardens of today there is much to be said for trees of narrow outline, though we must remember that with this reduction of spread all the luxuriant umbrageousness of a tree is lost. It becomes a mere column of greenery, and casts little in the way of enchanting shadow. However, narrow trees have many uses. Perhaps a building falls away, so to speak, at the end or side: a vertical line will help to give it balance. Or perhaps we need a pair of sentinels to grace our entrance gate, or to frame a view. Sometimes a columnar tree is needed just to create a contrast to the general rounded shapes of garden trees and shrubs; wherever they are they make a formal statement.

There is nothing we can do which will have a greater effect of lengthening a formal vista than to provide an avenue of slender columns. Repetition of the same vertical line at regular intervals can give an appearance of even greater length: a progression of sentinels is a means of calling attention to the walk we have to make to get to the end. I suppose no other plant has been used to bring this about in gardens so frequently as the Irish Yew (*Taxus baccata* 'Fastigiata'). It originated in Ireland towards the end of the eighteenth century and is a robust female plant displaying its crimson fruits to advantage. Narrow while young, it gradually becomes broad with age, though still of vertical growth. Fortunately, like all yews, it withstands severe clipping and thinning to keep it in shape; its very dark green is a contrast to almost anything else, and there is a beautiful golden form. Yews thrive on any soil except those that are water-logged.

Two other deciduous trees need a thought; one is *Koelreuteria paniculata* 'Fastigiata' and the other *Prunus* 'Amanogawa'. The latter, one of the Japanese cherries allied to *Prunus serrulata,* is charming while young, especially in blossom or autumn colour, but develops into a coarse and shapeless tree with age. The other, the *Koelreuteria,* is very slow-growing, narrow and neat; it is lovely in its spring or autumn tints, or when blessed with its airy heads of small yellow flowers at that nadir of the year for ornamental trees, the month of August.

While in Britain a yew of any kind will blend with all aspects of our gardens or countryside, I should be chary of introducing columnar or conical cypresses in open country districts. Such trees seem to me to need neighbouring buildings and built-up areas to be able to enter into garden design; there is much of an Italianate feeling among them. However, they provide a few narrowly columnar forms for use where they would be suitable, and foremost I would class *Juniperus scopulorum* 'Skyrocket', a slim grey-green tapering line, and *Thuja occidentalis* 'Malonyana', which unlike the parent-species remains a good green in winter. Neither of these is of overpowering size, whereas the so-called Incense Cedar (not remotely like a Cedar), *Calocedrus* (*Libocedrus*) *decurrens*, is of majestic size, a great dark green column. A splendid group is growing fast at the bottom of the Trials Field at Wisley; mature specimens contrast with the arching grace of *Parrotia* at Westonbirt in Gloucestershire, that great arboretum of such infinite variety.

Now let me call attention to two less generally accepted columns. There is, first, a very narrow-growing holly — not *Ilex aquifolium* 'Pyramidalis', which gets wide and ugly with age, but *I. a.* 'Green Pillar'. This is a slender, berrying female shrub or tree which makes a welcome change from the usual conifer and, like all hollies, is amenable to shaping by knife or secateurs. It would blend with the British countryside as well as the Irish Yew and will thrive on most normal soils.

The other offering I have to make is the use of vines trained up poles. This use of climbing plants — because I use the term "vine" very widely — is unaccountably neglected in our gardens. When once a climber has been trained up a tall pole, it can hang down very narrowly if a lax grower such as *Parthenocissus quinquefolia* or *P. henryana* be chosen. Alternatively, the true vines will make thrusting annual shoots and give quite a different outline. The common ivy and its varieties, *Hedera helix*, would be good evergreens for a few years but would tend to develop bunchy flowering shoots at the top which, though of great beauty in themselves in green or variegated varieties, would tend to spoil the achievement of a formal column. For such a purpose it is wisest, for long life, to use poles treated with a preservative.

But perhaps we should come down to earth, so to speak, and consider what might be used in our own small gardens. I can think of nothing better than *Juniperus communis* 'Hibernica', the Irish Juniper. (Strange how this and the best columnar Yew both come from Ireland!) It will ascend to some 6 feet or so but gets filled with dead, sharp needles and needs a good combing or shaking every few years. It thrives on acid or limy soil. Much smaller is *J. c.* var. *suecica*, and smaller still *J. c.* 'Compressa', but these are real miniatures for the least of companions, even on rock gardens and troughs. These lesser exclamation marks have been echoed in recent times by chance seedlings of *Berberis thunbergii* (for lime-free soils): 'Erecta' (green), 'Red Pillar' and 'Red Sentry' (of coppery tone). They bring some new ammunition to our armoury for small gardens and a close to these notes, which have ranged, as is my usual wont, from the great to the small.

Gertrude Jekyll. From F. Jekyll, *Gertrude Jekyll*, 1934.

Cutting Forty-Six —
Gertrude Jekyll

While studying the craft and science of horticulture in my early days in the late 1920s, I had also been captivated by the art. A friend lent me Gertrude Jekyll's *Colour Schemes for the Flower Garden* which fired my enthusiasm for graded colours in the herbaceous borders.

On coming to work in Chobham, near Woking in Surrey, in June 1931, I lost little time before I managed to get permission to visit her renowned garden. And so, on a warm Saturday afternoon, September 6th, I cycled all the way through Guildford and Godalming to Munstead. There was only a hand gate to her modest and charming home amongst the trees on the sandy rising ground. She received me sitting placidly in a chair, welcomed me and told me to walk around the garden, pick a piece of anything I wished to talk about and come back to the house for tea. My notebook reminds me of graceful bushes of *Leucothoë axillaris* (*L. fontanesiana*) and huge hummocks of *Gaultheria shallon*, with neither of which I was familiar, and a carpet of *Cornus canadensis* just coming into berry. Having been brought up in limy Cambridge I particularly remember these, and huge banks of azaleas and rhododendrons, kept well apart.

But it was the colour borders which enthralled me. I had never seen anything like them before, although I was a little prepared, in my imagination, by her writings. Since it was rather late in the summer, they were probably past their best, but a succession of colour was kept going by the expedient of putting in late-flowering plants grown in pots to prolong the season. The main flower border was a grand size, some 200 feet long by

14 feet wide, though reduced somewhat for planting by the shrubs at the back against the stone wall. Some of the shrubs augmented the colour scheming; others provided interest earlier in the year, for this big border was developed mainly to give colour through July until late September. I saw the Michaelmas daisy border, that took over after the main border, and those leading to the Hut where she pursued her crafts. What was so remarkable about the colourings in the main border — from cool to strong — and to cool again at the far end — was the solidity of the whole, bolstered by the shrubs and great clumps of *Yucca recurvifolia* and *Bergenia cordifolia* 'Purpurea'. I have not forgotten the wafts of scent from *Lilium auratum* and also the delicate pink *L. krameri* (*L. japonicum*) and *L. longiflorum*. Golden Privet, African marigolds, silvery *Senecio* and *Santolina* were all there contributing their bit, likewise cannas and dahlias. At the back was a group of the dignified *Helianthus orgyalis* (*H. salicifolius*) not yet in flower; it looked like some burgeoning lily. This I took indoors to ask about.

The much narrower pair of borders along the path leading to the Hut were about at their best. The gorgeous red, yellow and orange tones "hit" one and caused the eye to fly along them, coming to rest where the path was cleverly deflected to the left between hedge buttresses, the more easily to take in the striking change to silvery grey foliage and cool colours, contrasted by the sober dark green of fig, and bright blue of *Delphinium* 'Blue Fairy'. Another plant I picked to discuss with Miss Jekyll was the comparatively rare *Ophiopogon jaburan*, which I learned was pot grown and plunged in position where an annual plant had spent itself.

Then there were cool, damp positions graced by the new lemon-yellow *Primula florindae* and contrasting blue trumpets of *Gentiana asclepiadea*. And, of course, a combination of frailty with firmness, a froth of *Aster corymbosus* (*A. divaricatus*) draping over *Bergenia* leaves, a little feature I have often repeated. In those days hostas were practically unknown in gardens; at Munstead Wood one came across them grouped with ferns also standing in pots by one of the water tanks.

And so, in to tea. Miss Jekyll was still seated in the same chair, looking very like the portrait by William Nicholson, painted eleven years previously, her hair neatly parted in the middle. We examined my few specimens and I think she was rather surprised at how few there were. But though her garden was fully stocked it was at the time of summer flowers, well-tried plants, not rarities. In fact I had brought with me a few photographs, in monochrome, including that of *Lilium cernuum* and *L. alexandrae* (*L. nobilissimum*) which I had in my garden at Cambridge, and I felt she did not take much interest in them! But in after years I realised not only that her sight was poor — through those tiny spectacles — but that her interest was in plants that made *effect* in gardens, not botanical rarities. She had after all been making her garden pictures for forty years, and had assessed and assimilated all the salient points and uses of every plant she grew.

Our tea was brought and we had it on occasional tables near the sunny windows; thin white bread-and-butter and a preserve (I do not remember what) and some little cakes. Her mellow voice floated on through the words of wisdom she imparted about my samples, and I came away deeply moved by all I had seen and heard. It was a pleasurable visit, long anticipated, and a lucky one for me, because she died in 1932. William Robinson, her famous gardening contemporary, went to her funeral. We all have profited almost unbelievably from their examples and written words; most of what we do in our gardens today stems from their ideas.

Rose 'Nymphenburg' (top), *Rosa moyesii* (top right), Rose 'Penelope' (left), *Rosa filipes* 'Kiftsgate' (lower right), *Rosa rugosa* (bottom left), Rose 'Ormiston Roy' (bottom)

THE
FALL of
THE LEAVES

The birds that sing on autumn eves
Among the golden tinted leaves,
Are but the few that true remain
Of budding May's rejoicing train.
Like autumn flowers that brave the frost,
And make their show when hope is lost,
These 'mong the fruits and mellow scent
Mourn not the high-sunned summer spent.

— Robert Bridges, *Shorter Poems*

Cutting Forty-Seven —

Only Privet, but . . .

It is perhaps not generally realised that we malign a pair of good shrubs when we speak of "common privet". Correctly, Common Privet refers to a very respectable native of the chalk and limestone hills of Britain. It is evergreen in all but starved conditions, and after its summer display of tiny white flowers in spikes, it produces in autumn heads of shining coal-black berries which are ideal for picking with the pink fruits of the Spindle Tree and with wreaths of fluffy Travellers' Joy or Old Man's Beard, the wild *Clematis.* Such a bunch will rival in beauty anything bought from a florist. Years ago, when I was manager of a large wholesale nursery, this native Common Privet, *Ligustrum vulgare,* was still offered for sale by the hundred, but the Oval-leaf Privet, *Ligustrum ovalifolium,* introduced from Japan late in the last century, was offered by the thousand — indeed, it was not unusual to receive orders for many thousands at a time. It had superseded the Common Privet and was being planted almost by the mile for hedges around housing estates — so much so that, from being planted in untoward conditions and frequently neglected, it is often starved, in poor health, suffering from draughts, drains and tree roots, and is now in its turn called "common privet". Privet, indeed, has become an opprobrious term, tainting our appreciation of all the species in the genus.

While *Ligustrum vulgare* is not a first-class hedging shrub, *L. ovalifolium* is, and a well-groomed hedge of it used to be looked upon with envy by myself at a time when the parental hedge was of the true Common Privet. Used as hedges, of course, neither of the species produces flowers; but there was no comparison between the two when clipped, the Oval-leaf making a uniform light green hedge. The only snag is that Privet requires trimming twice during the growing season, at the end of May or early June, and again in September. Since these notes have started off with hedging, it may be as well to recall that both species make a mass of roots which spread into borders; such greed makes them unsuitable as a background to flowers — but of course, without this voracious feeding habit the Oval-leaf species would not be the success it is, in any position or soil up and down the British Isles.

It is unfortunate, to say the least, that privets should suffer from this opprobrium, because there are some superlative shrubs among the several species that have come to us since the end of the eighteenth century, when *Ligustrum lucidum* first reached our shores from China. On first sight, anything less like the hedging shrubs could hardly be imagined. In the south of England, at Kew and Wisley, Battersea Park and elsewhere, are magnificent shrubs or open-growing small trees, attaining some 30 feet or more, clothed with large lilac-like evergreen foliage and, according to the warmth of the summer, crowned with cream flower-spikes for several weeks from August to October. There is no doubt that this is one of the finest late-flowering shrubs or small trees for large gardens, parks and street planting, only outclassed by its two variegated forms, 'Excelsum Superbum', strongly marked with yellow, and 'Tricolor', striped and tinted with silvery grey, cream and pink.

Much more compact is another species from the Far East, *L. japonicum*. In spite of its having been brought to our gardens as long ago as 1845, it is seldom seen. This failure to take it to our gardener's heart is another example of the inhibiting stigma of "privet", for it is a magnificent dense-growing shrub with shiny dark lilac-like leaves, almost completely covered by its heads of white flowers in August. In actual flower-production it is perhaps outshone by *L. sinense*, introduced a few years later and appreciated only by the few, such as E. A. Bowles. It resembles *L. ovalifolium* in general but is much more spectacular in flower and has a wintry crop of dull black berries.

But my pride and joy of all the privets is *L. quihoui*, another Chinese species, known and grown since about 1860. Of them all this is at once the most spectacular in flower and the most worthy of our best gardens. My own plant is some 10 feet high and wide and annually gives me the utmost satisfaction in late summer, being a complete smother of airy spikes of tiny cream flowers, resembling some of the smaller-flowered lilacs (to which genus these species are closely related). Apart from the noble eucryphias and varieties of *Hibiscus syriacus*, no shrub can hold a candle to it in August. Visitors always gasp and exclaim and ask what it is. The tiny dull maroon berries are of little consequence, so the faded spikes are best removed in late autumn.

It is time to write something about fragrance. The Oval-leaf Privet has a rather stuffy smell which many object to, but these greater species are more refreshing. *Ligustrum quihoui* floods the garden with fragrance, and if it *is* a bit heavy we must bear in mind that the summer will soon be gone and no scented shrubs will open their blooms until autumn.

Going back to the hedging privets, we cannot pass by without noting the well-known Golden Privet, *L. ovalifolium* 'Aureum', striped with bright yellow and a great sight when covered with its creamy white flowers. In addition there is the white variegated 'Argenteum', a symphony of cool tints of green, grey and cream; when in flower in a partly shaded spot it can enthuse the most phlegmatic mortal. Supposedly a hybrid between this species and *L. vulgare*, the very vigorous 'Vicaryi' originated at Aldenham, Hertfordshire, in 1920. It is unique in being flushed with yellow all over, and at its best in full sun.

There are other highly ornamental tall-growing species, such as *L. compactum* and *L. chenaultii*. Both may be expected to achieve 12 feet or more. The handsome panicles of creamy flowers are followed by bunches of maroon berries. Brought from China in 1890, *L. delavayanum* has a dense growth and tiny dark, box-like leaves — so much so that I have been amused to see it trained into round-headed standards and sold as Box topiary. Apart from this intelligent use — because Box is much slower in growth — this little Privet has not much to recommend it.

There is no doubt that if we could once get rid of the commonplace tag of "privet", these shrubs would be more planted. They are so thrifty and anxious to please. It is a strange but noteworthy fact that many shrubs which we have to think of for late summer display have white or creamy flowers; nearly all the richer-coloured flowering shrubs open their blooms earlier in the year. Even so, I should not want to be without eucryphias, stuartias, elaeagnuses and osmanthuses, *Clethra tomentosa,* iteas, clerodendrons — and, of course, *Ligustrum quihoui,* standing in quality above most of them.

Cutting Forty-Eight —

Climbers in Trees

The ardent tree lover and planter will be likely to scorn the next paragraphs. The very thought of obscuring trunks and confusing the growth of upper branches with wayward trails of climbing plants fills him or her with horror — although tree planters are not asked to do anything of the sort: a tree has to be a minimum of twenty years old (according to the vigour of the specimen) before it is a suitable support for a climbing plant. Moreover it may be asked, Why should we want to plant climbers in trees? There are several answers to this question.

I think first we should call to mind the needs of a climbing plant. There is no doubt that, long ages before there were arches, pergolas, walls and the like, the only means that a climber had of reaching up into the sunlight and thus flowering and setting seeds was by means of a tree trunk, or a stone cliff. For the former support the climber had to overcome the competition of the tree's roots and contend successfully with shade in its young life. Thereafter, as it reached up into the sunlight everything was right for the climber: coolness at the root, abundant humus, and support for its weak branches. This is something we might all bear in mind when planting a rose in a windswept position in soil exposed to all sunshine: it is likely that all climbing roses would be better placed where their roots are in the shade. We have one British native rose, *R. arvensis*, the Musk Rose of Spencer and Shakespeare, which is usually found in bosky places. In fact, there is no doubt that this Synstylae group of roses, mainly natives of the Far East, are all much at home in places where their roots are in the cool, and this group is the cornerstone, so to speak, of the many Rambler roses in our gardens: hence the natural need of Rambler roses for some shade, at least at the root. The same rule must apply to all climbing plants, whether they are of the type that simply sprawl their branches through higher supports or those that swarm up the host's trunk to reach the sunlight.

Now we might ask ourselves why we want climbing plants to grow through our trees. It depends on the trees. If they are gaunt, bare stemmed, and of no great intrinsic importance but merely act as a screen against undesirable objects in the landscape, or perhaps as a windbreak, I consider they are suitable subjects for embellishment by means of climbing plants. In our smaller gardens of today we need to make use of all available space and opportunity to find homes for the plants we love, covet or acquire.

We have, of course, to suit the climber to the tree. In the rich soil *and cool exposure* at Kiftsgate Court in Gloucestershire, the rose named after the garden has a basal trunk of a foot or two and measuring several feet in diameter; the branches spread to about a hundred feet and ascend into a Copper Beech to about 40 feet. The weight of the rose branches has caused the Beech to give way and break in places. This is an exceptional example, but it does highlight the necessity of choosing suitable companions. The combination of this white-flowered rose with a wonderful fragrance reaching through the dark coppery purple of the Beech in July is worth a long journey to see.

Rambler roses are ideal for our purpose because they hang out of the tree branches, displaying their beauty to the utmost advantage. They need help in their young stages, getting their branches into position by means of a forked pole; their prickles will help to keep them in place. This is so different from the honeysuckles, which will rush up into the sunlight and stay there, out of sight. Wisterias are great and vigorous climbers which have the advantage of hanging their long trails down towards the admirer, but like the honeysuckles they need the initial support of wire or rope to get their trails aloft.

If it is the trunk of the tree which it is desired to embellish, and without going to the trouble of wiring it, then we need self-clinging climbers such as ivy and the climbing *Hydrangea petiolaris.* I have seen bold tree trunks of 40 feet in height enveloped in this plant's branches and covered with its corymbs of white flowers. It seems to flower quite well in shade, but is more showy in fair exposure. I wish its close relative, *Schizophragma integrifolia,* could be relied upon to climb a tree trunk; it needs a deal of help. Its flowers last in beauty in shade for over two months, whereas a fortnight is about the maximum period of the *Hydrangea.* As to the ivies, they do no harm to an old tree trunk; but only variegated varieties will show up in the shade, and I am not sure that variegation is the right touch for this sort of planting. In any case white (usually called "silver") variegation is the best for shade; yellow ("golden") variegation will succeed, but yellow-flushed, such as 'Buttercup', will remain plain green without sunlight. Such dictatorial plants can, however, be persuaded to give of their best in a varied planting with varied aspects of light filtering through the branches. Both the *Hydrangea* and the ivies will in time grow outwards to display their flowering branches, to a width of perhaps a three-foot radius from the trunk. In the fullness of time such growths combined with the tree branches can become a hazard whenever there are gales. There is never one easy answer to problems in gardening. As John Clare wrote,

> Dark creeping Ivy, with thy Berries brown
> That fondly twists on ruins all thine own . . .

There are many lovely climbing plants for embellishing trees. One of the most popular is *Clematis montana* and its pink varieties; they flower in late spring or early summer and, when once established aloft by means of their clinging leaf-stalks, may be left to their own devices, hanging in festoons out of every stout branch. Much later in the year, in early autumn, the yellow-flowered species headed by *C. tangutica* will delight our eyes. In the mild climate of Northern Ireland, at Mount Stewart, the stems of *Clematis* ✕ *jouiniana* remain exposed all the year, and as a consequence the small milky blue flowers in their lavish trusses have a great appeal in late summer; they are in marked contrast to the dark green of the parent Irish yews.

While on the subject of *Clematis,* let me add a note of warning about two rampageous plants which should not be let loose in gardens. One is our native *Clematis vitalba* — Travellers' Joy or Old Man's Beard. This is a mighty, woody climber whose beauty on our chalklands pulls trees down with the weight of its festoons; it has several close relatives which are apt to insinuate themselves into our gardens by means of their rarified names. The other is *Polygonum baldschuanicum,* the Russian Vine. There is danger here, from its twining and all-enveloping shoots which smother its supports, and also from the fact that it is known to some botanists as *Fallopia* or *Bilderdykia.*

One of the most stunning combinations I have seen was a tall holly in full berry, entangled with the arching branches of *Celastrus articulatus,* also in full berry; these berries are composed of orange seeds bursting from yellow capsules — a display of several weeks. It remains to ensure that a hermaphrodite form of *Celastrus* be obtained, or, failing that, a male as well as a female, to ensure a good crop of berries.

This brings us through till the autumn, which I think is the supreme moment for the display of climbers in trees. A memory remains with me of a Silver Birch, white stem showing and its leaves yellow, like dripping gold, threaded through with trails of *Vitis coignetiae,* whose leaves were like scarlet plates. Once again, this Cutting highlights the telling effect we get when it is not only contrast of colour that predominates, but contrast of size as well. The plates of scarlet against the glittering jewels of the birch leaves were seen in the clear air of late October, after rain. It is at such moments that we bless the waning year.

In fact, many of the vines (*Ampelopsis, Parthenocissus* and *Vitis*) excel in many ways: they take command and by means of their clasping leaf stalks make their way up trees, and when once they reach the forked branches, then hang down. But they are luxuriant, and liable to bring down their host plant's branches. There is the joy of seeing scarlet vine leaves among the yellowing of the tree leaves. This combination of colours is not difficult; most native British trees turn yellow or yellowish in autumn and many of our most noteworthy autumn displays are from vines whose leaves turn red. Take, for instance, the well known *Parthenocissus quinquefolia* whose long trails frequently depend to ground level; or *Vitis chaffanjonii, V. megalophylla* and others in rich colours; all will be the more appreciated when growing as nature intended, rather than when trained on various frameworks or walls.

Without full thought it is easy go go astray in our selection of host plant and guest. When I moved house I inherited a fairly tall Holly, and brought with me a self-sown seedling of *Clematis cirrhosa* var. *balearica.* Thinking how well the creamy green bells of the climber would look with the holly berries, I planted the Balearic evergreen to climb up the Holly — which it did very well and quickly, and started to flower. Only then, and after an interval of a few years, did I discover that the host plant was the yellow-berried *Ilex aquifolium* 'Fructu Luteo', which does not make much contrast!

Given, then, that we wish for a climber in a tree, and given that the tree is in a more or less open position and that its branches are not too umbrageous, how do we set about establishing the climbing plant in soil that will already be thickly filled with roots? The old method was to sink a half-cask (having removed its base) near the trunk of the tree and to fill it with nutritious soil. Today we should probably use a stout polythene bag (having again removed its base), filled likewise. To get to specific details about the position, I suggest that the bag be sunk at a distance from the tree trunk, say about twice the diameter of the trunk away, severing all the tree roots. Then lead the climber's main shoot towards the trunk. If it is a self-clinger, see that its adventitious roots or prehensile leaf stalks have the right sort of support within reach. Unless they are firmly and closely introduced they will not catch hold, but when once they have become attached it is surprising how quickly they will forge upwards. After all, it is what they would do in nature, and we are giving them every opportunity.

This method is the most natural we can give the young plant, and so much more sightly and effective than planting the climber at the perimeter of the tree's branches and leading the climber up to them by means of ropes. Only twining plants such as *Wisteria* would profit by the aid of ropes or wires. In fact, I have found it difficult to get *Clematis montana* to enter into the head of a holly, and there are many instances where the climber seems intent upon growing out towards the sun, and loth to grow into the head of branches. A little coaxing will be needed in early years to ensure that the trails do not all grow out too soon, before they are anchored firmly in the tree's head. Thereafter all should do well, and a fountain of beauty should result.

> On russet floors, by waters idle
> The pine lets fall its cone . . .
> And traveller's joy beguiles in autumn
> Hearts that have lost their own.
> — A. E. Housman (1860–1936)

Cutting Forty-Nine —

Ferns:
"Plain Green and No Flowers"

The facts implied in my title are only partly true. I could show you *Adiantum pedatum* var. *japonicum* with young fronds of soft coppery pink; *Osmunda regalis* in smoky purple; *Athyrium nipponicum* 'Pictum' with purple stipes and grey fronds; *Dryopteris erythrosora* in bright orange in spring turning to yellow, with scarlet indusia; to say nothing of the bright orange-brown fronds in autumn of the Royal Fern. In the spring in Cornwall, around the coasts, a clump of fern may stand out from all the rest because of its brilliant yellow-green, distinguishable even in the distance. This is *D. pseudomas* (*D. borreri*); it is also the predominant fern on long stretches of the west coasts of Scotland. The same exceptional colouring is found in *D. wallichiana*, a related species from the Himalaya. Its pale colouring in spring is accentuated by stipes which are covered with sepia scales and hairs; the unfurling fronds thereby acquire a simian appearance. Then there is the golden crested Hart's-tongue fern, now known as *Asplenium scolopendrium* 'Crispum Golden Queen'. In short, ferns for the outdoor garden are by no means all "plain green". But this is a rather indigestible first paragraph, and perhaps we should start at the beginning.

In considering ferns we must get used to some terms not used elsewhere in this book, such as "stipe" in place of stem and "frond" instead of leaf. The frond may be divided into "pinnae", and "indusia" are the tiny flaps on the backs of most fronds which protect the "spores", which is the name for fern seeds. The indusia may be of different shapes and sizes; those shaped like shields or "bucklers" give the name to various genera such as *Dryopteris* and *Polystichum.* When the spores ripen in summer, they blow away in their millions; those which alight on damp peaty or woodland soil or on absorbent rocks germinate, producing a tiny "prothallus", not unlike a Liverwort and often smaller. It is these minute growths which are the true fern plants; the sexes mate and produce what we know as the ferns in our gardens. These big

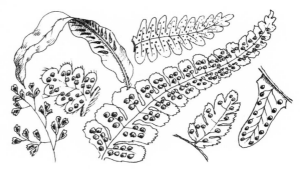

Under portions of fern fronds showing indusia

plants are comparable to mushrooms, which are similarly the spore-bearing part of a plant which lives most of its life underground.

I hope that this short paragraph has made clear the different phases in the life of a fern. We see it is true that ferns do not have flowers, and we have already disposed of the myth that all are plain green. Nevertheless, whatever may be the attraction of the other ferns mentioned, it is the evergreen species that have, I think, the most value in our gardens; and all ferns add an indefinable something to our plant groupings, in shape, line and texture. One of the boldest among reasonably hardy species is *Blechnum chilense.* This will achieve 8 feet in moist woodland, its arching stipes being set with a ladder-like array of thumb-wide, dark green pinnae. It is sometimes erroneously labelled *B. tabulare* or *Lomaria magellanica;* the Hard Fern, *Blechnum spicant,* is a much smaller version. Blechnums do not thrive in limy soils, which most ferns enjoy. In fact, a word on suitable soils would not come amiss. Ferns in general do not thrive in clay or chalk, but seem to prefer a loose, friable, limy soil with plenty of leaf-mould or other humus worked into it; the site should be at least partly shaded and on the moist side — though of all plants for dry shade, the species of *Dryopteris* and

Polystichum are most suitable. The common Male Fern will put up with dreadful rooty, dry places, in fact thrive in them — while I have seen *Polystichum setiferum* 'Acutilobum' alive and well for many years in full sun on a paved path.

Among our natives only *Blechnum spicant* and the well-known Hart's-Tongue fern can be called evergreen in British gardens, though many other species may keep their fronds in sheltered woodland conditions. We must go to the Far East and Far West to find those beautiful glossy dark green fronds which are all but evergreen with us, even in a hard winter.

The two species from North America which are evergreen are both known as Christmas Fern or Sword Fern; in the western United States these names apply to *Polystichum munitum*, and in the east to *P. acrostichoides*. (My plant of *P. munitum* was a self-sown sporeling from A. T. Johnson in North Wales, many years ago.) They both make fine clumps up to 2 or 3 feet and are simply pinnate — that is, without further divisions of the fronds — but whereas the former bears its spores in a regular array on the backs of the fronds, in the latter they are only borne at the tips, which are in addition much reduced, making (supposedly) the "sword". In the Far East there are several species of very high decorative value with equally shining, dark fronds, prettily arched and divided into small lobes. Such are *P. polyblepharum*, *P. squarrosum*, *P. discretum* and the smaller *P. tsussimense.* All are of the highest order. Many polystichums produce bulbils along the base of the stipes, but regrettably I have not seen them on any of these species. They are mostly found on forms of *P. setiferum*, and on no form in such freedom as *P. setiferum* 'Acutilobum'. This is one of the most exquisite and lacy of all hardy ferns and will keep its fronds in all but the most severe winter weather.

The other genus which will put up with dry conditions is *Polypodium; P. vulgare* thrives even on mossy tree branches, in the damper west of the British Isles. It makes admirable ground-cover and has several very appealing variants, such as 'Longicaudatum' and 'Cornubiense'. I prefer to cut them down in spring; it is a lovely surprise when the new fronds appear in full summer in verdant green.

There are several moisture-loving ferns, but they are not evergreen. At their head stands *Osmunda regalis,* achieving 5 feet or more in wet positions. The young fronds, covered with fawn wool, unfurl with great elegance. The smaller variant, *O. r.* 'Gracilis', with coppery tinted young foliage, is worth a long wait if you can at last acquire it. They all make peaty, rooty hummocks above the soil, reminiscent of a Tree Fern. The Lady Fern, *Athyrium felix-femina,* has very dainty forms but begins to look tired by August, and the same may be said of the Ostrich Plume Fern, *Matteuccia struthiopteris.* Few ferns are more beautiful in early summer or late spring. Whereas the lady ferns will seed themselves on any damp ground, *Matteuccia* spreads by underground runners. Margery Fish found the Japanese Holly Fern, *Cyrtomium falcatum,* hardy in Somerset, but it has never thriven for me. It is of bold beauty, and is frequently seen in conservatories. The other species, *C. fortunei,* seems to be quite hardy, but has none of the majesty of the former.

There are many smaller species of great charm: *Asplenium trichomanes* and *Ceterach officinarum* for the rock garden; dainty, divided treasures such as *Cystopteris* and *Onychium japonicum;* and invasive colonisers like *Gymnocarpium* and *Adiantum venustum.* Apart from the last, the hardy Maidenhair, however, they cannot be called evergreen, and as I set out to write about evergreen ferns, it would not do to enlarge upon these and others here. But if you make a point of looking at ferns in summer, I shall be surprised if you are not captivated by their beauty, unique in the plant world.

Cutting Fifty —

Ivies and Their Uses

It was William Robinson who wrote of the beauty of ivy in almost any position, even on trees, but he qualified his remarks by adding "so long as it is away from any kind of building". Ivy seems to cause very different feelings in different people. There are those who cannot tolerate it on trees, usually because they think its close-clinging stems are sucking nourishment from their hosts. This is not the danger, however. The only damage ivy can cause to a tree is by encasing its stem and branches in so dense a mass of interlacing shoots that they cannot expand; or, of course, by in the fullness of time becoming so bushy that it acts as a wind-hazard. As to buildings, ivy keeps them warm and dry but does damage to all but the hardest mortar. While it is in place, all is well, but if it is taken away the sucking roots pull off the smooth finish of the mortar, leaving it rough and absorbent and more open to damage by frost; moreover, only a wire brush will remove the dead but still attached roots from bricks, stone or concrete.

Ivy will rapidly swarm up a wall and invade gutters; it will also, by passing behind down-pipes, prise them off the walls as its shoots expand. Yet in spite of all these dire consequences I think it likely that gardeners will continue to plant ivies on their houses, because they are so very beautiful. They can be maligned or praised. I recall a joke in an old volume of *Punch* where an elderly German professor, admiring foliage in a corsage on the bosom of a *grande dame*, exclaimed, "Ach, so beautiful, Madame; it reminds one of ify clinging round an old ruin!" There is no doubt that the neat, regularly disposed leaves on an ivy shoot fingering its way up a wall endear it to us, regardless of the coarse growth of maturity. Let us see what they have to offer when not growing on house walls. Keeping to the usual procedure in these notes, we will appraise the largest first.

At the Royal Botanic Gardens at Kew, large areas in parts of the arboretum are given over to the Irish Ivy, *Hedera helix* var. *hibernica*. This is a most wonderful plant to use as completely weed-free ground cover, of richest dark green, which when fully established may be as much as 18 inches high. Like that terribly invasive dwarf bamboo *Pleioblastus pygmaeus*, it gives relief to close- or rough-mown grass, and weds that carpet of green to shrubs and tree stems in a highly satisfying way. Both will keep out dogs and children and add immeasurably to the scene. But used in this way the Irish Ivy is not for our smaller gardens; in fact, I would not use it at all in any but public gardens, despite its beauty of leaf. There are others of greater use and beauty, in particular *H. colchica*, whose extra dark, large, scarcely lobed leaves smell deliciously of lemon when crushed, as opposed to the bitter smell of all others. It makes a splendid screen or background when trained on stout trellis or rustic-work, which it will support by its own strength — in common with all other ivies — when the woodwork is getting weak.

I think I shall not be making an unpopular claim when I say that its variety 'Dentata Variegata' is the most spectacular and satisfying of all variegated climbers; one which, I might add, though yellow variegated, is of a bland primrose-tint contrasted with grey and green. It is handsome to a degree, and truly magnificent when growing on a support next to, say, purple varieties of *Clematis* or *Delphinium*. It is also a rapid ground-cover. I saw it once in winter, threading its way under large azalea bushes whose russet leaves already densely covered the ground. The contrast was stunning.

Another picture, also from the depths of winter, is of the sun catching a south-eastern facing wall, and showing up areas of what appeared to be scarlet and black: it was not berries, but the twigs of *Cornus alba* var. *sibirica* in bright red next to the very dark murrey-purple of *Hedera helix* 'Atropurpurea'. This is the better of the two varieties of Common Ivy which though green in summer become burnished and dark at the approach of cold weather. The less good one is 'Glymii'. I remember I longed for the opportunity to plant a Winter Jasmine next to them — what a trio they would have made, as bright as any summer grouping.

But if you do not relish the dust and dirt that accumulate in ivy on walls, and the sparrows and spiders that lurk, to say nothing of the wasps and bluebottles that love the flowers — mere greenish heads but of a special beauty, slowly turning into dark berries — do bear in mind that special value of ground-cover referred to earlier. The Common Ivy, *Hedera helix*, in its many varieties will effectively clothe the ground with a variety of tints. In the drear days of winter every ivy leaf is a picture of great beauty, in shape and tint, and seldom are two alike, being veined and coloured with great subtlety. One of the most vigorous is also one of the most neglected, 'Marginata Major', a lovely mixture of shades of grey-green and cream. I think I should choose 'Adam' for a more compact creamy white variegated form of startling colour and leaf-shape. 'Glacier' is wholly pale grey-green and vigorous. Among the yellow variegated forms none is more popular than 'Goldheart'; as its name suggests, the leaves are green with a large central area of yellow. Unfortunately it is apt to revert to plain green.

There are two wholly yellow — or "golden", as it is called — forms: 'Buttercup' and 'Chrysophylla'. The former is apt to "burn" in hot sun, while it remains green in shade: the difficulty is to find the right place for it. On the other hand, 'Angularis Aurea', with recurrent yellow-leafed shoots, does not "burn". All of these coloured forms, and the dark 'Atropurpurea', are of normal vigorous growth.

Down the scale in size we come to some gems. There is the long-fingered, small-leafed 'Sagittifolia' and its remarkable cream variegated form; 'Danny', a size smaller; and 'Little Diamond', a huddle of branches, almost a bush, ideal as a frontal plant. Through the kindness of its finder, I have a wholly yellow 'Sagittifolia', called 'Light Fingers', which scarcely burns at all. 'Très Coupé' is fairly vigorous, in dark green, but the ultimate must surely be 'Duckfoot': its tiny leaves are indeed the shape of a duck's foot, and it makes a delightful little hummock or a charming pot plant.

There are still two true dwarfs to be considered; one, 'Erecta' or 'Congesta', is bolt upright, even fastigiate, with acutely pointed leaves, and the other semi-procumbent, 'Conglomerata'. Together with 'Duckfoot' and 'Little Diamond' they are intriguing small plants for rock gardens or the edges of borders.

While all are quite hardy on wall, fence or rock, or flat on the ground, it must be admitted that these ivies sometimes suffer in hard winters when trained onto wires. Yet they can achieve a most unusual feature in making an ivy hedge on stout netting. Alternatively, they may be used on single wires or canes to develop into a lattice effect. I have also seen them used to mimic topiary; first the shape intended must be fashioned in wood or wire, and the long shoots be encouraged to cling to the framework. In this way you can have dark green or cream variegated shapes.

I mentioned ivy flowers earlier. They are not produced on the long growth-shoots; when the plants are fully established the dainty trails — the main attraction to most of us — will settle down and produce flowering shoots of a totally different character. These shoots will remain as bushes if taken off and rooted. Returning to the largest growers first, although one does see bushes of *H. colchica* and its yellow variety, both have the unfortunate habit of partly folding their apparently limp leaves, and look as though they are drooping, mournfully. As to the Irish Ivy, its arborescent form is almost too vigorous to consider, though a great sight in autumn when in flower. It is the more normal varieties, green or variegated, which are the most valuable in bush form. They are slow-growing, but gradually mound themselves into fine cumulous masses that are an asset to any garden.

In great contrast is a noble and large shrub, often seen covered with bunches of black berries in milder areas. This is *Fatsia japonica,* noted for its very large, tropical-looking, hand-like leaves in shining green. It does not resemble an Ivy, to which it is closely related botanically, until it flowers in autumn, when its ivory-white stems and drumstick heads of tiny blooms will be seen to be in the Ivy-image. *Fatsia* should be planted in shade for the greatest effect. "Its great, leathery palmate leaves stand buffeting by wind far better than might be expected . . . It produces in late autumn handsome panicles of white flowers arranged in globular heads, the whole suggesting carved ivory."

Cutting Fifty-One —

George Rowland Jackman

I imagine the answers would be very varied if it were asked in a quiz what the following plants had in common: *Fuchsia* 'Chillerton Beauty' — *Ruta graveolens* 'Jackman's Blue' — *Chamaecyparis lawsoniana* 'Pembury Blue' — *Clematis* 'Barbara Dibley' — *Ceanothus* 'Cascade'.

The true answer is that we owe them all to Rowland Jackman, who found or selected them, and propagated and distributed them from his nursery at Woking.

And the answer would be the same to a similar list: *Euonymus europaeus* 'Red Cascade' — *Yucca flaccida* 'Ivory' — *Chamaecyparis lawsoniana* 'Green Hedger' — *Agapanthus* 'Lilliput' — *Berberis gagnepainii* 'Fernspray'.

These two short lists contain ten shrubs and plants of quality which, with others of Rowland Jackman's selection, deserve to be in most gardens. Some of them are gradually becoming well known; it takes a long time, however, for a good shrub to emerge as a leader among the numerous species and cultivars in general production, and the fact that some of the plants Rowland selected are not better known is in part due to his modesty. He retired from his nursery — George Jackman & Son, Woking Nurseries Ltd — in 1972, and since then the nursery has been under different owner-ship. But I remember many a visit there from about 1938 onwards when, of an evening, we would wander round the frames and glass houses for a while and then see the nursery stock in the fields. After the war our steps would invariably lead to the stock ground where Rowland kept all his special plants for trial and study, ready for propagation if they proved worthy. I did not always agree with his findings, and this is probably what made a visit so interesting for both of us, but there is no doubt that many of his plants please many gardeners.

Take, for instance, any garden where foliage of a greyish hue — even blue in some lights — is sought: there you may be pretty certain to find 'Jackman's Blue' Rue. Its cloudy masses of filigree foliage are as beautiful in frost as in sun, and make a pleasant foil for the usual silvery-grey plants. Two of the other plants mentioned above, *Fuchsia* 'Chillerton Beauty', a plant of some 2½ to 3 feet with flowers of soft violet and a blush calyx,

George Rowland Jackman

CUTTINGS FROM MY GARDEN NOTEBOOKS

and *Agapanthus* 'Lilliput', a dwarf plant with flowers of darkest blue, would make a delightful late summer group with the Rue. Behind, achieving about 4 feet, could be the creamy spires of *Yucca flaccida* 'Ivory'. A grouping such as this would be an asset in any garden. In his own garden, in dense shade, associated with ferns, ivies and periwinkles, *Berberis gagnepainii* 'Fern-spray' was outstandingly beautiful, contributing the qualities which invoked its name. Its arching branches and narrow leaves add a good touch to a dark corner, and are augmented by pale yellow flowers in spring.

Nobody who wants a first-rate, fairly quick, dense evergreen hedge need hesitate about planting the excellent cultivar *Chamaecyparis lawsoniana* 'Green Hedger'. It seems to have all the attributes needed to make a good hedge; fortunately it is easy to propagate, and hence its price stands comparison with the inferior type species, of which no two seedlings ever match. Today many people choose the Leyland cypress (✕ *Cupressocyparis leylandii*) for its speed of growth, but unless they are looking for a tall unclipped screen of over 50 feet, they are likely to regret it in the future; it does not make a compact hedge, and its vigorous growth entails much clipping to keep it in line. Rowland's 'Green Hedger' is first-rate and a good rich green, and his 'Pembury Blue' is one of the best and most compact of the blue-grey forms of the same species. His slender *Cupressus macrocarpa* 'Golden Pillar' adds yellow tinting to these conifers.

Jackman's have always been famous for clematis, not only *C.* ✕ *jackmanii* itself, but for 'Belle of Woking', 'Jackmanii Superba', 'Lady Betty Balfour', 'Lady Northcliffe', 'Mrs George Jackman', and others; to these famous varieties Rowland added 'Barbara Dibley' and 'Barbara Jackman', both in the carmine/purple/petunia colouring, but distinct, vigorous and early flowering. He always recommended them for north-facing walls where the colours would not fade.

I well remember being shown the original plant of *Euonymus europaeus* 'Red Cascade', one of a dozen or more seedlings, many of which were much more brilliant and larger-fruited than the native spindle tree. It did not take long to realise that in this one he had a superlative autumn-fruiting tree, with large rosy crimson husks enclosing the usual orange seeds. And it is a tree for small gardens, for it does not achieve much more than 10 feet; unlike many *Euonymus* specimens, it seldom fails to crop when grown singly.

None of these plants was launched into the horticultural world without a great deal of thought and observation. A plant had to be very good — in every way — before it satisfied Rowland. Anything which did not measure up to his high standards was discarded, scrapped and thrown away, even after several years of trial and perhaps propagation.

How does one assess a plant? Each of us has different ideas, and plants have many differing and separate qualities. Apart from the obvious beauty of leaf, flower and fruit, there are the season's attractions — young leafage, glossy or matt adult foliage, autumn colour; the colour, shape, poise and duration of flower; the colour, shape and poise of fruit or seed pod; the mode of branching, and the plant's appearance in winter. Many of these attributes add up to the word usually used by plantsmen: the "habit". Those who have had the privilege in the past of spending an hour with Rowland will be unlikely not to have realised that with him this was the end-product. Though he was deeply conscious of the beauties of flower and leaf and humble in their greater moments, he did not claim great artistic ability. On the other hand, he was a craftsman of the first order: there was no skill connected with the growing and production of plants of which he was not a master. And this I think opened his eyes to the "habit" of a plant, enabling him to assess its finer points, and also to think out or to record captivating plant associations.

In the 1950s and 1960s there was not a better ordered nursery than his, though he would be the first to admit that something, every year, did not measure up to his ideals of good husbandry and quality stock. Anyone whose life is in the least affected by the weather will know to a certain extent the anguish one goes through in trying to defeat its vagaries and provide for one's stock. It is no easy life, and used to be a great deal more difficult in the days when the spade and hoe were trumps, and plastics had not been invented.

Practically all of Rowland's plants were selected simply because he had an eye trained in plant observance. Thus the Fuchsia was picked out in a garden at Chillerton on the Isle of Wight and proved to be known but not named. The Agapanthus and the Yucca were raised on the nursery from mixed seed; the Rue was growing in a Chertsey garden; of the cypresses, 'Pembury Blue' was picked up in a Kent nursery, but 'Green Hedger' was purchased under an erroneous name.

For a separate group, others of his plants could be chosen, such as *Potentilla fruticosa grandiflora* 'Jackman's Variety', which will produce brilliant yellow flowers in May and onwards, while *Ceanothus* 'Cascade' would be in contrasting blue on a wall behind it. For strong colour with the Potentilla later in the season one could plant *Helianthemum* 'Bengal Rose', a vivid colour over silvery leaves, and *Hypericum patulum* 'Goldcup'. On a wall the small-leafed Ampelopsis, *Parthenocissus tricuspidata* 'Beverley Brook', a foundling from a garden near Kingston upon Thames, would provide scarlet autumn colour. For spring flower and clear colour he selected *Ribes sanguineum* 'China Rose'.

In the field of trees Rowland also left us with some good things. A Rowan, *Sorbus aucuparia* 'Sheerwater Seedling' (commemorating a canal in Woking), makes a compact, tall head and regularly produces large bunches of scarlet fruits. A form of *Liquidambar styraciflua*, called 'Worplesdon' after that village, was chosen for its consistently good autumn colour on lime-free soils. The Common Pear, *Pyrus communis*, produced an erect seedling that caught Rowland's eye, and he named it 'Beech Hill', while a particularly graceful but erect-stemmed Silver Birch is named 'Silver Spire'. The last two occurred locally.

It was always Rowland's contention, apart from his innate modesty, that the giving of a non-committal name to a plant — rather than turning everything into a "Jackman" variety — would help to ensure its acceptance throughout the nursery trade. In this way he hoped the plants of his choice would become better known and grace more gardens. He was in command at Woking Nurseries from 1934 to 1967, the fifth George Jackman, working long hours with a devotion to his nursery, his staff, and his plants that few could rival. During this period his *Planters' Handbook* appeared annually, and is no doubt a treasured possession with many. The detailed but concise descriptions of trees, shrubs and plants are invaluable. I like to think that these publications will be as valued as the plants he selected for us all, well into the future. In the pages of the *Handbook* we find his discerning appraisal of the beauties and uses of plants.

I feel sure that these few words of recognition, inadequate though they may be, will be appreciated by the many whom he helped with instruction, advice and enthusiasm over the years. It is in this way that his personality, as well as his plants and his words, will live.

Cutting Fifty-Two —

Cultivars

By this rather unwieldly and hybrid name — a merging of *cultivated variety* — we designate a vast concourse of selected forms of plants, descended from one or even two species or hybrids, which have pleased gardeners and flower lovers enough to warrant their being propagated vegetatively. To raise them in the old way, from seeds, would open the door to considerable variation and even disappointment in some very variable species. Nurserymen, to protect their calling, have for long been raising stock for sale by means of cuttings or other methods such as grafting or layering, in order to preserve the special characteristics of each selected form, unique because of its growth, foliage or flower, its colour, size or fragrance.

The splendidly proportioned flowers of *Lilium candidum,* for instance, are not known in the wild but are the outcome of an appreciation of form and stance predating written history. Likewise certain roses — *R. alba, R. damascena* and the like — are not known as wild plants; the dahlias which were brought from Peru by the conquistadors were already a hybrid swarm selected by the Incas; and original importations from China contained ancient hybrids and unique garden forms such as *Jasminum* ✕ *mesnyi.* Mankind has for long been noting and carefully propagating many selected forms of garden and agricultural plants, in order to preserve noteworthy individuals for the future. Not all aberrant forms are healthy; some have dropped out, while others may carry their disease with them until, in these scientific days, their health can be restored.

It is all a case of selection by mankind, but quite different from the phrase "our selection" which used to appear in catalogues some fifty or a hundred years ago: this was a means of getting rid of plants which had not sold satisfactorily!

It may be as well to recall here that the plant kingdom is divided into Families and genera, species, botanical varieties, forms and cultivars. While species are often raised from seeds, with an attendant slight or large variation in appearance, the varieties, forms, cultivars and indeed hybrids are or should be propagated vegetatively in order to preserve the characteristics of each variation. In order that catalogue and book descriptions may be regarded as reliable, propagation must ensure that uniformity reigns. This is what is necessary in gardens; it would not do if one planted a group of, say, three plants under one label, only to find that they were widely different in habit, colour or other essential for making a garden picture.

Completely the opposite obtains when contemplating natural planting. If we look through hedgerows, spinneys and woods we shall note the wide variation of the trees and shrubs included; in fact, no two will be exactly alike in habit or leafage: a result of seed raising. I would go so far as to say that, while in hedges in gardens one needs the uniformity of vegetatively propagated stock, in the wilder application of the countryside completely the opposite should be the aim. That is what gives the irregular flushing of green in the spring and also the patches of colour in autumn. No woodland, planted from uniform stock, can compete in beauty with the natural variation of seed-raised individuals. But what we need in our smaller gardens is plants which can give a guaranteed effect and be garden-worthy, stalwart and long-lasting in their chosen sphere.

The same notes should cover the planting of bulbs; keep your "grandiflora" named varieties for the borders and for cutting, but where possible obtain seed-raised stock for naturalising. This applies mainly to species from the wild, which are after all the most appropriate for this work. Though the appearance in spring of clumps and drifts of grandiflora varieties of daffodils and narcissi is welcome and cheering, on our roadsides and in our parks, they seldom increase by seeding and thus never become naturalised but remain in their clumps.

As the centuries roll by, those concerned with the production for sale of trees, shrubs and plants — whether of annual or perennial duration — tend to be constantly looking for unique forms or hybrids (our "cultivars") which can be launched upon the public in the full knowledge that they will perform as described. Flowers with double or more rows of petals, as in many of the daisy breed, are particularly enmeshed in the pursuit of ever more impressive and showy garden forms. We have in great part accommodated our tastes to many double daisy-flowers, though I personally eschew the heavy, lumpy forms of some of them. Gigantic dahlias and gross chrysanthemums are not my ideals; the latter were described as "mops dipped in lobster sauce" by Reginald Farrer, that ardent lover of nature's miniature treasures. It seems that in order to pander to those with little taste for nature's unalloyed beauty, breeders will stoop to anything to achieve attention and notoriety: witness, for instance, such abortions of floral beauty as the narcissi with their coronas split open and folded back on to the outer segments. The trumpet of a daffodil or the cup of a narcissus is surely the essence of that unique spring flower, and needs no "improvement". To me, such achievements (if they may be so called) can only be looked upon as the prostitution of nature's beauty.

In the same category would come, I feel, those queer columbines called 'Clematiflora' which have no spurs — surely the character which lifts them above all other flowers and is accentuated in the species *Aquilegia longissima*; in a similar vein are the snapdragons (*Antirrhinum*) which have been bred without a throat and thus will not snap. When I was quite young they were always called "monkey-mouths" as well as snapdragons. Double-flowered hyacinths have no attraction for me, but I am inclined to take to heart the frilled sweet peas which were ushered in early in this century. There is something about a sweet pea which makes it essentially a flower for picking, and thus allows the flowers to be frilled and flounced, as opposed to the rather severe and enfolded shape of the original.

Frilled, flounced and goffered does not suit all flowers, however. I am sad to see how this style of hybridisation has affected the bearded irises. To my mind the modern cultivars, though so wonderful and divergent in their colours, have lost the essential *fleur-de-lys* shape of the originals, like two capital letter R's back to back. Here was something that manifestly did not want "improving". The frilling and goffering have destroyed the original shape in many cultivars today. And I am sad to see that some tastes are bowing before new shapes in day lilies. Not only are they being bred with short stems, resulting in the flowers scarcely overtopping the coarsened foliage, but breeders are producing flowers whose segments reflex almost into a ball, with total disregard to the lily shape. And must they have frilly edges, thus farther distancing them from the lily-like form? and do we really want those muddy violets and mauves? It is well known that the best scents — and the most telling garden pictures — accrue from the light yellows.

Long years ago, at the Cambridge University Botanic Garden, the Curator, R. Irwin Lynch, started to raise hybrid Transvaal daisies — strains of *Gerbera*, slightly hybridised. With their narrow ray-florets, they had a purity of daisy-outline unsurpassed: few daisies of any kind had so refined an outline or such delicacy of composition. Now, unfortunately, they have been debased into doubles and semi-doubles.

It will be some time before such travesties can be perpetrated on shrubs and trees. Even rhododendrons have so far resisted giving birth to any appreciable number of horrors, and other genera of shrubs, though being raised with considerable enterprise, retain their innate beauty. But I fear the worst; when commercialism invades our gardens too much, there may be a reversion in appreciating the beauties of nature. And who will declare that a double rose is more beautiful than a single? I am so steeped in roses that perhaps I should resist writing more about them. I would go as far as to claim that a half-open Hybrid Tea rose is an achievement which even Dame Nature did not attempt.

Cutting Fifty-Three —

Hedges

Except where a property is of limitless acreage with uninterrupted views, its boundary will usually be within sight and reach. This boundary should not be thought of as a final and hard line, but rather as a device to limit intruders. Some of us are lucky enough to have an old wall as a boundary, thereby adding immeasurably to the garden by providing a vertical backcloth against which all manner of lovely climbers and shrubs can be grown. It is a mistake to let the plants totally obscure the wall, however: the masonry should be allowed to grin through in contrast. This is not so with fences; they are not truly architectural and definite, but eventually bend and sag and decay, and are best covered completely.

Today's boundaries are often merely concrete posts connected with chain-link or other wire netting. Here again it is desirable to cover the erection with lax-growing plants, which will give the privacy of a hedge without the necessity of clipping, and the supports will be firm and permanent. There is another practical point to be considered, if wooden posts of any kind are used: in time they rot at ground-level and need renewing or supporting. Thus it is wise not to plant shrubs or climbers against the posts, but between them.

The next most obvious boundary-marker is a hedge. But I suggest that before planting one, the whole matter should be given deep thought. Hedges take up a lot of space, have greedy roots, and need a lot of work annually in clipping. It must be visualised that a hedge cannot be much less than 2 feet in width, and very often gets considerably wider. Furthermore, if in addition to being a boundary-marker it also is to act as a background to a border of assorted plants and shrubs, a space of at least 2 feet must be left as access for clipping. And in our small gardens today, four feet or more sliced off for the sake of a hedge may be deemed too great a loss. A fence of any sort covered with climbing plants would take less space.

Apart from practicalities, there are also the aesthetics to be considered. Do we want a hard and definite line around our property? Is not this the opposite of what we should like to achieve? Rather than plant a straight row of anything, should we not use our garden shrubs to create the background of our flower planting and at the same time provide an irregular screen over which trees and shrubs in neighbouring gardens can be seen and enjoyed? After all, the space needed for shrubs is not much more than is needed for a hedge, if the right things are chosen; and there will be no clipping, only occasional pruning. There is another thought: if a hedge is chosen, this presupposes that the neighbour will also clip his side and keep it in order.

Having cleared away some of the disadvantages and objections, let us now consider hedges. It is important to plant in clean soil, by which I mean free from perennial weeds. The planting should be at least one foot from the boundary, in a deeply prepared trench which should have humus and fertiliser mixed in its base; similar humus should be mixed with the topsoil around the roots. In windy sites it may be necessary to stake each plant individually, or tie them to a strained wire. But before these practical counsels comes of course the choice of the species, one or more.

Today, when even hedging plants are grown in containers, ready for instant impact, the choice will often be the Leyland Cypress in one of its forms, green or yellowish. It is about the quickest growing plant available, but requires clipping twice every year to keep it really trim. (Clipping anything once a year is quite enough for me!) Because it is so vigorous, it will speedily get too wide; we do not yet know whether it can be reduced with impunity, to "green-up" all over again. It would never be my choice, since there are other good species available; first I would recommend *Chamaecyparis lawsoniana* 'Green Hedger', selected originally by Rowland Jackman and grown from cuttings ever since. It is miles ahead of often cheaper seed-raised Lawson cypresses, which vary much in growth and colour. It seems to me that if we choose to plant a hedge, we need uniformity. There are many forms of Lawson cypresses available, in green, yellow and glaucous tones. The yellows can be very upsetting and inhibiting as backgrounds; the glaucous one is much more subtle. It is important to choose varieties with outward-growing fan-like shoots; those with erect twigs do not lend themselves well to clipping. This is rather the fault with the best Arborvitae (*Thuja plicata*), named 'Atrovirens', whose dark winter green is so good compared with the normal seed-raised species. The other Arborvitae, *Thuja occidentalis*, does not make so good a hedge and turns to a khaki-brown in winter, though there are some cultivars coming on the market of a richer green. The one great advantage these arborvitaes have over the Lawson cypresses is their pleasing odour of oranges, as opposed to the oily smell of the latter.

I think there is no doubt that our native English Yew makes the very best hedge. There is a general impression that it is slow growing, but with adequate preparation of the ground and good cultivation a young hedge will achieve a foot a year. When well clipped it has a smooth mossy appearance, ideal as a background to the garden. It is important to purchase seed-raised stock and if possible to select those of uniform growth; when raised from cuttings, the plants are often of wayward inclination.

The next most evident choice among evergreens is the Holly. It must be realised that while Holly makes an impenetrable hedge in maturity, and is again an admirable background, the very size of the leaf precludes it from ever making so smooth an effect as Yew. There is also a certain amount of glitter, which gives the surface of the hedge a less receding perspective. The usual choice is seed-raised *Ilex aquifolium*, but these are very variable and plants grown from cuttings of a female plant are more desirable. The freely berrying variety 'J. C. van Tol' is one often recommended, but while as an isolated plant it has few equals, its rather lax twigs are not ideal for hedges. Among all hollies none can really equal the hybrid *I.* × *altaclerensis* 'Hodginsii'. This is a very hardy, dark green, broad-leafed plant but bears no berries, being a male. However, there are innumerable cultivars of holly, small and large leafed, green and variegated, and all but the most lanky growers will make a good hedge.

While the ordinary *Lonicera nitida* — now known as 'Ernest Wilson' — is satisfactory for small hedges up to about 3 feet, if a taller form is required it is best to choose 'Fertilis' or 'Yunnan'.

There is no shortage of other evergreens. Any shrub with a reasonably bushy habit will respond to clipping into a hedge. In fact, it always amazes me that gardeners are not more venturesome. If one excepts the obviously cheap, mass-produced hedging plants such as Privet and *Lonicera nitida,* the cost of the greater range of shrubs should not be prohibitive. One of the best large evergreens for the job is *Cotoneaster lacteus,* a sombre evergreen responding well to knife or secateurs; it is quick growing and keeps its late maturing berries well. A lesser plant is the greyish leafed *C. franchetii; C. simonsii* is not evergreen but clips into a neat hedge and the birds do not usually take the berries, whose scarlet remains through the winter. I find *Berberis gagnepainii* somewhat dull in green, but it has a rare moment of autumn beauty from its purple, bloom-covered berries.

Of late years much work has gone into raising and selecting forms of *Pyracantha.* Those descended mainly from *P. atalantioides* are upright in habit and truly evergreen, and also carry berries. A few such are 'Dart's Red', 'Shawnee' and 'Teton', and there is also the old, compact 'Watereri'.

In mild and maritime regions, escallonias are very valuable. Comparatively hardy is 'Donard Seedling', not truly evergreen but bespangled with small pinky-white flowers through the summer and early autumn. Various hedging trials have shown 'Crimson Spire' and 'Red Hedger' very much to the fore, while for very mild districts the beauty from rich green leafage and lovely pink or crimson flowers of *E. macrantha* cannot be beaten.

And so we come down to the small shrubs for dwarf hedges within the garden design. Chief among them is Box — of which the best for hedging is what is known as *Buxus sempervirens* 'Glauca' (or 'La Chapelle'), with a close runner-up in the ordinary straightforward Common Box. But be sure to get plants from uniform stock — there are many types in nurseries — and avoid 'Handsworthensis', which though vigorous and comparatively fast growing has vertical twigs, and is thus not conducive to good clipping. *Euonymus fortunei* has some attractive variegated forms—'Emerald Gaiety', for instance — though no special plain green of bushy habit has come to the fore. Lavenders have long been used for hedging, but must be clipped in spring. *Lavandula angustifolia* ('Hidcote' is merely a named clone) is a rich colour and small growing. The plant known variously as 'Dutch' or 'Vera' is in reality a bushy, strong growing grey-leafed hybrid, *L.* × *intermedia*, and has a long flowering period, even into autumn in some seasons.

We will now take a look at deciduous hedging. First and foremost is, I suppose, Common Beech, *Fagus sylvatica.* It is exceptionally beautiful in young leaf and also retains its rich brown foliage through the winter. Against it is the fact that it usually harbours white fly in the summer, and has greedy surface roots. It is really only suitable for large hedges, since it can grow to 20 feet or more in height. Occasionally people are tempted to grow a hedge of Copper or Purple-leaf Beech. Though it is lovely in spring, all colour has to be clipped off in August, revealing merely a dead, dark tone. Another snag about beech hedges is that in spring the leaves fall off, littering the garden and making the hedges transparent for two or three weeks.

Hornbeam (*Carpinus betulus*), though less attractive in its winter garb, has the benefit of less greedy roots, no white fly, and prettily tinted young foliage. Hornbeam has another great asset: like all the above evergreen plants except the cypresses, it can be cut back to the main stems if it gets too large — a trimming that Beech scarcely tolerates, taking many years to make good.

This brings me to another big point. All trimming of hedges, from infancy, should be done to keep them as narrow as possible and with a surface leaning inwards from the base, nearly to the width of the leading shoots at the top. However hard they are clipped annually, they will slowly get wider, and sometimes have to be reduced drastically. Complete success will attend this effort with all the plants mentioned except Beech, cypresses and Lavender; Box is slow to respond, but sure in time. This necessary, even unavoidable, job can only be really successful when there is a good, straight, central row of plants. Therefore, never plant a 'staggered' row; it merely ensures a greater width of hedge to clip at the top, and as we all know this is the most time-consuming and awkward job. It is a different matter when planting a field boundary with Quickthorn and other natives; there a staggered row helps to make a bulky hedge.

There is sometimes a temptation to plant a mixture of things in a garden hedge. It *has* been done with success, witness the tapestry hedge at Hidcote — a mixture of Holly in both green and variegated varieties, Box, and Copper Beech. These have blended well. But the choice of, say, alternate yellow and green cypresses or golden and green privet is seldom successful because of the greater vigour of one; besides, it gives a bizarre effect. I have also seen great contrast achieved by interspersing panels of Box with upright pillars of Yew or Cypress: such an assortment creates a very dominant feature on its own, and is seldom to be used as a background to ornamental beds and borders.

The distance apart for planting is a variable matter. As a general rule 18 inches will suffice, but many of the stronger growers can be placed at 2 feet or even more, so long as they are plants well furnished to the ground. A very good and comparatively cheap hedge can be made by using Quickthorn at 1 foot apart with a Common Holly at every 4 or 5 feet. In time this will result in a dense, impenetrable hedge with Holly threading through it all.

I have already stated that the young hedge should be clipped from infancy, severely, tapering upwards. At 2 or 3 feet in height it should not exceed 9 inches in width at the base. Leading shoots should not be stopped until the hedge is 1 foot below the desired height, and then a pinching-out of the very tips is all that is required. Most hedges are best clipped in late

August or early September, but Lavender should be left until April, and Box I prefer to clip in mid May or towards the end of that month. The plants will immediately put on a mass of tiny growing tips and remain freshly green all the summer.

One is tempted to leave strong shoots to grow up on the top of the hedge to make finials, spheres or other topiary. They will entail much work with steps and ladders and, if one's time and energy are likely to run out, are best omitted. Hedges always make work in any case, and caring for one is a chore that becomes more arduous as the years pass.

Cutting Fifty-Four —

Shrubs for the End of the Season

Of course there is no such thing in gardening; one season leads imperceptibly into the next, and except for periods of severe frost, a dead season doesn't exist. And even when the ground is deeply frozen, coloured twigs and berries remain — to say nothing of the resilient evergreens.

The thought behind my title is really occasioned by the gradual demise of all the summer flowers. Many linger into autumn, such as *Aster* × *frikartii*, Japanese anemones and *Sedum* 'Autumn Joy', but I have given these some of their due notice in "After the Phloxes". The glory of the early summer shrubs has left the garden rather empty, though here again there are a few stalwarts. We call to mind buddlejas, the varieties of *Hibiscus syriacus, Hypericum* × *moserianum*, potentillas and hydrangeas, which with the fuchsias carry us on bravely into autumn and its first frosts.

Sir Herbert Maxwell used to jot down any combination of colours he particularly liked late in the year, such as: "A bevy of blue-purple *Crocus speciosus* pushing up through a carpet of *Cerastium tomentosum.* [I should choose *C. biebersteinii* instead, as being less rampageous and more silvery.] A tangle of *Polygonum affine* beside porcelain-blue *Geranium wallichianum.* A furnace of *Kniphofia aloides* [*K. uvaria*] in a sea of snowy *Anemone japonica* ['Honorine Jobert']. A crimson cascade of *Berberidopsis corallina* falling over *Crinum powelli* 'Album' at the foot of a wall."

Those of us who live in suitable districts may put some reliance on the shrubby *Hibiscus syriacus* varieties. They need good sunshine in August to bring them into flower when the nights are warm. Apart from the buddlejas no late summer shrubs can compete with their rich beauty, and they even excel in a blue form ('Blue Bird'), a rare tint in shrubs; otherwise, lilac, white and light crimson are the order of the day, each flower being lit by radiating veins of red, and cream stamens. To get the greatest beauty from them the hibiscuses need rich feeding and hard pruning as for a Hybrid Tea rose.

My own particular choice of September shrubs are two white-flowered species: *Ligustrum quihoui* and *Clethra tomentosa*. Both are richly fragrant, casting their scent freely over the garden. I have known the *Ligustrum*, a Chinese species of Privet, for many years as a denizen of old and played-out botanic gardens and parks, but have been astonished at its prowess in my ordinary garden soil where it has made a bush some 10 feet high and wide, completely smothered by small flowers in lilac-like sprays, up to a foot in length. Everyone who sees it gasps and wonders why they have not seen it before. The answer is, of course, that lovers of choice plants shy at the mention of the word "privet": that this is pure snobbery is evident the moment the beauty of *Ligustrum quihoui* comes into their ken, and much the same might be claimed for an equally spectacular though more stodgy species, *L. japonicum*.

As fragrant as these, in fact even more so, is *Clethra alnifolia* var. *paniculata*, which flowers in late July, and its close relative *C. tomentosa*, which does not open until September. The small spikes of tiny cream flowers are very sweet. While *C. alnifolia* and its superior variety *paniculata* are cream, there is also 'Rosea' in a pleasing cream-pink. All are more invasive at the root than *C. tomentosa*, and all need lime-free soil with humus.

It is worth looking carefully at the buddlejas. Apart from the well-known varieties of *B. davidii* — and specially including the splendid 'Pink Delight' — all of which have a fairly short summer season, there are the smaller and much less common *B. fallowiana* and its white form 'Alba', and *B. stenostachya*. These two species have comparatively small spikes of flower and are at their best in September. The first species has extra grey woolly stems and foliage accentuated by the white, orange-eyed flowers of 'Alba'. All of these can usually be found still in bloom in early October. *Buddleja fallowiana* is less hardy than *B. davidii* and is often killed to the ground in cold districts, but speedily sprouts again.

A good crop of late blooms will usually accrue on bushes of certain varieties of *Ceanothus*, particularly *C.* × *delilianus* 'Gloire de Versailles', in powder-blue; 'Henri Desfosse', dark blue; and 'Perle Rose' in warm pink. But, like the varieties of *Hibiscus,* they must be well fed. Other hybrid ceanothuses which have good late crops of blue are 'Autumnal Blue', which is pale, and 'Burkwoodii', rich blue. The last is not as hardy as the others mentioned, and they all like as much sun as they can get.

As to hydrangeas, everyone knows the numerous forms of *H. macrophylla,* both lace-caps and hortensias, which are all so sensitive to soil, only thriving in those free of lime, and determined to be blue in certain soils only, pink in others. There is a tremendous range of varieties, flowering from late June until autumn, when the white Hortensia 'Mme Mouillère' goes on producing its generous rounded heads until winter arrives. Nearly as sensitive to lime are the varieties of the more compact *H. serrata,* of which 'Preziosa' is a wonderful reddish pink Hortensia and 'Blue Bird' a good lace-cap. Equally sensitive is the Japanese species *H. paniculata,* which has pointed panicles of blossom, not rounded. There are some noted newcomers with very large heads, such as 'Pink Diamond', but I rather think I prefer 'Kyushu', a wild lace-cap, to the other overfed grandifloras.

The most superb of all hydrangeas belong to the group headed by *H. villosa,* which are tolerant of lime in all its forms, and have velvety leaves and extra large heads of lilac flowers in August and September.

One sunny corner of my garden is given to *Caryopteris* × *clandonensis,* a low little shrub with masses of lavender-blue flowers in early September, and its later relative *C. incana.* These are augmented by the true cobalt-blue of *Ceratostigma willmottianum,* a Plumbago which flowers for weeks on end, then usually dies to the ground in winter. All of these are loved by the butterflies.

Finally in our little catalogue of these late summer shrubs are a few climbers. There are many purple and violet varieties of large-flowered

Clematis, none so late as 'Lady Betty Balfour', a vigorous grower. By its side I should like to see *C. rehderiana,* whose pyramids of small bell-shaped blossoms are creamy coloured — and, if you think of cowslips, their fragrance will suggest these spring delights. It will go on flowering into October, at which time a lovely companion for its colour is the Trumpet Creeper, *Campsis* ✕ *tagliabuana* 'Mme Galen'. The handsome divided foliage is held on stems which attach themselves to a sunny wall and, just when you have despaired of ever seeing the flowers, erupt on every shoot into large trumpets of orange-red; *C. grandiflora* is even more spectacular but less prolific and reliable, and there is a yellow form as well.

There is no doubt that the final months of summer can be very rewarding if you look around for the unusual among our gardens' treasures.

The Green Room

When the horticultural history of the twentieth century comes to be written, I think it will be found that the garden at Hidcote Bartrim Manor, Gloucestershire has had more influence than any other on the design of gardens. This is probably especially true of the second half of the century, during which time it has been open almost daily under the aegis of The National Trust, enabling countless thousands of visitors to make their way round the garden. Its influence is not surprising when we remember that the garden, on a difficult site, was designed by an artist, Lawrence Johnston, who was also a connoisseur of plants; he had travelled through France absorbing ideas of design.

Many of the separate portions of the garden were the outcome of studying the "capabilities" — to borrow from Lancelot Brown — of the site: a large area of level land, after which, without reference to the siting of the manor, the ground fell away to a stream, and then rose up again to the skyline of fields. Johnston, in developing the garden over the earlier half-century, did not make a blue-print of the whole design; rather, he altered what was necessary, as he went along, always coming up with a new, convincing scheme. Much levelling, achieved with the aid of retaining walls, enabled him to make the direct, level progression that is such a triumph, parallel with but from the south side of the manor. There was only just enough space before the stream impinged upon the area, running off at an oblique angle.

The fulcrum of the whole design of the main flower garden and borders is of course the *rond-point* in the main vista, approached through handsome iron gates. The *rond-point,* at the top of the little sketch, has a grass central circle surrounded by a circle of brick paving. Outside this are borders of various shade-loving plants, such as hellebores and spring bulbs, overshadowed by *Syringa chinensis,* the so-called French Lilac, which is of graceful habit and does not bear all its flowers on its topmost branches, as do all the hybrids and forms of *S. vulgaris,* the Common Lilac. After its spring display the *rond-point* subsides into sober greenery while the Red Border beyond and the Old Garden nearer to the manor assume control.

On the south side of the circle is an opening between the lilacs with an intriguing view of a further formal scheme. Parting the lilacs, one goes through an arched opening in a hedge of Copper Beech. An area much the size of many a modern garden is before us, laid out with consummate care and providing much interest and inspiration. The immediate foreground is given to small brick paths edged with dwarf box. In the spring the beds are solidly filled with the blue of *Scilla sibirica,* followed in summer by dwarf, free-flowering hardy fuchsias of various colours. On one side this little garden has a border of pink-tinted flowers chosen to provide colour mainly between the tones of the scillas and the fuchsias. The border includes the seldom-seen rose 'd'Orsay', a hybrid of an American species. There was no space for an echoing border on the other side of the little beds, but the inspiration occurred to Johnston to give it a hedge of varied colouring and texture. Besides green and variegated hollies there is Box, and green and copper Beech, in all an intriguing mixture, able to be seen and appreciated for its full height of six feet or thereabouts

FIFTY-FIVE – THE GREEN ROOM

because the fuchsias are all short growers. A firm Box hedge finishes the end of the little garden, making way in the centre for three or four stone steps leading down into a sunken garden. The steps are guarded by a pair of obelisks topped by birds in yew topiary, once slim and sedate, now rather overgrown. The flanking borders contain a Magnolia, *Osmanthus delavayi* and white roses. But the surprise here is a sheet of water raised 2 feet above the surrounding circular path and featuring an ornamental fountain of putto and fish.

It is interesting here to note that the natural stream, flowing below, was piped so that only its initial gurgle is heard to disturb the placidity of the raised pool and fountain. Originally there was a scheme of a central sunken pool surrounded by radiating beds filled with flowers, but at some time Johnston decided to turn the whole central area into a bathing pool with one side deep enough for diving. (The new scheme occasioned the building of a thatched shelter at one side as a changing room.) This raising of the level of the water provided a mirror for the next feature. On top of a wall is a high hedge of yew, with centrally a fine architectural archway, apt for reflection. This leads to the ultimate in this series of excitements, the tranquillity of the Green Room reached by a short flight of steps composed of tiles on edge. The view gives into this, a circle of tiny leaved yew and box, with simply a small circular lawn and dark green painted iron seat. Lest you think this is a disappointing end to the journey, there are two side outlets to other areas.

I should have mentioned that below the hedge and wall there is a narrow border given to shade-loving plants in specially prepared peaty soil. Blue *Meconopsis* are followed by blue willow gentians (*Gentiana asclepiadea*) contrasted by yellow and white *Corydalis* in the wall.

Despite all its varied enchantments, the whole area covered scarcely exceeds an eighth of an acre, an area such as is given for children to play in round many a modern home. But what artistry and what intriguing ideas! The transition from the bold foreground of beds, with the middle distance a mirror for the arch and the progressive lessening of the size of foliage into the Green Room, is all a marvel if one stands to assimilate it. I believe it to be one of Lawrence Johnston's crowning achievements, along with the *palissades à l'italienne* of the main vista. Whereas that would require a lot of work in the making and the maintenance, the way to the Green Room is comparatively simple and might be a model for a similar rectangle in any plot today. But to see the shady hedges threaded up with scarlet Flame Flower (*Tropaeolum speciosum*) is an added treat for summer visitors to Hidcote alone.

Cutting Fifty-Six —

The Fall of the Leaves

The leaves are so light that they sidle on their going downward,
hesitating in that which is not void to them, and touching at last
so imperceptibly the earth with which they are to mingle, that
the gesture is much gentler than a salutation, and even more
discreet than a discreet caress. They make little sound, less than
the least of sounds.

The above is how Hilaire Belloc felt it, this transformation of our gardens in autumn. I think he could only have written those sentences when sitting idly under a clear blue sky, watching one leaf after another drifting downwards in the still air.

We know that each twig cuts off the supply of sap to achieve this transformation. Our native trees or shrubs have been giving us their final season's joy since life began. Apart from a mere handful of shrubs which give richer tones, our British trees turn mostly to yellow, enriched by the tawny gold of the oaks and the deep tones of the beeches. The autumn glory of leaves went unnoticed by gardeners and plant lovers through long centuries until newcomers to our shores lit the autumn with orange and flame and red. There was little for gardeners to regale themselves with after the flowers of June had gone, apart from the autumn excitement and satisfaction of gathering fruits and nuts.

Thanks to the enthusiastic scouring of the world for new plants for our gardens, we have today in Britain a very wide range of trees and especially shrubs whose leaf-fall is panoplied in gorgeous colour. During this century, mainly, with the wealth of Far Eastern shrubs and American trees, autumn colour has become an end-of-the-season delight with many of us and even an obsession with some. There is another important point: most of these imported foreigners change their tints earlier than our yellowing natives, which means that the garden can still be a heart-warming sight in St Luke's Little (Indian) Summer.

It so happens that this appraisal of leaf-colour has coincided with more adequate heating of our homes. Perhaps we take more kindly to brilliance outdoors if we sally forth well fed and warm. I know that at times I have wished the autumn season over, the leaves down and swept away, on some of the chill and rainy days that beset us in what in the United States is known as the Fall — a very suitable and easy word for the waning season.

The fall of the leaves covers a long season. Even by the end of June, in some years, a premonition of autumn will be felt when we look at *Parrotia persica.* There, at the extremities of the branches, we shall see a coloration of a bronzy or purplish tone, the forerunner of the brilliant tints that will invade the huge bushes from outside inwards until the whole is ablaze with red and yellow except for the outermost twigs, which by that time are bare. It is then that we shall first notice the buds of brown velvet which herald the crimson tassels of February.

Scarlet, as opposed to the yellowish tones of most natives, seems naturally to be the colour most desired. On a good clear day, nothing of summer's joys can approach the brilliance of a bush totally enveloped in red leaves. What can compete with, say, *Acer palmatum* 'Ozaka Zuki', *Aronia arbutifolia, Cotinus coggygria, Fothergilla, Vaccinium corymbosum* and the azaleas, to name but a few favourites?

I could quickly name a further lot: *Berberis thunbergii, Cotoneaster bullatus, Enkianthus perulatus, Viburnum furcatum, V. plicatum* and our own splendid British native, *V. opulus.* Some go soon and some late, but two of the latest to linger, usually well into November, are *Eucryphia glutinosa* and *Photinia beauverdiana,* and October's walls and arches will be ablaze with *Ampelopsis, Vitis* and *Parthenocissus.* One of the most noticeable shrubs is *Rhus typhina* whose long pinnate leaves, held horizontally and in blazing scarlet, lighten for a few brief days many a dull corner of bricks and mortar.

The first of autumn's fires among trees is firmly with *Prunus sargentii* — perhaps almost too soon, for all else is still green. The leaves have usually dropped before other trees turn red, trees such as *Acer rubrum, Quercus rubra* and two of the longest-lasting of them all, *Q. coccinea* 'Splendens' and the multicoloured *Nyssa sylvatica,* which may often still be in colour in November. *Liquidambar styraciflua* can also be a brilliant sight if you manage to get hold of one of the named forms noted for their colour.

It does not do, however, to concentrate wholly on these blazing fires. Aloft, our yellowing natives give us the clue: yellow must not be forgotten; it includes, among shrubs, *Rosa rugosa, Lindera* and *Clethra.* We need also some of darker tint, the blood red and murrey of *Disanthus cercidifolius,* and 'Atropurpurea' forms of *Berberis thunbergii* and *Prunus cerasifera* ('Pissardii'), whose deep tones of summer will enrich the flame of autumn.

I think by now you will all be satiated with red and flame and yellow and I suggest setting aside a corner for a fresh colour grouping. I have in mind pink and crimson and creamy tints. Taking the warmest tone first, there is the gorgeous and reliable *Euonymus alatus* in pure crimson without flame or orange. Next to it place *E. verrucosus,* which turns to pale pink and cream, and *Cotoneaster horizontalis* 'Variegata' in unvarying pink, fortunately without red berries. Something quite unusual is found in *Berberis dictyophylla,* whose reddish tones are muted by the white stems and pink berries, and in the uncommon *Orixa japonica,* almost the only shrub that turns to a very pale tint, which I can best describe as lemon-white. With the new blend thus conjured up, a carpet of vivid blue *Gentiana sino-ornata* would be acclaimed: it would seem there is no need for autumn to go out in unadulterated pyrolatry. There is room, too, for the subdued and long lasting orange-red tones of *Spiraea thunbergii,* whose wire-fine twigs will no sooner have lost their slender leaves at the end of December than its first minute white flowers appear with the turning year.

One cannot be sure of autumn colour, though most of the species cited are pretty reliable. For the best colour, it is said that you should ensure a light touch of frost at about the autumnal equinox, a good rain and then a spell of fine weather from mid October. But the soil should be neutral or even acid, friable and well drained, and of course Aeolus must be warned off.

Cutting Fifty-Seven —

Pines in the Garden

We do not generally think of pines for planting in gardens. To me, at least, they are trees very much of open spaces, where their rugged simplicity can take on a wild and windswept outline not assumed by any other tree.

> The loud wind through the forest wakes . . .
> And in yon gloomy Pines strange music makes,
> The bending Firs a mournful cadence keep.

These lines are from William Drummond of Hawthornden, writing in the early seventeenth century. There is no doubt that he was thinking of pines, correctly, as species of the genus *Pinus,* whereas 'Fir' is nowadays widely applied as much to pines as to spruces. A spruce is never made the more interesting by the caress or blast of wind — it tends to become pruned and shaped into something *not* "spruce" and symmetrical. A great conical pine tree, of even shape and usually furnished with branches to the ground, will prove an asset to most gardens of moderate size. The bunched and dense needles shimmer with the passing breeze or, on a still day, provide a subdued background reflecting little light.

I have never, since my earliest days, been able to resist the pull of the pine, near in the garden or far in the landscape. They have so much nobility and individuality. In the dry soil and landscape of my Cambridge childhood they thrive better than most conifers, and were among the first evergreen trees whose Latin names I memorised; the silky grey-green tresses of the great Himalayan Pine, *Pinus wallichiana,* the dense, bunched, dark green needles of the Swiss Pine, *P. cembra*, or the Bush Pine, *P. mugo*, in darkest green, so frequently seen on rock gardens. In later years I came to recognise its value in a totally different setting: as a dark foil in the Red Border at Hidcote. It was surely a master-stroke that led Lawrence Johnston to place this bush, the garden's darkest piece of greenery, to act as a complete contrast to all the vivid rich colours of the flowers. This is a most variable shrub — and cannot be called a tree, some selected modern forms, such as 'Gnom', being measured in inches rather than feet, and certainly not in yards. 'Corley's Mat' is intriguingly prostrate, rising perhaps to one foot.

Those most artistic of gardeners, the Japanese, have always held the pine in great veneration and admiration. Particularly do they honour the pine by selecting a pair to guard their garden gates, the rugged *P. thunbergii* on one side to represent the male element, and the softer, pliant *P. densiflora*, the female, on the other. Nobody who has a penchant for things Japanese could ever expect to be free of the influence of pines; not grown as a forestry specimen, but invisibly pruned and shaped into a representation of bent old age. No other conifer lends itself so well to this shaping, often supported by props to lessen the extended weight of the branches. In Japan, as elsewhere, their dense foliage and strong outline is a foil for the lacy filigree of maples and the rustling, pliant bamboos without which Japaneese gardens are never complete. A frequent choice is Thunberg's pine, which has never found much favour in Britain, our choice being wider and including pines from many parts of the world.

A close relative of the Swiss Pine is *P. pumila;* it holds its needles, in bunches of five, in which it also resembles the much larger and more luxuriant Himalayan Pine. It makes a lowly bush, like *P. mugo,* but is more dense in foliage and growth. In some seasons the bright crimson male cones decorate the soft, dark, grey-green bushes with a wonderful display. Also blessed with bunches of five needles is a small Japanese tree, *P. parviflora.* Its most appealing forms have distinctly grey-blue, curved needles whose light colour acts as a contrast to the dark cones which it produces at an early age.

A close relative of *P. densiflora* is the dwarf 'Umbraculifera', a Japanese garden variant which nevertheless breeds true to type from seeds. Its silky green needles are very appealing, carried densely over the top of the mushroom-shaped bushes. A specimen at Hidcote is a graft from a seedling raised from a plant I imported from the Yokohama Nursery Company when I was still a schoolboy. Thus have pines always held me.

Another unique pine of similar growth is *P. sylvestris* 'Moseri', raised by the French firm which also gave us two large-flowered clematises and a *Mahonia* named after it. The pine has the winsome merit of becoming flushed with brassy yellow in winter; there is a magnificent gnarled specimen on the old rock garden in the University Botanic Garden at Cambridge. At the Royal Botanic Gardens at Kew until recently, when it was removed when alterations were made to the rock garden, there had been growing for almost a century *P. strobus* 'Prostrata', a pleasing procumbent growth of the Weymouth Pine, whose needles are in bunches of three.

I will finally draw attention to two species whose great attraction is in the colour of their bark. The Chinese Lace-bark Pine sheds its bark regularly to reveal the creamy under-layer, in much the same style as the London Plane; its bark is its special redeeming feature, for its foliage is not specially attractive. I have left till last the British native Scots Pine, *P. sylvestris.* I venture to state that it is the most beautiful of all pines, perhaps of all conifers, though its ubiquity in dry soils in the south of the country and in the damper climate of west Scotland and the Lake District is apt to make us forget it when thinking of trees for the garden. It is true that we have to wait some fifty years before it can be fully appreciated. Then, if it has been planted so that the westering sun can shine upon it, the full glory and contrast of tints will be revealed, especially after rain. To the ineffably soft grey-green of its pairs of needles is coupled the warm orange-brown of the bark, even reddish after rain. The Scots Pine is a free seeder, and in the past was used as a hedging plant in the sandy wastes of the Breckland in Norfolk, hacked down to governable height, which has resulted in fantastically shaped trees alongside the roads.

Cutting Fifty-Eight —

The Apple Tree

More than any other kind of fruit tree, the apple has figured in poems, songs and the nostalgia for old gardens. It is the fruit which comes to perfection in the British climate. Vaughan Williams set to music the Dorset folk song 'Linden Lea', whose second verse contains the lines

> . . . brown leaved fruit's a-turning red,
> In cloudless sunshine overhead,
> With fruit for me, the apple tree
> Do lean down low in Linden Lea.

Just what an apple was doing in a meadow of Lime trees is not explained, but I suspect there are few of us who are not touched by the sentiment of the verse. There is something very appealing in the memory of an old, leaning apple tree — its trunk and branches a host to moss and lichen — hung with rosy red fruits, flushed, striped or plain green. And the Dorset song brings us right into October, when St Luke's "little summer" ushers in cloudless days and the season for gathering the apples. When the weather allows, it is a golden moment of fulfilment and promise, not equalled in the gardener's year. Is there anything to surpass the fresh flavour of a choice dessert apple, picked at the moment of ripening — ascertained by lifting the fruit and finding the stalk easily separating from the leafy branch — among all the treasures of the year? It is something that has been with us all, ever since fruits of quality were raised by selection from seeds from the wild stock, over hundreds of years ago. The seeds, or pips, gave rise to the name of "pippin" by which many apples are known, not the least being 'Cox's Orange Pippin', raised in 1830.

Good seedling apples have always been treasured for their flavour, their keeping quality when gathered, or their abundant cropping and freedom from disease. In days long ago, when one could not go to the store for fresh apples every week, they were gathered with tender care and stored in cool, damp, frost-proof fruit rooms for use in due season. Today but a handful of varieties are found in the shops, instead of a succession of varieties which would be at their best from August until early summer in the following year. Each would have not only its best season, but also a different flavour and texture. But today, in our tiny gardens, there is little room for even one traditional tree, let alone a fruit-store. Efforts are being made by the breeders, however, to produce suitably dwarfing rootstocks to take new varieties of controlled growth. There is no doubt that this is highly desirable, and, when the object has been achieved in all ways, we may be able to grow a dozen toothsome kinds in a dozen yards. In this way we shall avoid having to cope with a surplus of any variety at one time.

In contemplating these gustatory delights we perhaps forget the other great benefit of apples — their blossom. During this century the beauties of flowering crab apples and Japanese cherries have been extolled almost *ad nauseam;* before their advent I am sure that along with laburnums and thorns, apples and crabs were valued for their blossom. Much as I love the lacy loveliness of the Japanese trees, they bear no fruit, give sparingly of autumn colour, and their roots play havoc with lawns and borders. If apples be reassessed, I think we shall find that they more than hold their own if grown as trees for blossom and fruit. While a few cherries have some scent, notably *Prunus* × *yedoensis* and 'Jonioi', *all* apples are fragrant with a warm sweet attar unlike that of anything else. And the scent is shed freely by the flowers, silky yet downy, in many varieties warmly coloured with rosy flush in closed bud, and opening to blush white, a dappling of tints over each tree.

Foremost among apples for rich tinting of bloom are 'Sunset', a richly flavoured variety of Cox's derivation, 'Lord Derby' and 'Arthur Turner', two useful culinary varieties, and 'Upton Pyne', which has the largest flower of any apple, and sweet fruits.

It is good to feel that these are all still available from specialist firms. They and others remind us that the apple is especially the fruit which comes to perfection in England where it has been grown for many hundreds of years, from way back in those centuries when, apart from fruits and vegetables, there were few plants of any kind that gave delight after June.

Cutting Fifty-Nine —

Tools

It might be claimed that a man's work is only as good as his tools. Over the centuries a perfection has been reached, whereby garden tools have been so polished and streamlined in shape that they may be said to fit the human frame. If they do not, owing to cheap or unthinking design, they will be awkward to hold and use, and work done with them will, though perhaps unwittingly, be impaired.

Take the scythe, which we might call the most human of tools; it is adjustable to fit the human frame of whatever size or poise this may be. Anyone who has heard the swishing of the blade through damp grass, or the scream of the stone along the blade during those minutes when the back straightens up to allow for re-sharpening, will realise there is a great partnership between craftsman and tool. "The pen thinks for you; and so does the scythe mow for you if you treat it honourably and in a manner that makes it recognize its service." This is from *Hills and the Sea* by Hilaire Belloc, a great writer and scythesman.

In the few remaining large areas of rough grass in our shrunken gardens the scythe has been replaced by chugging machines. There are indeed many machines available today which turn gardening at weekends into a noisy and smelly occupation — machines for mowing, sawing, clipping and shredding. All save time and labour, and the finished product is usually good, but only for those who like tending and using machines will there be enjoyment; for those whose walk of life does not embrace machines there will be frustration, resulting in "things going wrong". But I am not intending to write about these machines: I will leave them to those who are more conversant with them, confessing my experience to be limited to mowing and clipping.

The scythe's smaller relative, the sickle or hook, is invaluable for the cutting down of herbaceous plants in autumn.

The smaller the garden the more it depends upon hand-tools, and therefore the quality of these tools assumes great importance. Beware of getting tools too large for your frame of body. I am of about average size, and have found by experience, through a long life of gardening, that more and better work can be done more easily by using tools of small to moderate size. Not for me are large spades and forks and shovels — I leave them to the navvies of gardening.

The spade might well be called the king of garden tools. So many other jobs with other tools depend on initial work by the spade — the digging, the levelling and the planting. It is so much better to dig a bed or border thoroughly than to use a mechanical tool, which does not cultivate very deeply. In years of drought, it is well-dug borders in which signs of lack of moisture have been least apparent. Except in heavy clay soils I should always use a spade, whereas on clay it may be better to use a strong-tined fork. It is surprising how the rudiments of digging are not taught or observed — the opening of a trench and keeping it open to the end of the operation, when the original soil from the first trench is used to fill in the last excavation. In this way all small weeds get well buried. If you are right-handed, the heel of the left foot should aid the arm in pressing the blade into the soil. To use the sole or instep is bad for the shoe and the foot, and the pressure is less ready. I am still using a spade purchased more than sixty years ago: because it was a well-known make, straight, and had a well-strapped shaft — with the metal bands reaching two-thirds of the way up to the handle — the original ashwood handle is still unbroken, and the blade is gently worn into a curve at the cutting edge. The upper edges have narrow metal "shoulders" to protect the shoe. As a spade is to be a friend for life it pays to buy the best, which today would be of stainless steel — one such would have saved me hours of cleaning during and after work, for of all tools this is most important to keep clean: a clean blade prevents clogging.

I remember a visit to Sissinghurst Castle soon after I assumed the responsibility of advising on that noted garden. I remarked on the excellent level digging over the beds and how lucky Pamela Schwerdt — then head gardener — was to have a staff who could make such a good job of the heavy clay soil. "But we do it all ourselves," she said! Much the same remark was made to me when I had dug over the entire front garden of my new property. "How nicely *they* have dug it," said a visitor. . . . A good bit of digging gives a lot of satisfaction, both during and after the work. It is just sad that on heavy or stony soils a fork has to be used instead of a spade. But the level tilth is there just the same.

Shovels are not so dictatorial. Here again, the largest size will not be found the most advantageous: a large shovelful of soil or sand or whatever is a back-breaking weight. When once the heap to be moved has dwindled, always shovel from the base of the heap and use the right knee to give an extra push to the handle.

While it is a great boon and luxury to have stainless steel tools, it is not quite so important with shovels and forks as it is with spades: except in very sticky soil they do not clog so easily. And of course, ideally on sticky soils one should wait, hopefully, for a drying day: clay should not be handled when wet, but the weather is not always co-operative. In general, for most gardens and gardeners, I think broad-bladed forks are better than square-tined ones. Although I keep a fairly large one, I also have what is known as a "lady's fork", a smaller edition with square tines. It was given to me some 75 years ago and has many uses: it is rather worn down, but sharp. It has had one new handle; the breakage was due to carelessness and impatience. It often happens that one tine of a fork is pulled out of alignment, and this is the time to cut off both outer tines to leave a two-pronged implement, just right for prising off portions of herbaceous plants, seedings, et cetera, to give to friends. E. A. Bowles was the first gardener I knew who made regular use of such a tool. I would not be without a fork, but I find that almost all work can be done just as well with my spade. One is apt to titivate the soil with a fork or a hand-fork, and this has the result of helping weed-seeds to germinate.

If you find it necessary to have a hand fork, I recommend the three-pronged, flat-tined version with a short 6-inch handle; never one with a long handle, or tines like a grating — they collect clods and weeds. I have never used a hand fork, doing all small work with a stainless steel trowel, which is one of the greatest boons for gardeners. Here again, get a well-known make, with a short handle; one has less purchase with a long handle.

Generally in late spring there comes a short spell of dry weather which is just right for quick work with the hoe, to kill weeds and also to thin those delectable plants that seed themselves too freely. Here again, a small tool is more useful for getting between other plants. My most useful one has a sharp blade for push-ing and the two shoulders — on either side of the central handle — are also sharp, for pulling; it has therefore only half the drag on weeds found in the most usual type, in which the blade is only sharp in front and has two supports. I also keep a small swan-neck or carrot-hoe for certain intimate jobs; but in general I am not a hoe-user, believing that they bring more weed-seeds to the surface.

Rakes have been revolutionised by plastic models, shaped to the soil or grass at any angle. Moreover, the tines do not tear foliage or twigs of heathers and other lowly plants when used to remove infestations of fallen leaves. Rakes should be broad and long-tined; when leaf-raking, you can pick up the leaves with them. I think these plastic-tined ones largely surpass the wire and other metal rakes, except for soil-raking in preparation for seed sowing. As to the besom broom, made of a bundle of twigs fastened to a handle, are its days numbered? A besom is the sort of thing that, like a scythe, tends to be neglected for modern inventions, but if I still had a large lawn I should use one in preference to a rake or leaf-sweeper.

As with digging, there is immense satisfaction to be had from the proper use of a besom. One must  bend one's back to almost horizontal; the broom should be near the ground for most of its length and be given a slight turn of the handle after each stroke. This ensures that the broom will keep or assume a paint-brush shape, and not become bent or one-sided as it would without the turning, or when used from a more-or-less upright position. The more horizontal the broom is, the greater the power and thrust against the leaves. On a windless day, with a supple back, merrily go the leaves. For gathering up the leaf heaps there is nothing so efficacious as a pair of wire rakes with their handles much shortened.

It irks me very much to see an amateur — and sometimes trained gardeners — using edging shears without fully understanding the art of their use — for it is an art. Do not stand facing the edge and take bites, so to speak, with both hands. The shears should be held and guided by an almost stationary left hand, while the right hand does the work of cutting. Face obliquely to the direction (to the left) where the work is proceeding. It is quite surprising how the working right hand more or less propels the shears along.

Sometimes the grass abuts onto paving, with no cutting verge: the edging shears can be forced along, but it is not easy. It is probably better to use the half-moon cutter, suitably sharpened, cutting along with a sawing motion impelled by the arms and not by the foot. The half-moon turf-cutter goes hand in hand with the turf-lifter. Unless the former is needed for edging, as above, the two are not usually found in small gardens, but generally indicate that there is moving of turf to be done. Pressure is mainly from the right knee, as with the shovel.

As to secateurs or clippers and all cutting implements, keep them well oiled and see that the blade is at right angles to the branch or twig to be cut, to avoid straining the blade. The modern light-weight, metal-handled parrot-bill pruners are most useful for shoots that are too large for secateurs. They are ideal, too, for pruning or thinning prickly roses and other shrubs. And a pair of long-arm pruners is needed in most gardens, for high shrubs and trees.

Most barrows are made today with understanding; that is to say, the wheel is as near to the bulk of the load as possible, to avoid too much weight depending on the arms. Metal or plastic water cans, on the other hand, are designed and made today without much thought. Fortunately one can still buy the real professional thing, a Haws can, with a long spout and a variety of brass roses. There is no substitute for these; I have had my galvanised model for more than forty years and it is still in mint condition. It is well to have a coloured plastic can reserved for the use of weedkillers on paths and drives.

In a garden like mine, of a quarter of an acre, all the tools mentioned above are needed at some time of the year, including long-arm pruners and a pruning saw. It pays to buy the right thing of an approved make, and to look after it.

Cutting Sixty —

The Dark Colours

It must be forty or more years since I first went to St Nicholas, a renowned garden at Richmond in Yorkshire, so ably run by The Honourable Robert James. My visit was primarily to see his collection of old garden roses — the word "garden" was always included in those days, to differentiate them from roses such as the Hybrid Perpetuals which were bred for the show-bench. He showed me many treasures, including the wild single *Rosa gallica* and what we now call (without foundation) 'Empress Josephine', which he had been given by Miss Ellen Willmott. His garden was very much on show in early July and abounding in colour. I particularly remember groups of very dark wine-red Sweet Williams, a strain which he had been at pains to select and reselect over the years. I remember his words: "It is all very well keeping to soft and light colours; they are the joy of a garden, but you must have plenty of dark tones here and there to show them up, like the bass notes in an orchestra." There is no doubt he was right; it was the reason behind his repeated use of dark roses of the Gallica group, such as 'Tuscany' and 'Charles de Mills'; the rich crimsons of the peonies; some of the darkest oriental poppies, followed by *Veratrum nigrum* in chocolate brown, and the darkest purple phloxes. Without such a balance a garden can look weak and even insipid. We only have to conjure up Bach's great 'Sanctus' to find in our minds those velvety deep notes of the accompanying organ which bring such majesty to the piece, when we have already experienced the richness of the orchestra and voices.

The little group of plants mentioned above contains some well tried favourites, but are all summer flowering. Curiously, spring flowers, other than rhododendrons and camellias, are mostly of light colours. Our first deep note of the season comes from the so-called "black" tulips; they have a profound effect because in the early year they give us the first opportunity to splash about with strong colours. The black tulips — 'La Tulipe Noire' and others — have an extraordinary effect of acting as a foil to clearer colours and even uniting disparate tints. There comes a memory of this tulip's use with orange *Cheiranthus* and pink 'Clara Butt' tulips under the seventeenth-century wing of Lanhydrock House, Cornwall, where the colours seemed to be reflected by the ancient stonework — though it was in reality warmed by a covering of similarly tinted lichen, caught by the sun. The picture lives in my mind very vividly.

After the tulips come the old double crimson peonies. No flower of the year makes quite such a gorgeous bowl of richness. With them are the hybrid lilacs; however much we love the whites and cool mauves, their soft beauty is redoubled by a plant of one of the darkest, such as 'Souvenir de Louis Späth' or 'Mrs Edward Harding'. Companions at that time are found in the darkest bearded irises, so satisfying against the light yellows and lavender blues, and the dark plum-coloured lupins, followed by delphiniums. Do not however, get it wrong: the bulk of all these plants should be of the lighter colours — these are the tones from which garden pictures are made, but the occasional bass note is needed as well as brilliance or softness.

A bunch of sweet peas can appear weak and frilly without a few of the dark purple and wine-colours. During the summer months free use can be made of the darker penstemons, and *Hemerocallis* 'Stafford' and 'Missenden', so decisive against 'Dorothy McDade' and 'Marion Vaughn' in light yellow. Among roses alone there are wonderful colours of a rich darkness, unsurpassed in the Climber 'Guinée', the Floribunda 'Dusky Maiden' and the older 'Souvenir du Docteur Jamain' — though this last suffers from scorching of the petals in hot weather. Later there is a wealth of tints in dahlias, and some richly toned clematises of noted depth — 'Madame Édouard André', for instance, or the still darker *C. viticella* variety, 'Royal Velours', a dusky note which looks particularly well on mellow stone.

With a specially long flowering season is *Knautia macedonica*, which used to be called *Scabiosa rumelica*. Its pompon-like flowers of pure crimson continue to be produced from early July till autumn and look pleasing with the lighter blue *Agapanthus campanulatus* forms, which are quite hardy; they will enliven a border after early roses have passed over, as at Mottisfont Abbey near Romsey in Hampshire.

One way of introducing dark colour into mixed borders — which is what I am visualising — is by the use of what we call coppery purple foliage; we all know what we mean by this term, but anything less like copper-colour (or purple) would be hard to find. As a frontal plant for a sunny but not-too-dry border, there is the invaluable creeping *Ajuga reptans* 'Atropurpurea' (I should always avoid all the speckled and multicoloured variants) whose metallic beetroot-tinted leaves are decorated by five-inch spikes of blue flowers in spring. And then, when the warm days of May and June arrive, we can bless that splendid *Heuchera micrantha diversifolia* 'Palace Purple', grown and named at Kew by Brian Halliwell. The flowers are of little effect, but the clump of rich darkness is just what is needed to show up white campanulas.

Many people today attempt gardens filled with white flowers. The fashion started at Hidcote Manor long ago, but has really caught our imaginations because of the splendid area devoted to white at Sissinghurst Castle. In Scotland much the same result has come from the white borders at that other garden of consummate colour-work by the late Lady Burnett of Leys at Crathes Castle, Kincardineshire (Grampion). Here the borders of white and green were given backdrops of hedges of *Prunus cerasifera* 'Pissardii'. It is quite astonishing how the coppery purple foliage purifies the whites, for I need hardly remind you that true white is a rare colour, most being tinted with cream, blue, yellow or blush, giving an overall white effect. I have seen this striking combination of the very dark with white only at Crathes, but I long now to make a white garden with some dark-visaged shrubs interspersed here and there. Only the richest colours would be chosen: many coppery-purple bushes, such as *Berberis thunbergii*

'Atropurpurea', are too heavy and dark. The dwarf-growing 'Atropurpurea Nana' has a good colourful rich tone, as has 'Ottawensis Superba'. Prickly berberises are not, however, everyone's choice, and a better recommendation would be *Cotinus coggygria* 'Royal Purple'. *Prunus* ✕ *cistena* will achieve some 5 to 6 feet and has leaves of a lively dark tint, and considerably taller is the comparatively new *Cercis canadensis* 'Forest Pansy'.

Let me finally offer a word of warning. Alluring though this dark foliage is, it can easily be overdone. One has only to see several copper beeches or the usual prunus trees together to realise that their value is not enhanced by grouping, only when used in isolated planting, in carefully chosen sites with due consideration to the light that falls on them. As with dusky dark flowers, so with dusky dark leaves: they owe ninety per cent of their beauty to light, and, moreover, without full light the richest colouring will not materialise.

Cutting Sixty-One —

Heathers in the Garden

In many ways heaths and heathers are looked upon as ideal plants for the gardens of today. Their advantages are varied. They provide admirable ground-cover, last a long time in flower in different periods of the year, have a wide palette of colours, are easy to propagate by cuttings or layers, and will grow in open soils containing some humus, but mostly without lime. They need open positions, do not thrive when obscured by the autumn fall of leaves, and as a general rule are averse to encroaching shrubs and trees. It is therefore not difficult to select gardens where they will thrive and be an asset. Even so, unless conditions are to their liking they will not succeed, but become a liability.

It is no use being small-minded about planting these little shrubs. How often does one see a collection of a dozen or so different sorts planted in a prescribed area, all distinct in colour and growth. This is the worst sort of planting for them, brought about by our acquisitive tendencies and a desire for variety coming to the fore in our minds after a visit to a garden centre. The old maxim, to decide on what you want first, is much, much better than choosing attractive individual plants, then coming home and wondering where to put them. I doubt whether any plants are so prone as the heathers to such mistaken thought as this. Of all plants, they owe much to association and grouping — grouping not only in their own sphere, but in association with their surroundings. Heathers spell the open air, the moorland, the wide sweeps of hill and dale, and the companionship of grasses and small-leafed shrubs and little trees. They bring to the garden, if rightly used, a smell of the wild open country. This is not so fanciful as it may seem, for even in a comparatively small garden a wide grouping of these invaluable little plants can give a totally different effect from the ubiquitous rose-beds and mixed borders, or the very different woodland planting. The three ideals are miles apart and in my opinion do not mix well, neither in aesthetic appeal nor in cultivation.

I am well aware that few of us have the space in our gardens of today to imitate a stretch of moorland; my answer would be not to attempt it, but to concentrate on conventional planting. A little assembly of heathers of various colours and seasons is merely a sop to one's greed, not gardening in its wider applications. But let us look around and use what is available for different purposes.

First, there is the soil to be considered. Though a few species will tolerate or even thrive on limy soil with adequate humus, it is best not to attempt a heather garden or grouping of these plants in such soils, especially on chalk; they are not so particular about magnesium limestone. On the subject of soils and humus, it should be remembered that leaf-mould derived from trees growing in limy soil will not be of much use to such lime-haters: as a rule we must use peat. And I have learnt that this does not need to be dug into the soil, but can be spread on the surface; worms and the heathers' surface rooting habit will do the rest. On very dry soils the hybrids of *Erica carnea* and *E. erigena* (*E. mediterranea*) will be found most tolerant of extreme drought. Known as *E.* × *darleyensis*, they contribute nobly to the winter display of heathers, being usually the first to open in November, and last in flower until early May. They are far more drought-tolerant than *E. carnea* itself and, in fact, than the true heathers or *Calluna* variants; their only rivals in droughty conditions are *E. terminalis* and *E. arborea* 'Alpina'. For moist positions, *E. tetralix* and *E. ciliaris,* their forms and hybrids, should be chosen.

Having cast from our minds the undesirable thought of a few diverse kinds mixed in with other flower-garden planting, we might next consider the use of heathers in a comparatively large garden where the area available is sufficient to create a real moorland effect. There must be enough of each kind to foster the illusion of limitless space. More often than not, the effect is of a patchwork quilt or, at worst, an echo of carpet-bedding — which is probably far removed from the thoughts of the planter. Yet they are often planted thus, all equally spaced and clipped over, keeping them in neat compartments. Is this what we should do? An alternative is to make a spotty planting of a dozen or so named kinds repeated in mixture over an area; this again is artificiality undefeated — it cannot be described as creating a bit of wild scenery. In fact, in my opinion it is no use to attempt a wild effect with approved, distinct cultivars: they simply do not make a natural blend. There is only one way of achieving this and it is by raising the plants from seed, so that full variation is the result.

This will mean at least two years' preparation, and a certain amount of disappointment in the quality of the resultant flowers. But believe me, the result will be much nearer to the desired effect than any amount of mixing of distinct cultivars. Even dud seedlings can be tolerated; they show up the qualities of the best.

And then it must be remembered that to create a wild effect, a mixed planting of whatever heathers cannot be just placed on an undulating piece of terrain in a garden without linking it suitably to its surroundings. Birch trees and Gorse at once spring to mind, but birches make large rooty trees in time and Gorse is an undesirable neighbour in a garden, in spite of its glorious fragrance. Rather should we choose shrubs with small leaves, such as the larger so-called tree-heaths, escallonias and cistuses (if your garden will prove sufficiently sheltered for these two genera), lavenders, sages and the like. These all have comparatively small leaves and thus tend to make a blend. In my own garden a great and unexpected success has been the grey-glaucous *Hebe pinguifolia* 'Pagei'. Its growths are of similar vigour to that of *Erica carnea* varieties and thread through them in an unlimited way, contributing grey to the carpets of pink flowers of the heaths, and also a sheet of tiny white flowers just when the *carneas* are going over. Quite unexpectedly they are followed by *Penstemon scouleri*

'Albus', which flowers a bit later and has threaded its way through all, likewise.

Dwarf and spreading Broom and flat-growing junipers are all eligible, except that most brooms (*Genista* and *Cytisus*) have very strong yellow flowers and do not always make a happy blend; but we will come to colours later. Prostrate junipers, such as varieties of *Juniperus horizontalis* and *J. squamata* — but avoiding the over-planted *J.* × *media* 'Pfitzeriana' and its derivatives — are admirable and suitable companions, as are the really dwarf and prostrate pines. Prostrate too, *Arctostapylos uva-ursi* and *A. nevadensis*, the spreading dwarf Birch, *Betula nana*, and some of the dwarf procumbent willows, will all help to make a varied moorland blend. The main artistry in planting such a mixture with *Erica* and *Calluna* included is in the placing, for some will require a yard or two of space, others would be much smaller. To plant the whole lot a foot or two apart would be a disaster and lead to overcrowding very quickly. The ideal is a sea of growth, excluding all weeds after a few years' establishment, and creating a varied blend of greenery bespangled with flowers in due season.

Ericas and callunas require clipping over after flowering. I think this is most easily done with long-handled shears with horizontal blades. One can walk over the dwarf shrubs with impunity and, if it is done every year, the clippings will be short, need not be picked up and will soon be obscured by the new growths. The other shrubs will seldom require clipping. This clipping serves several purposes: it keeps plants compact and thus more resilient to autumn's fallen leaves, and it tidies away the dead flower spikes; furthermore, by circumspect use of the clippers an undulating natural effect can be achieved, some plants demanding closer clipping than others. But in this large garden of our imagination nothing should be sudden; all should blend with the surroundings.

This brings me to the colours of the flowers of heaths and heathers. All flowers of these two genera — *Erica* and *Calluna* — make a good assortment in their different seasons, but there is great danger in winter if some of the brilliant yellow- and-orange-leafed forms of *Calluna* and even one or two

Erica variants are included with *Erica carnea* and *E.* × *darleyensis* varieties. Their pink-tinted flowers clash horribly with the extraordinary brilliance of the callunas' leaves, and what perhaps started with the idea of brightening up the winter garden develops into a medley of disparate colour. We should not succumb to this in our summer gardens; why then give way in winter? It is at variance with all sensitivity, and also with the quiet tones of winter, and is further aggravated by the bright brown tints of faded flowers of both the genera concerned, if these are not clipped off betimes. One of the most difficult contenders in this category is the redoubtable *E. terminalis* itself, whose bright brown dead flowers last through the winter, an unpleasant reminder of summer in the early year.

Some of the *E.* × *darleyensis* varieties are of fairly large growth and will reach up to meet *E. terminalis* in due course. 'Brightness' and 'W. T. Rackliffe' come to mind, growing up to 3 feet, and densely bushy; 'Arthur Johnson' will achieve the same, and judging by its young growth in my garden, the notable 'Irish Dusk' will do likewise. This is a plant of fresh, even new, colour among the heathers: it has a pleasing touch of coppery pink. A word about white heathers for winter: 'Springwood White' remains the best and clearest, with good green foliage; 'Silberschmelze' is a greyish white and is shamed by the former. The newer 'White Perfection' is a good white but is later, flowering mainly in spring with 'Irish Dusk'. Whites are in strong demand for winter effect, to balance the numerous pink varieties.

Mahonia bealei

But perhaps I am going too far. It may be that some intending planters will desire just those contrasts which I seek to avoid. They will ask for the contrast of broad foliage such as *Bergenia* and *Viburnum davidii, Mahonia, Pachysandra procumbens, Yucca* and *Phormium* and want to bring in all that today's enthusiasts for texture and diversity can devise. This is another type of the art of planting, and I think should be left for a separate occasion.

> They will come again, the leaf and the flower, to arise
> From squalor of rottenness into the old splendour,
> And magical scents to a wondering memory bring;
> The same glory, to shine upon different eyes,
> Earth cares for her own ruins, naught for ours,
> Nothing is certain, only the certain spring.
>
> — Laurence Binyon (1869 – 1943)

Cutting Sixty-Two —

Pruning

"When should it be pruned?" is a question frequently asked after the purchase of a shrub. I am bold enough to add that it is one asked mainly by the idle-minded and unobservant gardener: shrubs do not all require pruning, and it is only by observation of their habits and peculiarities that it can be ascertained whether pruning is necessary. Pruning is an enjoyable occupation, for it establishes our superiority over the shrub, telling it that its exuberance is unnecessary, that it must flower more freely, or that it must be allowed to set its berries.

In short, there is *one* rule for pruning: if pruning is necessary, it should be done in late winter or earliest spring for those species which flower after, say, midsummer; or immediately after flowering for those species which flower before midsummer. Let me elaborate a little on this for the benefit of those who have not studied the performance of their shrubs: those which flower before midsummer do so, mostly, on short or very short shoots which grow out from the branch of last season's growth. It follows, therefore, that the shrub needs to be encouraged to produce good growths from which short shoots will accrue in abundance early in the following year. On the other hand, those which flower after midsummer, or thereabouts, depend on vigorous shoots being produced which will flower well in the same growing season. Examples of the former group are *Prunus glandulosa* and the various hybrid weigelas; of the latter group, *Hibiscus syriacus* varieties and *Buddleja davidii* varieties. There are many exceptions, such as *Forsythia* 'Spectabilis', which flowers best on the second year's side shoots, and many varieties of *Philadelphus,* which flower in June or July but still need pruning immediately the flowers are shed.

Certain shrubs may be said to do their own pruning; their flowers are terminal and thus prevent the shoots from growing too far; an example is *Viburnum × juddii.* Then there is the long list of shrubs grown wholly or in part for the beauty of their berries; at whatever time they flower, pruning cannot be done until the birds or the weather have taken the fruits. There is also shaping to be considered — but I think we must start from the beginning.

A young shrub, purchased, or grown from seed or cuttings or a layered branch, will usually have two or three weak basal branches. After establishing itself, getting its roots well down, it will usually throw up one or more much stronger shoots, which will form the beginning of the future shrub; to encourage these new shoots, the original weaklings should be removed.

It is very rare that every shrub in the garden has enough space to allow it to expand fully; we are all avid for as much variety in our gardens as possible, and almost invariably plant too closely. The time inevitably comes when some reduction is necessary. It is a sad job, and the shrub never looks as good again; moreover, the job almost always needs repeating after a few more years, with consequent loss of beauty of flower or fruit, and of line and deportment. Therefore let me make a plea to plant circumspectly and thinly; temporary intervening spaces can be filled with quick-growing, short-lived species such as *Cytisus* (brooms), *Lavatera, Cistus,* tree lupins and the like, which can be dispensed with as the slower growing permanencies develop.

Watchfulness and understanding are the key words to successful pruning. Rhododendrons are notorious for leading enthusiasts astray into too-close planting. Fortunately they can usually be thinned out and moved to fresh spots with complete success if lifted with a sufficiently large root-ball. In common, I think, with all other evergreens, those with rough dark brown bark can be reduced if necessary to bare branches with every prospect of success; those with smooth light brown or flaking bark do not usually respond.

There are certain rules against pruning: woolly- or downy-leafed shrubs are best not touched until late spring. A trap here for the unwary is Lavender. By all means remove the flower stalks as soon as they are spent, but never clip over the bushes until late spring, and never cut into the old wood (without leaves). It is again a matter of understanding, for almost all woolly- or downy-leafed shrubs come from hot climates and should not be checked in autumn, which might result in premature young shoots. In addition, I should always choose the spring for planting them, when the soil is warming up and there is less danger of severe frost.

There is no doubt that severe annual pruning of such shrubs as *Weigela*, *Philadelphus*, *Tamarix* and *Deutzia* is a considerable drain on their energies, and they should be helped by nourishing them with a fertiliser. The same might be said of *Buddleja*, but these seem to thrive with a minimum of nourishment. The mention of *Tamarix* raises an interesting point because some species flower, on last year's branches, in the spring — for example, *T. parviflora* (*T. tetrandra*) — and need to have their flowered shoots reduced immediately, whereas the favourite summer-flowering species *T. ramosissima* (*T. pentandra*) needs cutting back in earliest spring to produce its best spikes. Much the same may be said about certain hydrangeas: *H. paniculata* needs hard pruning (and feeding) early in the year to encourage good flower heads, whereas those of the *H. villosa* group seldom need any reduction.

It will be seen therefore that the work needs constant thought, and that there will be some things needing attention in almost every week of the year — evergreens respond well to winter pruning. And apart from specific jobs as outlined above to encourage maximum production, the secateurs should be taken round the garden every week, to do a little shaping or dead-heading as soon as the need for it becomes evident. "A little and often" is the watchword that will obviate wholesale reduction by the use of long-handled pruners and the pruning-saw.

Cutting Sixty-Three —

The Restoration of Gardens

Most of the Cuttings in this book have been written to help those who are about to design or plant a garden; here is one which may help those who have the daunting task of renovating an old garden.

A garden, however perfect it may appear to be, is never static. Even in the most naturalistic of garden styles, nature's progress is being arrested by cultivation and maintenance. Schemes of quick-maturing plants may need a great deal of renewal during the many years that a tree, or even a shrub, is growing to its full beauty. For this reason, a garden of many parts and containing a considerable range of plants never matures as a whole, but is always in some part deteriorating. We gardeners seek to arrest the decay and do our best to keep a garden in good heart. When the gardener relaxes or, worse still, is absent, then nature assumes control and rapidly defeats the designer's ideas. More gardens than any other form of art must have deteriorated from neglect, but even so it is surprising how little has been written about their restoration. These notes are therefore offered as a pattern for the restoration of gardens, of all sizes.

An initial survey of a derelict garden would reveal certain things in need of immediate attention, such as blocked drains, crumbling masonry, danger from decrepit trees and fallen branches, insidious weeds, broken fences giving entrance to trespassers, and the like. Very often it is possible to administer first aid to such, even if in a temporary manner.

Before any major work is considered, it is advisable to study archives of all sorts. Aerial photographs taken in early morning or late evening often reveal traces of ancient layouts. County Record Offices, old maps, family photograph albums and old books may show interesting details, all of which should be taken into consideration when assessing the work to be done. It is not until every morsel of historic evidence has been studied that a scheme for restoration can be considered in full. So many facets have a bearing on what should or can be attempted. Few gardens owe their being to one designer or owner; as likely as not, a garden will show the influence of many, each swayed by the fashion of his time. A complex garden attached to an ancestral home in Britain may well have Tudor walls, gatehouses and other masonry, plus the severe lines of avenues, canals and walls dating from the Stuart period; in some gardens much of this may have been swept away by the fashion in Georgian times of creating an open landscape to be viewed from the house, with clumps of trees and serpentine lakes and cascades, grottoes and follies. In Victorian times were born both the ornamental shrubbery and gardening on the lawns, and great conifers were planted; then, during this century, "flowering" trees and shrubs may well have been added. With a shrinkage of resources, anything left as a memorial to the ideals of previous centuries will have been modified, or have become merely neglected. And during the whole time the walled or kitchen garden will have burgeoned, reached full maturity and luxuriance (complete with greenhouses, frames, potting sheds, elaborately trained fruit trees and flower borders), to be more and more neglected as this century has progressed. Here and there, in almost every old garden, there are one or more rare old plants to be safely preserved.

There are two questions that arise when the archival work is finished. One is that of deciding to what date or dates the restoration work is to be keyed, and the other is how much labour will be available for maintenance. Usually there must be much give and take about the first; there are so many loved layers of history in evidence that one can seldom boldly sweep all away so that the design conforms to one period only. In scheduling restoration it is essential to assess the amount of maintenance that will be required; it is pointless to restore and then find that funds are not forthcoming for the required staff.

Meanwhile, it is necessary to study what may be called the given quantities: the climate and micro-climate; pollution of the air; the soil, the water table and the drainage. To these must be added a history of dire troubles that will be known to local people, such as floodings, direction of strong winds, the prevalence of vermin, deer, et cetera. (Yews and other evergreens will quickly reveal whether deer browse on them in winter; in this connection, *Lonicera nitida* proves to be distasteful to deer and is a useful, quick-growing evergreen shrub for underplanting the verges of nibbled evergreens.) As likely as not *Armillaria mellea* (honey fungus) will be present, but little can be done about this in a big way on account of cost; assuring good growing conditions and bolstering the fertility of the soil may combat it successfully. Badly drained soil is usually reflected in bad growth of certain trees.

Apart from all historical matters, we have today a different outlook on our gardens than was the custom in years gone by. Whereas in earlier centuries stress was so often upon shaded alleys and arbours — the outcome perhaps of wearing thick stuffy costumes — today we are mostly sun-worshippers. This brings to mind the thought that our restored garden should be a sheltered place — sheltered from cold and prevailing winds, with sunny corners for sitting. This is something that is by no means always evident in garden designs of the past, and it may be that the restoration of woodland belts and tree clumps needs rethinking. The landscape designers of the past were not necessarily always right. One can have a splendid view, or shelter; seldom both. It is surprising how even a fairly distant belt of trees will reduce wind, whereas a near wall has little effect. With regard to belts and woodlands, it is as well to decide whether they shall be composed of deciduous broad-leafed trees, or conifers, or both; the choice is bound up in the history of the place. A mixture should always be chosen in preference to a pure plantation, to avoid the ravages which a disaster such as Dutch Elm disease can wreak. Gardens in Europe and North America which depended on elms for their shelter have been turned into windswept heaths.

Having decided on the type and extent of restoration, it is time to attend to relevant details. In a large garden, access must be provided for tree surgery and the extraction of timber, the dredging of lakes and ponds, and for contractors' vehicles. Before any machinery or vehicles are allowed entry, certain sacrosanct areas should be clearly marked and roped off. This particularly applies to historic features, shallow-laid drains, and all trees and shrubs that are to remain. Their root-area, stems and overhanging branches should not be left unguarded, and their careful preservation should be written into any contract. Contractors' bonfires often burn overhead tree branches, and no bonfires should be made on land intended for the planting of rhododendrons and their relatives.

With regard to the dredging of ponds and lakes, usually the excavated material will have to be accommodated. Sometimes it is possible to shrink a large informal lake by slightly revetting or campshedding the margins (building them up with a facing of piles and boarding), behind which the silt can be placed and graded for sowing with grass or other planting. Silt is of a strange nature; sometimes it takes a couple of years to dry, and this process will reveal large cracks. To guard against future silting, catchment pits can sometimes be installed.

With regard to tree surgery and the reduction of overgrown shrubs, it is necessary to know what species will respond sufficiently well to pruning to make surgery or pruning worthwhile. Trees such as Beech and Birch are unresponsive to pruning, whereas Sweet Chestnut and Oak react well. In the case of shrubs it is better to be very severe and reduce nearly to ground level many strong-growing deciduous bushes; the same applies to the commoner evergreens. Results will be better and more quickly achieved thus than by merely shortening big awkward branches.

Hedges often need attention. Over the years they gradually get wider and taller, no matter how closely they are clipped, and often their bases are infested with ivy and other weeds. If it is desired — either from a sense of design and proportion or merely for reduction of annual clipping — to reduce a hedge in width and height, it is essential that the shrubs should be in full health. Drainage should be considered, and the fertility of the soil checked. It is normal procedure to reduce *back to the main stems* the top and one side, preferably in early spring, and to wait for two or three years before tackling the second side, giving the stems time to sprout and make a close green cover. The reason for reducing the top in the first instance is to admit light and rain into the massed branches. Meanwhile, both sides of the hedge should continue to receive nourishment. In spite of the fact that their health-giving shoots are clipped away every summer, it is noteworthy that hedges are seldom given any nourishment over the years, whereas other parts of the garden are manured annually. Probably the most favoured hedging plant within a garden is the English Yew, and fortunately this is usually responsive to hard pruning. Occasionally some very old yews will die, in which case the hedge must be patched with youngsters. Hornbeam is equally amenable. Holly and Box are slow, but eventually succeed; and the least satisfactory is the Beech. Old stems of Beech sometimes refuse to sprout, and it is therefore wise, during the reduction, to save as many tractable thin branches as possible to tie back into the new alignment. Such reduction of a hedge alongside a lawn also necessitates the reinstatement of the grass. This is best left until some years later, so that fertilisers can continue to be applied to the roots of the hedge.

In addition to giving attention to growing things, there are repairs to be made to walls, steps, curbs, summer-houses, and garden ornaments. In assessing damage to garden ornaments, a decision should be taken as to whether the ornament is of a material to withstand the ravages of weather, or whether it needs airy, dry protection in winter. I will not go further into the niceties of the repairing of masonry and brickwork, which are each special skills.

An assessment of working conditions as well as of aesthetics should be made. In the old days, gardeners' time was not considered; today it is of vital importance. And so we have to ask, Whether the service areas (that is to say, the production department, bonfire and compost corners) are placed advantageously to the main paths? Do the paths still lead to the right places? Sometimes old Victorian paths are not necessary and can be grassed over. Are certain steps a nuisance for the total mechanisation of the garden?

When all destructive work, and repair work to fences, walls, masonry, et cetera, is done it is time to think of resurfacing paths, rejuvenating lawns, and new planting. Old garden paths were surfaced with gravel "as dug" — or with the largest stones sifted out — and in many places such gravel is still to be found. The term "hoggin" is sometimes used for it; it contains rounded pebbles and binding material, and results in a smooth surface, comfortable to walk upon. The gravel most easily bought today is usually of crushed stones, resulting in a harsh, noisy walking surface.

Before laying any sort of gravel, grass verges should be inspected for alignment. As likely as not the paths will be too wide, due to annual use of the half-moon edging tool. The best way of restoring verges is to lift the verge of grass; turn it round, and place the newly cut edge where it should be at the side of the path; then fill the gap in the lawn with soil and sow grass seed. Old lawns sometimes contain a delightful mixture of "weeds", and some tolerance should be given to them. A dense covering of daisies on a very large lawn or an admixture of Thyme on chalky soils are both to be considered for their beauty, as against a pure culture of grass. The application of a fertiliser plus weedkiller to old-established lawns should therefore be made with circumspection. On the other hand, flowery weeds in small grassed areas are apt to destroy the tranquillity which we desire of our lawns.

Considering how long a tree takes to establish itself and to make any contribution to the landscape, it is obvious that the least possible time should be lost in planting them. The same applies in a lesser degree to shrubs. Unless specially prepared specimens of large size are available, little is gained by planting in excess of the normal nursery size. Thorough preparation of the planting stations is of great importance; a hole with a minimum width of three feet and a depth of 18 inches is desirable for normal sized trees and shrubs, and immediate staking is advisable on windy sites. Nor should protection, where necessary, against rabbits, hares and deer be delayed.

Before replanting old beds and borders, especially of roses and herbaceous plants, it is wise to empty them completely, healing into the ground elsewhere anything that is to be saved, after freeing the roots of all soil. While the weather is still warm a dressing of a disinfectant such as dazomet ("Basamid") should be applied to free the ground of fungus diseases, pests and weeds. The soil will be ready for replanting during the following spring; an analysis will provide information regarding fertility. As likely as not archive material will provide a history not only of the design, but also of previous colour schemes. This may well need separate consideration.

The restoration of an old garden to something that can be maintained today, with a minimum of labour plus all suitable machinery, is a great challenge. Photographs taken before, during and after the work are very revealing and are a source of great interest in after years.

ENVOI

... every day brings to a gardener its special interests.
There is always something worthy of his care and admiration,
some new development of beauty,
some fresh design to execute, some lesson to learn,
some genial work to do.

— Dean Hole, *A Book about the Garden*, 1892

SOURCES

Many of the plants described in these cuttings should be readily available from local nurseries and garden centres, provided that they are hardy to the regions in which you garden. To find some of the more unusual plants, the gardener will need to search further afield. In the United Kingdom, by far the best place to find suppliers of particular plants remains *The RHS Plant Finder*, published every two years and available in most bookstores. In the United States, Barbara Barton's *Gardening by Mail* provides a comprehensive list of specialist nurseries.

In addition, the following mail order nurseries in the United States are some, though by no means all, of the growers in different geographic regions who specialize in varieties of plants which are not yet commonly available.

Antique Rose Emporium
Route 5, Box 143
Brenham, TX 77833
Old garden roses

Canyon Creek Nursery
3527 Dry Creek Road
Oroville, CA 95965
Perennials

Fairweather Gardens
P.O. Box 330
Greenwich, NJ 08323
Ornamental trees & shrubs

Forestfarm
990 Tetherow Road
Williams, OR 97544-9599
*Western natives, perennials,
    trees & shrubs*

Gardening by Mail
Barbara J. Barton
Tusker Press
Houghton Mifflin Company
A directory of mail-order resources

Gossler Farms Nursery
1200 Weaver Road
Springfield, OR 97478-9691
Trees & shrubs

Heronswood Nursery
7530 288th Street NE
Kingston, WA 98346
Ornamental woody plants & perennials

Kurt Bluemel, Inc.
2740 Greene Lane
Baldwin, MD 21013-9523
Ornamental grasses, sedges,

Langenbach Fine Tool Co.
P.O. Box 453
Blairstown, NJ 07825
Garden tools & accessories

Nuccios Nursery
P.O. Box 6160
3555 Chaney Trail
Altadena, CA 91001
*Sedges, rushes & bamboos,
Camellias & azaleas*

Pickering Nurseries, Inc.
670 Kingston Road (Highway 2)
Pickering, ON, Canada L1V 1A6
Roses

Roses of Yesterday & Today
803 Browns Valley Road
Watsonville, CA 95076-0398
Roses

Siskiyou Rare Plant Nursery
2825 Cummings Road
Medford, OR 97501
Alpine & rock garden plants

Wayside Gardens
P.O. Box 1
Hodges, SC 29695-0001
Ornamental trees & shrubs, perennials & roses

We-Du Nurseries
Route 5 Box 724
Marion, NC 28752
Rock garden & woodland plants

CHECK LIST OF PLANTS
WITH USDA HARDINESS ZONES

Because it would have been impossible to have given all the facts necessary to intending planters in my somewhat discursive pages, I have thought it well to provide a list of those facts in easily assimilable form. Further details can be obtained from catalogues and books devoted entirely to plants. This index therefore indicates in columns the following facts:

1 Plant Name
2 USDA Hardiness Zone
     See map on page 330 for zone areas and temperatures
3 Evergreen or Deciduous
     D = deciduous } some small plants seem to hover between the two categories
     E = evergreen
4 Plant Type
     T = tree
     S = shrub
     P = perennial
     B = bulb
     R = rock plant
     A = annual
5 Flower Colour
6 Autumn Color, Fruits or Berries
     AC = autumn colour
     F = fruits or berries
7 Propagation
     C = cuttings
     D = division
     G = graft or budding
     L = layering
     R = root cuttings
     S = seeds
8 Page Number (asterisk indicates illustration)

PLANT HARDINESS ZONES
IN THE UNITED STATES

Cold tolerance is the major factor governing plant hardiness and the zone numbers beside each entry in the plant index indicate the geographical survival range for this specific factor. The accompanying Hardiness Zone Map is based on average winter minimum temperatures and indicates the geographical extent of each zone. In addition to cold hardiness, other factors such as high day and night temperatures, humidity levels, soil type, drainage, and the presence or absence of winter snow cover affect hardiness levels. There are, in addition, microclimates within each zone, therefore hardiness recommendations should be interpreted in the broadest sense, allowing adjustments for prevailing conditions.

The research for the plant Hardiness Zones has been carried out by John E. Elsley, Director of Horticulture, Wayside Gardens, who has kindly given permission for its use here.

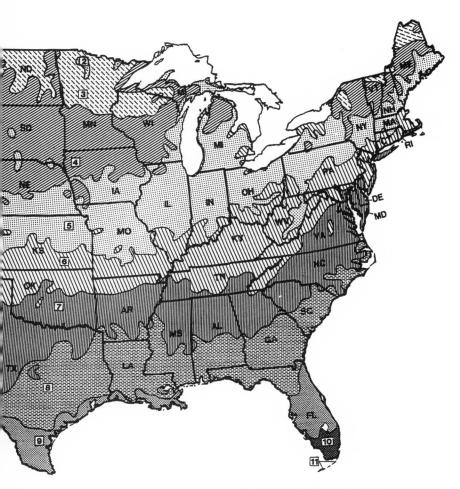

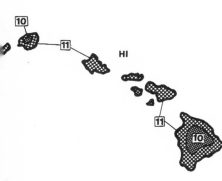

RANGE OF AVERAGE ANNUAL MINIMUM
TEMPERATURES FOR EACH ZONE

	Fahrenheit	Celsius
ZONE 1	Below −50	−46
ZONE 2	−50 to −40	−46 to −40
ZONE 3	−40 to −30	−40 to −34
ZONE 4	−30 to −20	−34 to −29
ZONE 5	−20 to −10	−29 to −23
ZONE 6	−10 to 0	−23 to −18
ZONE 7	0 to 10	−18 to −12
ZONE 8	10 to 20	−12 to −7
ZONE 9	20 to 30	−7 to −1
ZONE 10	30 to 40	−1 to 4
ZONE 11	Above 40	Above 4

Plant Name	USDA Hardiness Zone	Evergreen or Deciduous	Plant Type	Flower Colour	Autumn Colour (AC) Fruits or Berries (F)	Propagation	Page (*Illustration)
Abies magnifica	5–8	E	T				195
Acer palmatum and varieties	6–8	D	S/T	reddish	AC	CG	98
— — 'Senkaki'('Sangokaku')	6–8	D	S		AC	CLG	132, 195
— *pseudoplatanus* 'Brilliantissimum'	5–7	D	T			G	98
— *rubrum*	4–9	D	T	reddish	AC	LS	292
Aconitum x *arendsii*	3–8	D	P	lavender-blue	F	D	176
— *carmichaelii*	3–8	D	P	lavender-blue	F	DS	176
— *japonicum*	5–8	D	P	lavender-blue		DS	164, 176
Adiantum pedatum var. *japonicum*	3–8	D	P			D	256
— *venustum*	4–8	D	P			D	259
Aesculus chinensis	6–8	D	T	white		GS	221
— *neglecta* 'Erythroblastos'	5–8	D	T	pale		G	67, 98
Agapanthus 'Liliput'	8–10	D	P	blue	F	D	265, 267, 269
Ajuga reptans 'Atropurpurea'	4–8	E	R	blue		D	105, 178, 308
Alchemilla mollis	4–8	D	P	yellow		DS	158
Amelanchier lamarckii	5–9	D	T	white	AC	CL	130
Ampelopsis chaffanjonii	5–8	D	C		AC	CL	204
— *megalophylla*	5–8	D	C		AC	CL	204
Anaphalis triplinervis	4–9	D	P	white		D	95
Anemone apennina	6–8	D	B	blue		DS	23, 183
— *blanda*	4–8	D	B	various		DS	23, 183
— × *hybrida* ('Japanese')	4–8	D	P	pink		DR	175, 282
— *japonica* 'Honorine Jobert'	4–8	D	P	white		DR	175, 282
Anthemis cupaniana	5–8	E	R	white		CD	33
Apple 'Arthur Turner'	5–8	D	T	blush	F	G	298
— 'Cox's Orange Pippin'	5–8	D	T	blush	F	G	298
— 'Lord Derby'	5–8	D	T	blush	F	G	298
— 'Sunset'	5–8	D	T	blush	F	G	298
— 'Upton Pyne'	5–8	D	T	blush	F	G	299
Aquilegia alpina	4–7	D	P	blue		S	33
— 'Hensol Harebell'	4–7	D	P	blue		S	33
Arabis caucasica (*A. albida*) 'Variegata'	4–7	E	R	white		CD	5, 158

Plant Name	USDA Hardiness Zone	Evergreen or Deciduous	Plant Type	Flower Colour	Autumn Colour (AC) Fruits or Berries (F)	Propagation	Page (*Illustration)
Aristolochia macrophylla (*A. durior, A. sipho*)	5–8	D	C	brownish		CL	203
Armeria maritima	4–7	E	R	pink		D	212
Aronia arbutifolia	5–9	D	S	white	AC F	DLS	291
Artemisia stelleriana	4–8	E	P	yellow		CL	195
Arum italicum var. *italicum* ('Pictum')	6–9	D	B	pale	F	DS	4, 9, 133
Asplenium scolopendrium	4–8	E	P			DS	159, 206
– – 'Crispum Golden Queen'	4–8	E	P			D	10, 256
– *trichomanes*	4–8	D	P			DS	259
Aster divaricatus	4–8	D	P	white		D	242
– *forrestii*	5–8	D	P	lavender-blue		DS	197
– × *frikartii* 'Mönch'	5–8	D	P	lavender-blue		CD	14, 176
– – 'Wunder von Stäfa'	5–8	D	P	lavender-blue		CD	176
– *thomsonii* 'Nanus'	4–9	D	P	lavender-blue		CD	176
Athyrium filix-femina	4–9	D	P			DS	259
– *niponicum* 'Pictum'	3–8	D	P			D	256
Aucuba japonica 'Sulphurea Marginata'	7–10	E	S	brown		C	95
Balm, Lemon, 'Allgold'	4–9	D	P	white			227
Begonia grandis (*B. evansiana*)	6–9	D	P	blush		D	179
Berberidopsis corallina	8–9	E	S	red	F	C	282
Berberis darwinii	7–9	E	S	orange	F	CS	31, 130
– *dictyophylla*	6–9	D	S	yellow	AC F	C	115, 130, 292
– *gagnepainii*	7–9	E	S	yellow	F	CS	278
– – 'Fernspray'	7–9	E	S	yellow	F	C	265, 267
– 'Goldilocks'	8–9	E	S/T	yellow		C	220
– *thunbergii* 'Atropurpurea'	5–8	D	S	yellow	AC F	CS	104, 292, 308
– – 'Atropurpurea Nana'	5–8	D	S	yellow	AC F	C	97, 213, 309
– – 'Erecta'	5–8	D	S	yellow		C	239
– – 'Red Pillar'	5–8	D	S	yellow		C	239
– – 'Red Sentry'	5–8	D	S	yellow		C	239
– *valdiviana*	8–9	E	S/T	yellow		CS	220
Bergenia	3–8	E	P	various		D	315

Plant Name	USDA Hardiness Zone	Evergreen or Deciduous	Plant Type	Flower Colour	Autumn Colour (AC) Fruits or Berries (F)	Propagation	Page (*Illustration)
— *cordifolia* 'Purpurea'	3–8	E	P	pink		D	5, 242
— *crassifolia*	4–8	E	P	pink			8
— *purpurascens*	3–8	E	P	pink			8
— 'Sunningdale'	3–8	E	P	pink		CD	5, 158
Betula papyrifera	3–6	D	T	catkins		GS	110
Bilderdykia, see *Polygonum baldschuanicum*							
Blechnum chilense (*B. tabulare*)	8–10	E	P			DS	257
— *spicant*	4–8	E	P			DS	257, 258
Brachyglottis rotundifolius	9–10	E	S	white		C	82
— 'Sunshine'	9–10	E	S	yellow		C	82
Brunnera macrophylla	4–8	D	P	blue		DS	32, 85, 92, 182
Buddleja auriculata	8–9	E	S	cream		C	121, 283
— *fallowiana* 'Alba'	8–9	D	S	white		C	114, 120, 283, 284
— *stenostachya*	7–9	D	S	lavender		C	283
Bupleurum falcatum	4–9	D	P	green		DS	185
Buxus sempervirens 'Handsworthensis'	6–8	E	S	yellow		CL	279
— — 'Glauca' ('La Chapelle')	6–8	E	S	yellow		CL	279
— — 'Suffruticosa'	6–8	E	S			CD	212
Callicarpa bodinieri 'Profusion'	6–8	D	S	mauve	F	C	10
Calluna vulgaris 'Barnett Anley'	5–7	E	S	lilac		C	35, 111, 311, 313
— — 'Hiemalis'	5–7	E	S	mauve		C	66
Calocedrus (*Libocedrus*) *decurrens*	5–8	E	T			S	238
Camassia leichtlinii	4–10	D	B	various		D	33
— — 'Electra'	4–10	D	B	lilac		D	33
— — 'Eve Price'	4–10	D	B	violet		D	33
— — 'Plena'	4–10	D	B	cream		D	33
Camellia sasanqua	3–9	E	S	various		C	3
Campanula latiloba	4–8	E	P	lilac/white		D	5, 92, 186
Campsis grandiflora	7–9	D	C	orange-red		C	109, 205, 285

Plant Name	USDA Hardiness Zone	Ever-green or Decid-uous	Plant Type	Flower Colour	Autumn Colour (AC) Fruits or Berries (F)	Propa-gation	Page (*Illus-tration)
— × *tagliabuana* 'Mme Galen'	5–9	D	C	reddish		CL	205, 285
Caragana arborescens 'Pendula'	3–7	D	S	yellow		G	233
Carex buchananii	6–9	E	P	brown		D	105
— *morrowii* 'Variegata'	7–9	E	P	white		D	5
Carpenteria californica	8–9	E	S	white		CL	196
Carpinus betulus	5–8	D	T	cream	AC	S	279
Caryopteris × *clandonensis*	6–9	D	S	lavender	F	C	284
— *incana*	7–9	D	S	lavender		C	284
Ceanothus 'A. T. Johnson'	8–10	E	S	blue		C	66
— 'Autumnal Blue'	8–10	E	S	blue		C	182, 205, 284
— 'Burkwoodii'	8–10	E	S	blue		C	182, 284
— 'Cascade'	8–10	E	S	blue		C	265, 269
— 'Delight'	8–10	E	S	blue		C	205
— × *delilianus* 'Gloire de Versailles'	8–10	D	S	blue		C	284
— — 'Henri Desfosse'	8–10	D	S	blue		C	284
Cerastium tomentosum	2–7	E	P	white		D	282
Ceratostigma willmottianum	7–10	D	S	blue		S	184, 284
Cercidiphyllum japonicum	5–8	D	T		AC	LS	179
Ceterach officinarum	4–8	E	P			DS	259
Chaenomeles (*Cydonia*) 'Phylis Moore'	5–8	D	S	flame pink		R	193
Chamaecyparis lawsoniana 'Allumii'	5–8	E	T			C	104
— — 'Green Hedger'	5–8	E	T			C	265, 267, 269, 276, 277
— — 'Pembury Blue'	5–8	E	T			C	265, 267, 269
Cherry, 'Morello'	5–8	D	T	white		G	186
Chimonanthus praecox 'Luteus'	7–9	D	S	creamy		GS	116, 117*
Chionodoxa forbesi (*C. lucilleae*)	4–9	D	B	blue		DS	22
— *sardensis*	4–9	D	B	blue		DS	22, 182
Choisya ternata 'Sundance'	8–10	E	S	white		C	6, 37

Plant Name	USDA Hardiness Zone	Evergreen or Deciduous	Plant Type	Flower Colour	Autumn Colour (AC) Fruits or Berries (F)	Propagation	Page (*Illustration)
Chrysanthemum 'Anastasia'	5–9	D	P	old rose		CD	179
– 'Dr Tom Parr'	5–9	D	P	brown		CD	179
– 'Emperor of China'	5–9	D	P	pink		CD	179
– 'Mei-Kiyo'	5–9	D	P	old rose		CD	179
Cimicifuga racemosa	3–8	D	P	white	F	DS	176
– *simplex*	4–8	D	P	white		DS	176
– – 'Brunette' ('Atropurpurea')	4–8	D	P	white		D	176
– – 'Elstead Variety'	4–8	D	P	mauve/white		D	196
Clematis alpina	6–9	D	C	various		CS	32, 204, 205
– 'Barbara Dibley'	4–9	D	C	pink		CG	265, 267
– 'Barbara Jackman'	4–9	D	C	heather		CG	267
– 'Belle of Woking'	4–9	D	C	lavender-blue		CG	267
– *cirrhosa* var. *balearica*	7–9	E	C	cream		CS	9, 254
– × *jackmanii*	4–9	D	C	purple		CG	267
– 'Jackmanii Superba'	4–9	D	C	purple		CG	267
– 'Lady Betty Balfour'	4–9	D	C	purple		CG	267, 285
– 'Lady Northcliffe'	4–9	D	C	lavender		CG	267
– *macropetala*	6–9	D	C	various		CS	32, 197, 204, 205
– *montana*	6–9	D	C	white/pink		CL	204, 252, 255
– – *wilsonii*	6–9	D	C	white		CL	204
– 'Mrs George Jackman'	4–9	D	C	white		CG	267
– *rehderiana*	6–9	D	C	yellow	F	CLS	285
– *tangutica*	6–9	D	C	yellow	F	CS	133, 252
– × *vedrariensis*	6–9	D	C	pink		CL	204
– *vitalba*	4–9	D	C	cream			253
– *viticella* 'Abundance'	5–9	D	C	heather		CG	204
– – 'Alba Luxurians'	5–9	D	C	white		CG	204
Clethra alnifolia var. *paniculata*	4–9	D	S	white		C	120, 283, 292
– – 'Pink Spire'	4–9	D	S	pink	AC	CD	120
– *tomentosa*	4–9	D	S	white	AC	CD	120, 249, 283
Colchicum speciosum 'Album'	6–8	D	B	white		D	178
Convallaria majalis	4–9	D	P	white		D	57

Plant Name	USDA Hardiness Zone	Evergreen or Deciduous	Plant Type	Flower Colour	Autumn Colour (AC) Fruits or Berries (F)	Propagation	Page (*Illustration)
– – 'Fortin's Giant'	4–9	D	P	white		D	57
– – 'Rosea'	4–9	D	P	mauve		D	57, 181
Convolvulus cneorum	8–10	E	S	white		C	184, 195
Cornus alba	2–7	D	S	white	AC	C	26
– – 'Kesselringii'	2–7	D	S	white	AC	C	26
– – var. sibirica	2–7	D	S	white	AC	C	26, 261
– canadensis	3–6	E	R	white	F	DS	241
– kousa	5–8	D	S	cream	AC F	CLS	132
– mas	5–8	D	S	yellow	F	CS	38*, 132
– sericea stolonifera 'Flaviramea'	2–8	D	S	white		C	26
Corylopsis, species	6–8	D	S	yellow		CL	21
Cotinus coggyria (Rhus cotinus) 'Royal Purple'	5–8	D	S	purplish	AC	CL	97, 132, 133, 291, 309
Cotoneaster bullatus	6–8	D	S	white	AC F	CS	291
– conspicuus	7–8	E	S	white	F	CS	2, 130
– franchetii	7–9	E	S	cream	F	CS	278
– 'Gnom' ('Gnome')	6–8	E	S	white	F	C	10, 205
– horizontalis	5–7	D	S	white	AC F	S	2
– 'Hybridus Pendulus'	5–7	D	S	white	F	CG	233
– lacteus	7–9	E	S	cream	F	CS	278
– simonsii	6–8	D	S	white	F	S	2, 278
– × watereri 'John Waterer'	6–8	D		white	F	C	220
– – 'Exburiensis'	6–8	D		white	F	C	220
Crambe maritima	6–9	D	P	white	F	DR	228
Crassula sarcocaulis	8–9	D	R	reddish			49
Crataegus orientalis	5–7	D	T	white	F	GS	221
– oxyacantha (C. laevigata)	5–7	D	T	various	F	G	216, 223
– – 'Gireoudii'	5–7	D	T	white		G	223
Crinum powellii 'Album'	7–10	D	B	white		D	282
Crocosmia × crocosmiiflora	5–9	D	P	apricot		D	175
– masonorum	5–9	D	P	fiery		D	175
– – 'Firebird'	5–9	D	P	fiery		D	175
– – 'Lucifer'	5–9	D	P	fiery		D	175
– – 'Solfatare'	5–9	D	P	apricot		D	105

Plant Name	USDA Hardiness Zone	Ever-green or Decid-uous	Plant Type	Flower Colour	Autumn Colour (AC) Fruits or Berries (F)	Propa-gation	Page (*Illus-tration)
Crocus byzantinus							
(C. iridiflorus)	5–9	D	B	violet		DS	59, 179
— *goulimyi*	5–9	D	B	lilac		D	178
— *laevigatus* 'Fontenayi'	5–9	D	B	lilac		DS	3, 11, 121
— *speciosus*	5–9	D	B	violet		D	121, 282
— — 'Artabir'	5–9	D	B	violet-blue		D	121
— — 'Oxonian'	5–9	D	B	violet-blue		D	121
— *tomasinianus*	5–9	D	B	mauve		DS	58*, 116, 178
Cupressus macrocarpa 'Golden Pillar'	7–9	E	T			CG	267
Cyclamen hederifolium							
(C. neapolitanum)	5–9	D	B	pink		S	11
— *repandum*	7–9	D	R	pink		S	117, 118
Cynoglossum nervosum	5–8	D	P	blue		S	164
Cyrtomium falcatum	7–9	E	P			DS	259
— *fortunei*	6–9	E	P			DS	259
Cystopteris fragilis	2–7	D	P			D	259
Cytisus 'Johnson's Crimson'	6–8	D	S	crimson		C	65
Daphne cneorum 'Eximea'	5–7	E	S	pink		CL	65
— *mezereum* 'Autumnalis'	5–8	D	S	pink		SG	4
— *odora*	8–9	E	S	white		C	117
— *pontica*	7–8	E	S	green		C	117
Delphinium 'Blue Fairy'	3–8	D	A	blue		S	242
Dendranthema, see *Chrysanthemum*							
Dendromecon rigida	9–10	D	S	yellow		C	196
Dianthus 'Lord Chatham'	4–8	E	P	salmon		C	162
Dicentra formosa	4–8	D	P	mauve		D	32
— *spectabilis*	3–8	D	P	pink		DS	32, 92
Disanthus cercidifolius	6–8	D	S		AC	CLS	292
Dryopteris erythrosora	5–9	D	P			DS	256
— *pseudomas* (*D. borreri*)	4–8	D	P			DS	256
— *wallichiana*	6–8	D	P			DS	256
Elaeagnus commutatus	2–6	D	S	cream		CDS	163
— — 'Gilt Edge'	7–10	E	S	cream		CL	10, 95, 120
— *macrophylla*	8–10	E	S	cream		CL	120

Plant Name	USDA Hardiness Zone	Evergreen or Deciduous	Plant Type	Flower Colour	Autumn Colour (AC) Fruits or Berries (F)	Propagation	Page (*Illustration)
— *pungens* 'Maculata Aurea'	7–10	E	S	cream		C	161
Elsholtzia stauntonii	5–8	D	S	mauve		C	28
Enkianthus perulatus	6–8	D	S	white	AC	CS	291
Epimedium colchicum	5–9	E	P	yellow		D	159
— × *perralchicum*	5–9	E	P	yellow		D	159
— *perralderianum*	5–9	E	P	yellow		D	39, 159
Eranthis hiemalis	3–7	D	B	yellow		DS	58
Erica carnea	6–8	E	S	pink		CL	214, 311, 312, 314
— *cinerea*	6–8	E	S	pink		CL	214
— × *darleyensis*	6–8	E	S	pink		CL	311, 314
— — 'Arthur Johnson'	6–8	E	S	pink		CL	10, 65, 314
Erigeron glaucus	5–8	E	P	mauve		CS	83
Erythronium citrinus	4–8	D	B	citron		DS	59
— *dens-canis*	2–7	D	B	lilac		DS	53*, 54, 58
— *giganteum* (*E. grandiflorum*)	5–9	D	B	cream		DS	59
— *hendersonii*	5–8	D	B	lilac		DS	55, 59
— 'Pagoda'	5–8	D	B	citron		D	53*, 54, 59
— *revolutum*	5–8	D	B	pink		DS	54, 55, 59
— 'White Beauty'	5–8	D	B	cream		D	54, 59
Escallonia 'Crimson Spire'	7–9	E	S	crimson		C	82, 278
— 'Donard Seedling'	7–9	E	S	blush		CL	278
— × *edinensis*	7–9	E	S	pink		C	205
— 'Gwendoline Anley'	7–9	E	S	pink		C	111
— *macrantha*	9–10	E	S	pink		CL	278
— 'Red Hedger'	7–9	E	S	crimson		C	82, 278
Eucryphia glutinosa	8–10	D	S	white	AC	CS	131, 291
Euonymus alatus	5–9	D	S	green	AC	CLS	292
— *europaeus* 'Red Cascade'	6–8	D	S	green	F	CL	265, 267
— *fortunei* 'Emerald Gaiety'	5–9	E	S	green		C	9, 95, 279
— — 'Emerald 'n' Gold'	5–9	E	S			C	5, 95
— — 'Variegata'	5–9	E	S			CL	213
— *verrucosus*	6–9	D	S	green	AC	CLS	292
Euphorbia myrsinites	5–8	E	R	yellow		CS	40, 158, 162
— *polychroma* (*E. epithymoides*)	4–9	D	P	yellow		CD	32, 158
— *wulfenii*	7–10	E	S	green		CS	5, 32
Exchorda 'The Bride'	5–9	D	S	white		CL	33, 186, 205

Plant Name	USDA Hardiness Zone	Evergreen or Deciduous	Plant Type	Flower Colour	Autumn Colour (AC) Fruits or Berries (F)	Propagation	Page (*Illustration)
Fagus sylvatica	5–7	D	T		AC	S	279
– – 'Dawyck'	5–7	D	T	catkins		G	236
– – 'Dawyck Gold'	5–7	D	T	catkins		G	236
– – 'Dawyck Purple'	5–7	D	T	catkins		G	236
– – 'Pendula'	5–7	D	T			GL	231
Fallopia, see Polygonum baldschuanicum							
Fatsia japonica	8–10	E	S	white	F	S	185, 190, 263, 264
Festuca glauca	4–8	D	R	grey		D	212
Fig 'White Marseilles'	7–9	D	T		F	C	110
Foeniculum vulgare purpureum	4–9	D	P	brownish		S	105
Fothergilla major	5–8	D	S	white	AC	CLS	131, 291
Fraxinus excelsior 'Pendula'	5–7	D	T	brown	F	GL	231
– *mariesii*	6–8	D	T	white	F	GS	221
Fuchsia 'Chillerton Beauty'	8–9	D	S	pink		C	265, 266, 269
– 'Riccartonii'	8–9	E	S	crimson	F	C	204
Galanthus caucasicus 'Hiemalis'	5–8	D	B	white		D	3, 11
– *reginae-olgae*	4–7	D	B	white		D	3
× *Gaulnettya* 'Wisley Pearl'	7–9	E	S	white	F	C	214
Gaultheria shallon	6–8	E	S	blush		CDS	241
Gentiana sino-ornata	6–7	D	R	blue		CD	292
Geranium endressii 'Rose Clair'	4–8	D	P	salmon		D	66
– – 'A. T. Johnson'	4–8	D	P	pink		D	66
– × *himalayense* (*G. grandiflorum*)	4–8	D	P	violet-blue		D	66, 164, 197
– 'Johnson's Blue'	4–8	D	P	lavender-blue		D	66, 158, 159, 164
– *malviflorum*	6–8	D	P	violet		D	5, 31, 40
– *pratense*	4–8	D	P	lilac		DS	66
– *psilostemon*	4–8	D	P	magenta		D	197
– *sanguineum* 'Glenluce'	4–8	D	R	pink		DR	66
– *wallichianum*	5–8	D	P	mauve/blue		DS	282
Gleditsia sinensis 'Brussels Lace'	5–8	D	T			G	104

Plant Name	USDA Hardiness Zone	Evergreen or Deciduous	Plant Type	Flower Colour	Autumn Colour (AC) Fruits or Berries (F)	Propagation	Page (*Illustration)
Griselinia littoralis	9–10	E	S			CS	82
Gymnocarpium dryopteris	3–8	D	P			D	259
Hamamelis mollis	6–8	D	S	yellow	AC	G	116, 195
Hebe albicans	9–10	E	S	white		C	5
– – 'Sussex Carpet'	9–10	E	S	white		C	162
– 'Green Globe'	8–10	E	S	white		CL	213
– *pinguifolia* 'Pagei'	8–10	E	S	white		C	5, 162, 206, 312
– *rakaiensis* (*H. subalpina*)	8–10	E	S	white		C	6, 160, 206, 213
– *topiaria*	9–10	E	S	white		CL	213
Hedera colchica	6–9	E	S	green		CL	203, 261, 263
– – 'Dentata Variegata'	6–9	E	S/C	green		CL	9, 203, 261
– *helix* 'Adam'	5–9	E	S/C	green		CL	9, 214, 262
– – 'Angularis Aurea'	5–9	E	S/C	green		CL	262
– – 'Atropurpurea'	5–9	E	S/C	green		CL	9, 261
– – 'Buttercup'	5–9	E	S/C	green			252, 262
– – 'Caenwoodiana'	5–9	E	S/C	green		CL	214
– – 'Chrysophylla'	5–9	E	S/C	green		CL	262
– – 'Conglomerata'	5–9	E	S			CL	263
– – 'Duckfoot'	5–9	E	S			CL	262, 263
– – 'Erecta' ('Congesta')	5–9	E	S			CL	263
– – 'Glacier'	5–9	E	S/C	green		CL	262
– – 'Goldheart'	5–9	E	S/C	green		CL	262
– – 'Marginata Major'	5–9	E	S/C	green		CL	262
– – 'Light Fingers'	5–9	E	S			CL	262
– – 'Little Diamond'	5–9	E	S			CL	262, 263
– – 'Sagittifolia'	5–9	E	S			CL	262
– – 'Très Coupé	5–9	E	S/C	green		CL	262
– – var. *hibernica*	5–9	E	S/C	green		CL	261
Helianthus orgyalis (*H. salicifolius*)	6–9	D	P	yellow		D	242
Helleborus foetidus	6–9	E	P	green		S	5, 40
Hemerocallis 'Happy Returns'	4–9	D	P	yellow		D	128
– 'Stella d'Oro'	4–9	D	P	yellow		D	128
Hepatica × *media* 'Ballardii'	5–8	E	P	blue		D	110

Plant Name	USDA Hardiness Zone	Evergreen or Deciduous	Plant Type	Flower Colour	Autumn Colour (AC) Fruits or Berries (F)	Propagation	Page (*Illustration)
Heuchera micrantha diversifolia 'Palace Purple'	4–8	D	P	brown		DS	104, 105, 161
Hibiscus syriacus	6–9	D	S	various		C	248, 282, 316
Hippeastrum x *acramanii*	9–10	D	B	pink		D	196
Hippophaë rhamnoides	4–7	D	S		F	DS	114
Hosta fortunei hyacinthina	3–9	D	P	lilac		D	163
– 'Halcyon'	3–9	D	P	lilac		D	163
– *plantaginea*	3–9	D	P	white		D	180
– – 'Aphrodite'	3–9	D	P	white		D	180
– *sieboldiana elegans*	3–9	D	P	lilac-white	F	DS	125, 163
Hyacinthoides hispanica	4–9	D	B	various		DS	31
– *non-scripta*	4–9	D	B	blue		DS	31
Hydrangea petiolaris	5–8	D	C	white	AC	CL	205, 252
– *macrophylla* 'Mme Mouillère'	6–9	D	S	white		CL	284
– *paniculata* 'Kyushu'	4–8	D	S	white		C	284
– – 'Pink Diamond'	4–8	D	S	pink		C	284
– *serrata* 'Blue Bird'	6–8	D	S	blue		CL	284
– – 'Preziosa'	6–8	D	S	reddish		CL	284
– *villosa*	7–9	D	S	lavender		CLS	284, 317
Hypericum inodorum 'Elstead'	7–9	D	S	yellow	F	CL	133
– *kouytchense*	6–9	D	S	yellow	F	CS	163
– × *moserianum*	7–9	D	S	yellow		C	28, 128, 129*, 282
– *patulum* 'Goldcup'	6–7	D	S	yellow			269
Ilex aquifolium	7–9	E	S	white	F	CS	277
– – 'Green Pillar'	7–9	E	S	white	F	C	238
– – 'J. C. van Tol'	7–9	E	S	white	F	C	277
– × *altaclerensis* 'Hodginsii'	7–9	E	S	white		C	278
Indigofera heterantha (*I. gerardiana*)	7–9	D	S	mauve		CS	28
Ipheion uniflorum	5–9	D	B	pale blue		DS	23
– – 'Wisley Blue'	5–9	D	B	blue		D	23
Iris 'Arabi Pasha'	4–9	D	P	violet		D	111
– *aurea*	5–9	D	P	yellow		DS	19

Plant Name	USDA Hardi- ness Zone	Ever- green or Decid- uous	Plant Type	Flower Colour	Autumn Colour (AC) Fruits or Berries (F)	Propa- gation	Page (*Illus- tration)
– 'Austrian Sky'	4–9	D	P	lavender		D	18
– *bucharica*	4–9	D	B	yellow		DS	18
– *chamaeiris*	4–9	D	P	various		DS	18
– *ensata*	5–9	D	P	various		DS	19
– *foetidissima*	5–9	E	P	mixed	F	DS	14
– *fulva*	5–9	D	P	brown		DS	19
– × *fulvala*	5–9	D	P	plum		D	19
– *graminea*	5–9	D	P	purplish		DS	118
– 'Green Spot'	4–9	D	P	white		D	18
– *histrioides* 'Major'	5–9	D	B	violet		D	18
– *laevigata*	5–9	D	P	violet		DS	19
– – 'Rose Queen'	5–9	D	P	pink		D	19
– 'Langport Carnival'	4–9	D	P	red-purple		D	18
– 'Mirette'	4–9	D	P	lilac		D	111
– *missouriensis*	7–9	D	P	lavender		DS	17*, 19, 164
– *orchioides*	4–9	D	B	yellow		DS	18
– *orientalis*	4–9	D	P	white		DS	19
– *pallida dalmatica*	4–9	D	P	lavender		D	92, 113, 162
– *pumila*	4–9	D	P	various		DS	18
– *spuria*	5–9	D	P	various		DS	19
– *unguicularis* (*I. stylosa*)	7–9	E	P	various		D	3, 10, 16
– – 'Nancy Lindsay'	7–9	E	P	purple		D	145
Jasminum humile	8–10	D	S	yellow		C	137
– – 'Revolutum'	8–10	D	S	yellow		C	137
– × *mesnyi* (*J. primulinum*)	8–9	D	S	yellow		C	136, 271
– *nudiflorum*	6–10	D	S	yellow		CL	9, 134*, 135
– *officinale*	8–10	D	S	white		C	136
– – *affine* ('Grandiflorum')	8–10	D	S	white		C	136
– *parkeri*	7–9	E	S	yellow		CL	137, 196
– *polyanthum*	9–10	D	S	white		C	136
– × *stephanense*	8–10	D	S	pink		C	136
Juniperus communis 'Compressa'	3–7	E	S			C	239
– – 'Hibernica'	3–7	E	S		F	C	239

Plant Name	USDA Hardi-ness Zone	Ever-green or Decid-uous	Plant Type	Flower Colour	Autumn Colour (AC) Fruits or Berries (F)	Propa-gation	Page (*Illus-tration)
— — var. *suecica*	3–7	E	S			C	239
— *scopulorum* 'Sky Rocket'	4–7	E	T			C	238
Kerria japonica 'Guinea Gold'	5–9	D	S	orange		C	31
— — 'Variegata'	5–9	D	S	orange		C	31
Kniphofia aloides (*K. uvaria*)	5–9	E	P	red/yellow		D	282
— *rooperi* ('C. M. Pritchard')	6–9	E	P	red/yellow		D	178
— *triangularis*	6–9	D	P	red		D	178
— — 'Brimstone'	6–9	D	P	yellow		D	178, 179
— — 'Galpinii'	6–9	D	P	apricot		D	178, 179
— — 'Macowanii'	6–9	D	P	red		D	178
— — 'Nelsonii'	6–9	D	P	red		D	178
— 'Underway'	6–9	D	P	apricot		D	179
Koelreuteria paniculata 'Fastigiata'	5–9	D	T	yellow	F	G	237
+ *Laburnocytisus adamii*	5–7	D	T	various		G	86, 87
Laburnum alpinum	5–7	D	T	yellow		S	84, 85
— *anagyroides*	5–7	D	T	yellow		S	84
— — 'Aureum'	5–7	D	T	yellow		G	86
— — 'Pendulum'	5–7	D	T	yellow		G	86
— *caramanicum*	8–9	D	S	yellow		CS	87
— 'Newryensis'	5–7	D	T	yellow		G	85
— × *watereri* 'Vossii'	5–7	D	T	yellow		G	84, 85, 86, 202
Lathyrus aureus	6–9	D	P	amber		DS	141
— *latifolius*	5–9	D	P	magenta		S	138
— *magellanicus*	3–10	D	P	blue		S	141
— *nervosus*	3–10	D	P	blue		S	139*, 141
— *pubescens*	3–10	E	S	blue		CS	140, 141
— *rotundifolius*	5–10	D	P	coppery		D	140
— *tuberosus*	5–9	D	P	pink		DS	140
— *undulatus*	7–9	D	P	purplish		DS	140
— *vernus*	5–9	D	P	various		D	141, 142
Lavandula angustifolia 'Hidcote'	5–9	D	S	purple		C	159, 206, 212, 279

CUTTINGS FROM MY GARDEN NOTEBOOKS

Plant Name	USDA Hardiness Zone	Evergreen or Deciduous	Plant Type	Flower Colour	Autumn Colour (AC) Fruits or Berries (F)	Propagation	Page (*Illustration)
— × *intermedia* ('Dutch'; 'Vera')	5–9	E	S	lavender		C	279
— 'Munstead'	5–9	D	S	purple		C	212
— 'Nana Alba'	5–9	D	S	white		C	213
— 'Twickel Purple'	5–9	D	S	purple		C	159
Lespedeza thunbergii	5–9	D	S	magenta		CD	28
Leucojum aestivum 'Gravetye Giant'	4–9	D	B	white		D	32
Leucothoë axillaris (*L. fontanesiana*)	5–8	E	S	white	AC	CLS	241
Leycesteria formosa	7–9	D	S	white	F	CS	27
Ligustrum chenaultii	8–9	E	S	white	F	CS	248
— *delavayanum*	8–9	E	S	white	F	CS	248
— *japonicum*	7–10	E	S	white		C	247, 283
— *lucidum*	8–10	E	T	white		C	247
— — 'Excelsior Superbum'	8–10	E	S	white		C	247
— — 'Tricolor'	8–10	E	S	white		C	247
— *ovalifolium*	6–8	E	S	white		CS	46, 247
— — 'Argenteum'	6–8	E	S	white		C	248
— — 'Aureum'	6–8	E	S	white		C	248
— *quihoui*	6–9	E	S	white	F	C	248, 249, 283
— *sinense*	7–9	E	S	white	F	C	247
— 'Vicaryi'	7–9	E	S	white		C	248
— *vulgare*	5–8	E	S	white	F	CS	246, 248
Lilium auratum	5–8	D	B	white		S	242
— *krameri* (*L. japonicum*)	5–8	D	B	pink		S	242
— *longiflorum*	5–8	D	B	white		S	242
— *martagon*	4–8	D	B	mauve/white		DS	59
Lindera obtusiloba	6–9	D	S		AC F	CLS	292
Liquidambar styraciflua 'Worplesdon'	5–9	D	T		AC	CGL	269
Liriodendron tulipifera 'Fastigiata'	5–9	D	T	yellowish		G	236
Lonicera japonica 'Halliana'	5–9	E	C	cream		C	204
— *nitida* 'Ernest Wilson'	7–9	E	S			C	278, 321
— — 'Fertilis' ('Yunnan')	7–9	E	S			C	278
Lunaria annua 'Munstead'	6–9	D	M	magenta	F	S	30

Plant Name	USDA Hardiness Zone	Evergreen or Deciduous	Plant Type	Flower Colour	Autumn Colour (AC) Fruits or Berries (F)	Propagation	Page (*Illustration)
— rediviva	6–9	D	P	lilac-white	F	S	30
Luzula maxima	6–9	E	P	green		DS	185
Lysimachia ephemerum	7–9	D	P	grey		DS	163
Magnolia x veitchii	7–9	D	T	blush		GL	63
— virginiana	6–9	D	S	cream		CLS	121
— × watsonii (M. x wieseneri)	6–9	D	S	cream	F	GL	195
Mahonia japonica	6–8	E	S	yellow	F		4, 10, 22*, 190
— x media 'Charity'	7–9	E	S	yellow		C	4
— — 'Lionel Fortescue'	7–9	E	S	yellow		C	4
— — 'Underway'	7–9	E	S	yellow		C	4, 9
— 'Moseri'	5–8	E	S	yellow		C	4, 10, 35, 58, 90, 96, 124, 296
Malus x atrosanguinea	4–8	D	T	pink	F	G	223
— 'Dartmouth'	4–8	D	T	white	F	G	129, 223
— 'Excellenz Thiel'	4–8	D	T	pink		G	233
— floribunda	4–8	D	T	pink	F	G	223
— 'Golden Hornet'	4–8	D	T	white	F	G	223
— ioensis 'Plena'	3–8	D	T	pink		G	221
— 'John Downie'	4–8	D	T	white	F	G	129, 223
— 'Red Jade'	4–8	D	T	white	F	G	233
Marjoram, Golden (Origanum)	4–8	D	T	pink		D	227
Matteuccia struthiopteris	2–8	D	P			D	259
Meconopsis betonicifolia (baileyi)	7–8	D	P	blue		DS	69, 70, 71, 72
— cambrica	6–8	D	P	citron/orange		S	71
— chelidonifolia	6–8	D	P	citron		DS	68*, 72
— grandis	7–8	D	P	purplish		DS	69, 70
— integrifolia	7–8	D	P	citron		S	72
— paniculata	8–9	E	A	yellow		S	72
— punicea	7–8	D	P	red		DS	71
— quintuplinervia	7–8	D	P	lavender		DS	71
— regia	8–9	E	A	red/yellow		S	72
— × sarsonsii	7–8	D	P	ivory		D	72
— × sheldonii	7–8	D	P	blue		D	70
— — 'Archie Campbell'	7–8	D	P	blue		D	71

Plant Name	USDA Hardiness Zone	Evergreen or Deciduous	Plant Type	Flower Colour	Autumn Colour (AC) Fruits or Berries (F)	Propagation	Page (*Illustration)
– – 'Branklyn'	7–8	D	P	purplish		D	183
– – 'Ormswell'	7–8	D	P	azure		D	71
– – 'Quarriston'	7–8	D	P	lavender		DS	71
– – 'Slieve Donard'	7–8	D	P	blue		D	70, 71, 183
– simplicifolia	7–8	D	P	blue		DS	69
– villosa (Cathcartia villosa)	7–8	D	P	citron		S	72
– wallichii	8–9	E	A	blue		S	72
Mimulus guttatus 'A. T. Johnson'	8–10	D	P	yellow/brown		CD	66
Morus alba 'Pendula'	5–8	D	T		F	G	231, 232
Muscari armeniacum	4–8	D	B	blue		DS	23
– – 'Blue Spike'	4–8	D	B	blue		D	23
– – 'Heavenly Blue'	4–8	D	B	blue			23, 183
Narcissus 'Actaea'	4–9	D	B	white		D	16
– asturiensis (N. minimus)	4–8	D	B	yellow		DS	15
– 'Barrii Conspicuus'	4–9	D	B	yellow		D	118
– 'Beersheba'	4–9	D	B	white		D	16
– bulbocodium	6–9	D	B	yellow		DS	15, 54
– – 'Romieuxii'	6–9	D	B	citron		DS	15
– 'Cantatrice'	6–9	D	B	white		D	16
– 'Cedric Morris'	4–8	D	B	yellow		D	11, 12*, 14, 15
– 'Cheerfulness'	4–9	D	B	yellow		D	16, 118
– cyclamineus	6–8	D	B	yellow		DS	15
– 'February Gold'	5–8	D	B	yellow		D	15, 22
– 'Hawera'	4–9	D	B	yellow		D	32
– 'Jana'	4–9	D	B	yellow		D	12*, 15
– moschatus	4–9	D	B	cream		D	16
– obvallaris	4–9	D	B	yellow		D	15
– pallidus 'Praecox'	4–9	D	B	citron		DS	16
– papyraceus	4–9	D	B	white		D	118
– poeticus var. recurvus	4–9	D	B	white		D	12*, 30
– pseudonarcissus	4–9	D	B	yellow		DS	15
– 'Rijnveld's Early Sensation'	4–9	D	B	yellow		D	15
– 'Rockery White'	4–9	D	B	citron		DS	15
– 'Silver Chimes'	4–9	D	B	white		D	16
– 'Thalia'	4–9	D	B	white		D	16

Plant Name	USDA Hardiness Zone	Evergreen or Deciduous	Plant Type	Flower Colour	Autumn Colour (AC) Fruits or Berries (F)	Propagation	Page (*Illustration)
— 'Tittle Tattle'	4–9	D	B	yellow		D	16, 23, 30
— triandrus	4–9	D	B	white		DS	16, 23
— watieri	4–9	D	B	white		DS	15
Nerine bowdenii 'Fenwick's Variety'	8–10	D	B	pink		D	178
Nothofagus antarctica	8–9	D	T		AC	CS	195
— dombeyi	8–9	D	T		AC	CS	195
Omphalodes cappadocica	6–8	D	R	blue		D	32, 182, 206
Onychium japonicum	7–9	D	P			DS	259
Ophiopogon jaburan	7–9	E	P	lilac-white	AC	D	242
— planiscapus nigrescens	6–9	E	P	blush		D	178
Orixa japonica	7–9	D	S		AC	CLS	292
Osmanthus ilicifolius	7–9	E	S	white		C	120
Osmunda regalis	3–9	D	P			S	256, 259
— — 'Gracilis'	3–9	D	P			DS	259
Othonnopsis cheirifolia	8–10	E	R	yellow		CD	162
Pachysandra procumbens	5–9	E	P	white		CD	158, 159, 315
Paeonia 'Early Bird'	4–8	D	P	crimson		D	31
— 'L'Espérance'	5–8	D	S	yellow		G	197
— officinalis	3–9	D	P	various		D	31
— 'Souv. de Maxime Cornu'	5–8	D	S	orange		G	197
— tenuifolia	4–8	D	P	crimson		DS	31
Papaver commutatum	3–9	D	A	red		S	105
Parrotia persica	5–8	D	S	red		CL	291
Parthenocissus henryana	7–9	D	C		AC	CL	204, 238
— tricuspidata 'Beverley Brook'	5–8	D	C		AC	C	269
Passiflora caerulea	8–10	E	S	blue		FC	133
Pennisetum orientale (P. setaceum)	6–9	D	P			D	105
Pernettya mucronata	8–9	E	S	white	F	CD	131
— — 'Davis Hybrids'	8–9	E	S	white	F	CLD	131
Perovskia 'Blue Spire'	6–9	D	S	lavender		CD	27
Philadelphus coronarius 'Aureus'	5–8		S				37, 39, 317

Plant Name	USDA Hardiness Zone	Evergreen or Deciduous	Plant Type	Flower Colour	Autumn Colour (AC) Fruits or Berries (F)	Propagation	Page (*Illustration)
– *microphyllus*	7–9	D	S	white		C	119
Phlomis chrysophylla	9–10	E	S	yellow		CS	6
– *russeliana*	4–9	E	P	yellow		DS	92
Phlox 'Benito'	4–8	E	R	lilac		CD	32
– 'Fujiyama' ('Mt Fuji')	4–8	D	P	white		DR	174, 186
– 'Mia Ruys'	4–8	D	P	white		DR	174
– 'September Schnee'	4–8	D	P	blush		DR	174
Phormium cookianum	9–10	E	P	bronze	F	DS	82
– *tenax*	9–10	E	P	bronze	F	DS	5, 82
– – 'Purpureum'	9–10	E	P	bronze	F	D	105
Photinia beauverdiana	6–8	D	S/T	white	AC	C	221, 291
Picea breweriana	6–8	E	T		F	S	195
– *omorika*	5–7	E	T		F	S	195
Pieris 'Forest Flame'	7–8	E	S	white		CL	132
Pinus cembra	5–7	E	T		F	S	295
– 'Corley's Mat'	4–7	E	S			G	295
– *densiflora*	4–7	E	T		F	S	192, 295
– – 'Umbraculifera'	4–7	E	S		F	GS	296
– *mugo*	3–7	E	S		F	S	104, 295
– – 'Gnom'	3–7	E	S			G	295
– *parviflora*	5–7	E	T		F	S	295
– *pumila*	2–7	E	S			S	295
– *strobus* 'Prostrata'	4–8	E	S			G	296
– *sylvestris*	3–7	E	T		F	S	296
– – 'Moseri'	3–7	E	S			G	296
– *thunbergii*	6–8	E	T		F	S	192, 295
– *wallichiana*	6–7	E	T		F	S	294
Poliothyrsis sinensis	7–8	D	S/T	white		CS	221
Polygonum baldschuanicum	5–8	D	C	white			253
Polypodium vulgare	5–8	E	P			DS	206, 258
– – 'Cornubiense'	5–8	E	P			D	258
– – 'Longicaudatum'	5–8	E	P			D	258
Polystichum acrostichoides	3–9	E	P			DS	258
– *discretum*	6–8	E	P			DS	258
– *munitum*	5–8	E	P			DS	10, 258
– *polyblepharum*	5–8	E	P			DS	258
– *setiferum* 'Acutilobum'	5–8	E	P			D	258
– *squarrosum*	6–9	E	P			DS	10, 258

Plant Name	USDA Hardiness Zone	Evergreen or Deciduous	Plant Type	Flower Colour	Autumn Colour (AC) Fruits or Berries (F)	Propagation	Page (*Illustration)
— tsussimense	6–8	E	P			DS	258
Populus simonii 'Fastigiata'	2–8	D	T	catkins		C	236
Potentilla alba	5–8	D	R	white		DS	212
— fruticosa grandiflora 'Jackman's Variety'	3–7	D	S	yellow		C	269
Primula alpicola var. luna	6–8	D	P	cream		S	119
— florindae	6–8	D	P	yellow		S	242
— sikkimensis	6–8	D	P	citron		S	119
Prunus 'Amanogawa'	5–7	D	T	blush		G	237
— cerasifera 'Lindsayi'	4–8	D	F	pink		C	143
— — 'Pissardii'	4–8	D	T	pink		G	216, 292, 308
— 'Cheal's Weeping' ('Kiku Shidare Sakura')	4–7	D	T	pink		G	233
— dulcis (P. communis)	7–9	D	T	pink	F	G	216
— 'Jonioi'	7–8	D	T	white	AC	CS	129, 298
— laurocerasus	7–8	E	S	white		C	122
— — 'Magnoliifolia'	7–8	E	S	white	F	CS	126
— lusitanica	8–9	E	S	white	F	CS	122
— — var. azorica	8–9	E	S	white		C	122
— mume	6–9	D	T	various			117, 190
— sargentii	5–7	D	T	pink	AC	G	129, 292
— 'Shimidsuzakura' ('Oko Miyako')	5–7	D	T	white		G	129, 233
— subhirtella 'Autumnalis'	5–8	D	S	white/pink		CG	3
— — 'Pendula'	5–8	D	T	pink		G	232
— × yedoensis	6–8	D	T	blush	AC	CG	298
— — 'Shidare Yoshino'	5–7	D	T	blush		G	233
Pulmonaria saccharata (P. picta)	4–8	D	P	blue/pink		DS	159
Pulsatilla vulgaris	5–7	D	R	various		S	110
Pyracantha atalantioides	6–9	E	S	white	F	C	10, 220, 278
— 'Dart's Red'	6–9	E	S	white	F	C	278
— rogersiana	7–9	E	S	white	F	C	130
— 'Shawnee'	7–9	E	S	white	F	C	278
— 'Teton'	7–9	E	S	white	F	C	278
— 'Watereri'	7–9	E	S	white	F	C	278
Pyrus communis 'Beech Hill'	5–8	D	T	white	F	G	269
— salicifolia	5–7	D	T	white	F	SG	195

Plant Name	USDA Hardiness Zone	Evergreen or Deciduous	Plant Type	Flower Colour	Autumn Colour (AC) Fruits or Berries (F)	Propagation	Page (*Illustration)
— — 'Pendula'	5–7	D	T	white	F	G	109, 232
Quercus coccinea 'Splendens'	5–9	D	T	catkins	AC	GL	292
— *robur* var. 'Fastigiata'	5–8	D	T	catkins		GL	236
— *rubra*	5–8	D	T	catkins	AC	S	292
Rhododendron alabamense	7–8	D	S	blush	AC	CLS	77
— *albrechtii*	5–8	D	S	magenta	AC	CLS	74
— x *altaclerense* ('Smithii'; 'Russellianum')	8–9	E	S	reddish		GL	126
— *amagianum*	7–8	D	S	reddish	AC	CLS	77
— 'Angelo'	6–8	E	S	white/pink		L	44
— *arboreum*	7–8	E	S	red		GLS	126
— *arborescens*	5–7	D	S	white	AC	CLS	76, 77, 119
— *augustinii*	6–8	E	S	lavender		CL	41, 98
— *auriculatum*	6–8	E	S	white		LS	44, 45
— *austrinum*	7–9	D	S	pink	AC	CLS	76
— 'Blue Diamond'	7–9	E	S	lavender		C	33
— *bureavii*	6–8	E	S	pink/white		GL	126
— *calendulaceum*	5–7	D	S	orange	AC	LS	76
— *callimorphum*	7–8	E	S	pink		CGL	126
— *calostrotum* 'Harry White' ('Gigha')	6–8	E	S	cherry red		CL	125, 131
— *campanulatum* subsp. *aeruginosum*	5–8	E	S	lilac		CL	125
— — 'Graham Thomas'	6–8	E	S	lavender blue		GL	33
— *canescens*	5–9	D	S	white	AC	CLS	76
— *catawbiense*	5–8	E	S	pink		LS	123, 126
— *cinnabarinum*	6–8	E	S	various		CL	125, 131
— *concatenans*	6–8	E	S	yellow		CLS	125, 131
— 'Countess of Haddington'	6–8	E	S	white		CL	41
— 'Damaris Logan'	6–8	E	S	citron		GL	33
— *dauricum*	5–6	E	S	mauve		CL	41, 44, 161
— *edgeworthii*	9–10	E	S	white		CL	41
— 'Elizabeth Lockhart'	6–8	E	S	rosy		CL	124
— *falconeri*	9–10	E	T	creamy		GLS	127
— *fictolacteum*	7–8	E	T	creamy		GLS	127
— *fortunei*	6–8	E	S	mauve		LS	43, 44
— — subsp. *decorum*	6–8	E	S	white/pink		LS	43, 44

Plant Name	USDA Hardiness Zone	Evergreen or Deciduous	Plant Type	Flower Colour	Autumn Colour (AC) Fruits or Berries (F)	Propagation	Page (*Illustration)
––– *discolor*	6–8	E	S	white/pink		LS	43, 44
– 'Fragrantissimum'	8–9	E	S	white		CL	41, 119
– *griffithianum*	8–9	E	S	pink		GL	43, 44, 126
– 'Ightham Yellow'	6–8	E	S	citron		GL	33
– *johnstoneanum*	7–9	E	S	white		CL	41
– *lepidostylum*	6–8	E	S	yellow		CLS	125, 131
– *lindeyi*	9–10	E	S	white		CL	41
– × *loderi* 'King George'	7–9	E	S	blush		L	43
–– 'Pink Diamond'	7–9	E	S	pink		L	43
– *lutescens* FCC form	7–9	E	S	yellow		CL	124
– *luteum* (*Azalea pontica*)	5–8	D	S	yellow	AC	LS	75, 131
– *macabeanum*	8–9	E	T	yellow		GLS	127
– *mollis*	7–9	D	S	various	AC	CLS	74
– 'Moser's Maroon'	7–9	E	S	dark red		GL	124
– 'Mrs A. T. de la Mare'	7–9	E	S	white		L	44
– Nobleanum 'Venustum'	7–9	E	S	pink		CL	8
– *occidentale*	6–9	D	S	various	AC	LS	76
– *pentaphyllum*	7–9	D	S	pink	AC	CLS	74
– *periclymenoides*	4–8	D	S	white	AC	CLS	76
– 'Polar Bear'	7–9	E	T	white		L	45
– *ponticum*	6–8	E	S	mauve		LS	122, 123, 126
–– subsp. *baeticum*	6–8	E	S	mauve		LS	123
–– 'Foliis Purpureis'	6–8	E	S	lilac		L	8, 95, 96, 124
– 'Princess Alice'	6–8	E	S	white		CL	41
– *prunifolium*	6–9	D	S	orange-red	AC	CLS	77
– *quinquefolium*	6–8	D	S	white	AC	CLS	74
– *reticulatum*	6–8	D	S	crimson	AC	CLS	74
– *rex* subsp. *fictolacteum*	7–9	E	T	creamy		GLS	127
– *saluenense* subsp. *chameunum*	6–8	E	S	purplish		CL	41, 124, 125, 131
– *schlippenbachii*	5–7	D	S	pink	AC	CLS	74, 77
– *serotinum*	6–8	E	S	pink		LS	45
– *sinensis*	7–9	D	S	various	AC	CLS	74
– *sinogrande*	8–9	E	T	creamy		GLS	127
– *souliei*	6–8	E	S	pink/white		GL	126
– *thomsonii*	6–8	E	S	red		GL	126
– *vaseyi*	5–8	D	S	pink	AC	LS	33, 74

Plant Name	USDA Hardiness Zone	Evergreen or Deciduous	Plant Type	Flower Colour	Autumn Colour (AC) Fruits or Berries (F)	Propagation	Page (*Illustration)
— *viscosum*	4–9	D	S	white	AC	CLS	76, 77, 119
— *weyrichii*	5–8	D	S	blush	AC	CLS	77
— 'White Wings'	6–8	E	S	white		CL	41
— *xanthocodon*	6–8	E	S	yellow		CL	125
— 'Yellow Hammer'	7–8	E	S	yellow		CL	8, 45, 128, 130
Rhus typhina	4–8	D	S/T		AC F	DRS	291
Ribes laurifolium	8–9	E	S	creamy		C	197
— *odoratum* (*R. aureum*)	5–7	D	S	yellow	AC	CL	133
— *sanguineum* 'China Rose'	6–8	D	S	pink		C	269
Robinia hispida 'Macrophylla'	6–8	D	S/T	pink		G	221
— *pseudacacia* 'Fastigiata'	4–8	D	T	white		G	236
— — 'Frizia'	4–8	D	T			G	95
Romneya	8–10	D	S	white		R	163
Rosa alba	4–8	D	S	white/pink	F		144, 271
— × *anemonoides*	7–9	D	S	pink		C	20
— *canina*	5–8	D	S	pink	F	S	51, 196
— *centifolia*	5–8	D	S	pink			170
— *chinensis* var. *spontanea*	8–9	D	S	crimson		CG	152
— *damascena*	4–9	D	S	pink	F	G	165, 271
— — var. *semperflorens* (or *bifera*)	4–9	D	S	pink		G	165, 166*
— *eglanteria*	4–9	D	S	pink	F	S	229
— *foetida*	5–8	D	S	yellow		G	156
— *gallica*	4–9	D	S	pink		CDG	99, 151, 165, 167, 306
— — var. *officinalis*	4–9	D	S	crimson-pink	F	CDG	167, 168
— — 'Versicolor' (or Rosa Mundi)	4–9	D	S	striped	F	CDG	165
— *gigantea*	7–9	D	C	yellow		CG	151, 152
— *glauca* (*R. rubrifolia*)	5–8	D	S	pink	F	S	95, 132
— *moschata*	7–9	D	S	white		CG	120, 136, 150*, 151, 152, 165, 167
— *moyesii*	5–9	D	S	red	F	G	132, 187, 244*

Plant Name	USDA Hardiness Zone	Evergreen or Deciduous	Plant Type	Flower Colour	Autumn Colour (AC) Fruits or Berries (F)	Propagation	Page (*Illustration)
– – 'Geranium'	5–9	D	S	red	F	G	132
– multiflora	5–9	D	S	white	F	C	102, 120, 147
– – 'Russeliana' or 'Scarlet Grevillea'	5–9	D	C	crimson			147
– phoenicea	6–9	D	S	white	F	GS	151, 165
– pimpinellifolia	4–9	D	S	various		DS	82, 196
– rugosa	3–9	D	S	various	AC F	C	20, 82, 244*,
– – 'Alba'	3–9	D	S	white	AC F	CG	132
– – 'Fimbriata' ('Dianthiflora' or 'Phoebe's Frilled Pink')	3–9	D	S	pink		CG	196
– – 'Fru Dagmar Hastrup'	3–9	D	S	pink	AC F	CG	132
– stellata mirifica	6–9	D	S	pink		DG	196
Rose 'Albéric Barbier'	5–9	E	C	creamy		CG	203
– 'Alister Stella Gray'	7–9	D	C	buff		CG	156
– 'Amberlight'	7–9	D	S	brownish		G	105
– 'Bengal Crimson'	7–9	D	S	crimson		C	152
– 'Blanc de Vibert'	4–9	D	S	white		G	168
– 'Blush Noisette'	6–9	D	C	pink		CG	153, 156
– 'Brownie'	6–9	D	S	brownish		G	105
– 'Buff Beauty'	5–9	D	S	buff yellow		CG	204
– 'Café'	6–9	D	S	brownish		G	105
– 'Céline Forestier'	7–9	D	C	yellow		CG	154
– 'Champneys' Pink Cluster'	7–9	D	C	pink			153
– 'Claire Jacquier'	7–9	D	C	buff		CG	156
– 'Comte de Chambord' ('Mme Boll')	4–9	D	S	pink		G	168
– 'Crépuscule'	7–9	D	S	apricot		CG	156
– 'Delambre'	4–9	D	S	lilac		G	169
– 'Desprez à fleur jaune' ('Jaune Desprez')	7–9	D	C	peach		CG	153
– 'Devoniensis'	7–9	D	C	cream		CG	154
– 'd'Orsay		D	S	pink			287
– 'Fragrant Cloud'	5–9	D	S	red		CG	119
– 'Frühlingsgold'	5–9	D	S	yellow		C	20
– 'Gloire de Dijon'	7–9	D	C	yellow		CG	154, 155
– 'Gloire de Guilan'	5–9	D	S	pink		CG	144, 145

Plant Name	USDA Hardiness Zone	Ever-green or Decid-uous	Plant Type	Flower Colour	Autumn Colour (AC) Fruits or Berries (F)	Propa-gation	Page (*Illus-tration)
– 'Golden Wings'	5–9	D	S	yellow	F	G	114, 163
– 'Indigo'	4–9	D	S	murrey		G	169
– 'Ispahan'	4–9	D	S	pink		CG	144
– 'Jacques Cartier'	4–9	D	S	pink		G	168
– 'Kronprinzessin Viktoria'	6–9	D	S	white		CG	197
– 'Lady Hillingdon'	5–9	D	C	apricot		CG	155, 196
– 'Lamarque'	5–9	D	C	cream		CG	153, 154
– 'Mme Alfred Carrière'	5–9	D	C	white		CG	155
– 'Mme de Sombreuil'	5–9	D	S/C	white		C	9
– 'Marbrée'	4–9	D	S	purplish		G	169
– 'Maréchal Niel'	5–9	D	C	yellow		CG	155
– 'Mary Queen of Scots'	4–9	D	S	purplish		DG	197
– 'Mermaid'	6–9	D	S	yellow		CG	110
– 'Moonlight'	5–9	D	C	white		CS	204
– 'Mrs Herbert Stevens, Climbing'	6–9	D	C	white		CG	155
– 'Nathalie Nypels'	5–9	D	S	pink		C	9
– 'Old Blush'	7–9	D	S	pink		CG	152
– 'Panachée de Lyon'	4–9	D	S	striped		G	169
– 'Parks's Yellow '	7–9	D	C	yellow		CG	152, 154
– 'Parsons's Pink China'	7–9	D	S	pink		CG	151, 152, 153
– 'Pax'	5–9	D	C	white		CG	204
– 'Penelope'	5–9	D	S	creamy	F	CG	105, 244*
– 'Pergolèse'	4–9	D	S	purplish		G	169
– 'Perle d'Or'	7–9	D	S	buff		CG	156
– 'Portland' ('Portlandica')	4–9	D	S	red		CDG	168
– 'Quatre Saisons'	4–9	D	S	pink		G	165, 167, 170
– 'Quatre Saisons Blanc Mousseux'	4–9	D	S	white		G	170
– 'Rembrandt'	4–9	D	S	speckled		G	169
– 'Rêve d'Or'	7–9	D	C	yellow		CG	155
– 'Rose de Resht'	4–9	D	S	purplish		CG	144, 145, 147, 169
– 'Rose d'Hivers'	4–9	D	S	white		CG	144
– 'Rose du Roi'	4–9	D	S	crimson		G	144, 169
– 'Sharastanek'	4–9	D	S	pink		CG	144
– 'Slater's Crimson'	7–9	D	S	crimson		CG	152

Plant Name	USDA Hardiness Zone	Ever-green or Decid-uous	Plant Type	Flower Colour	Autumn Colour (AC) Fruits or Berries (F)	Propa-gation	Page (*Illus-tration)
— 'Souvenir de la Malmaison'	7–9	D	S	blush		CG	120, 154, 196
— 'Souvenir de St Anne's'	7–9	D	S	blush		CG	114, 120, 196
— 'Sultane Favourite'	5–9	D	S	pink		G	169
— 'Tom Brown'	5–9	D	S	brownish		G	105
— 'Vesper'	5–9	D	S	brownish		G	105
— 'Whisky Mac'	5–9	D	S	yellow		CG	119
— 'Willmott's Crimson'	7–9	D	S	crimson		C	152
Rubus biflorus	6–9	D	S	white		CL	27
— *cockburnianus*	6–9	D	S	white		CL	27
— *deliciosus*	5––8	D	S	white		CL	31
— *flagelliflorus*	7–9	E	C	white	F	CL	205
— *henryi*	6–9	E	C	white	F	CL	205
— *subornatus* var. *melanadenus*	6–9	D	S	white		DL	27
— *thibetanus*	7–9	D	S	white		D	27
Rudbeckia maxima	6–9	D	P	yellow		D	162
Ruta graveolens 'Jackman's Blue'	5–9	E	S	yellow		C	5, 159, 162, 212, 213, 265, 266, 269
Salix alba 'Britzensis'	2–8	D	T			C	25
— — var. *vitellina*	2–8	D	T			C	26
— *caprea*	5–8	D	S	catkins		C	83, 230
— — 'Kilmarnock'	5–8	D	T	catkins		CG	230
— × *chrysocoma* ('Ramulis Aureis')	5–8	D	T	catkins		C	37, 230
— *fargesii*	6–8	D	S	catkins	AC	CL	195
— *purpurea* 'Pendula'	4–7	D	T	catkins		CG	230
Salvia lavandulifolia	8–9	E	S	violet		C	159
Santolina chamaecyparissus	7–9	E	S	yellow		C	159, 212, 213
— — 'Nana'	7–9	E	P	yellow		C	213
— *pinnata neapolitana*	7–9	E	S	yellow		C	159
— — — 'Edward Bowles'	7–9	E	S	cream		C	159
Satureia montana	6–10	E	P	white		CD	212, 229
Schisandra rubriflora	7–9	D	S	red	F	CL	205

Plant Name	USDA Hardiness Zone	Evergreen or Deciduous	Plant Type	Flower Colour	Autumn Colour (AC) Fruits or Berries (F)	Propagation	Page (*Illustration)
Schizophragma integrifolia	6–8	D	C	white	AC	CL	205, 252
Schizostylis coccinea	6–9	D	P	various		D	178
Scilla bifolia	4–8	D	B	blue		DS	22, 182
— *messeniaca*	8–9	D	B	blue		DS	22
— *sibirica*	2–8	D	B	blue		DS	22, 182, 287
— — 'Spring Beauty'	2–8	D	B	blue		D	22, 23, 182
— *verna*	7–8	D	B	blue		DS	65
Sedum 'Autumn Joy' ('Herbstfreude')	3–10	D	P	coppery		CD	282
— *maximum* 'Atropurpureum'	4–9	D	P	bronzy		CD	104
Senecio doronicum	5–9	E	P	yellow		C	195
— *pulcher*	8–10	D	P	magenta		D	179
Skimmia japonica, female	7–9	E	S	white	F	C	6, 10
— × *reevesiana* 'Rubella'	7–9	E	S	white		C	6, 8, 117
Sophora japonica 'Pendula'	5–8	D	T	white		G	231
Sorbus alnifolia	4–7	D	T	white	F	G	222
— *cashmiriana*	5–7	D	T	pink	F	GS	221
— × *hostii*	6–7	D	T	pink		G	222
— *aucuparia* 'Sheerwater Seedling'	4–6	D	T	white	F	G	269
— *vilmoriniana*	6–7	D	T	white		G	221
Spiraea japonica 'Anthony Waterer'	4–9	D	S	crimson		C	29, 133
— — 'Fastigiata'	4–9	D	S	creamy		C	29
— — 'Goldflame'	4–9	D	S	pink		C	98
— — 'Walluf'	4–9	D	S	crimson		C	29
— — 'Macrophylla'	4–9	D	S	pink	AC	CL	29, 133
— *prunifolia* 'Plena'	5–8	D	S	white	AC	CL	133
— *thunbergii*	5–8	D	S	white	AC	CL	292
Sternbergia lutea 'Angustifolia'	6–8	D	B	yellow		D	178
Stipa gigantea	6–9	D	P	straw		DS	104
Styrax japonica	6–8	D	S/T	white/pink	F	C	221
Symplocos paniculata	5–8	D	S	white	F	CS	10
Syringa × *chinensis*	4–7	D	S	lilac		CL	118, 287
— *microphylla* 'Superba'	5–8	D	S	pink		CL	129
— *vulgaris*	4–8	D	S	lilac/white		CDS	118, 287

Plant Name	USDA Hardiness Zone	Evergreen or Deciduous	Plant Type	Flower Colour	Autumn Colour (AC) Fruits or Berries (F)	Propagation	Page (*Illustration)
Taxus baccata 'Fastigiata'	6–7	E	S		F	C	237
Teucrium chamaedrys	6–8	E	R	mauve			212
Thalictrum speciosissimum	6–9	D	P	yellow		DS	163
Thuja occidentalis	3–7	E	T			C	277
– – 'Hoveyi'	3–7	E	S			C	104
– – 'Malonyana'	3–7	E	T			G	238
– – 'Rheingold'	3–7	E	S			C	213
– *plicata* 'Atrovirens'	6–7	E	T			C	277
Thymus vulgaris	5–8	E	R	mauve		CD	212
Tilia miqueliana	4–7	D	T	cream	F	GS	221
Tropaeolum speciosum	7–9	D	P	scarlet	F	DS	186, 289
Tulipa batalinii	5–8	D	B	various		DS	31
– 'Generaal De Wet'	5–8	D	B	yellow		D	118
– *sprengeri*	3–8	D	B	red		DS	59
– *whittallii*	5–8	D	B	bronzy		DS	108
Ulmus glabra 'Camperdownii'	5–7	D	T	green	F	G	231
Vaccinium corymbosum	3–8	D	S	blush	F	CLS	291
– *vitis-idaea* 'Koralle'	5–7	E	S	blush	F	C	214
Veronica teucrium (*V. austriaca*) 'Trehane'	5–8	D	R	blue		CD	197
– – 'True Blue'	5–8	D	P	blue		D	164, 183
Viburnum carlesii	5–8	D	S	white		CG	118
– 'Chesapeake'	6–8	D	S	cream		CL	31
– *davidii*	8–9	C	S	white	F	CL	134, 315
– *farreri* (*V. fragrans*)	6–8	D	S	blush	AC	CL	3, 9
– 'Fulbrook'	6–8	D	S	white		CG	118
– *furcatum*	4–7	D	S	white	AC	CLS	291
– *grandiflorum*	7–9	D	S	pink		CL	195
– *lantana*	4–8	D	S	cream	AC F	S	86
– *opulus*	4–8	D	S	white	AC	CLS	291
– – 'Roseum' ('Sterile')	4–8	D	S	white	AC	L	86
– *plicatum*	6–8	D	S	white	AC	CLS	291
– *tinus*	8-10	E	S	white	AC	CL	6
Viola 'Irish Molly'	6–8	D	P	brown		C	105
Vitis vinifera 'Black Cluster'	6–9	D	C		AC	CL	203
– – 'Purpurea'	6–9	D	C		AC	CL	203

Plant Name	USDA Hardiness Zone	Evergreen or Deciduous	Plant Type	Flower Colour	Autumn Colour (AC) Fruits or Berries (F)	Propagation	Page (*Illustration)
Wisteria macrobotrys (*W. multijuga*)	5–9	D	C	lilac	F	L	203
— sinensis	5–8	D	C	lavender	F	L	85, 130, 202, 203
— venusta	6–8	D	C	white	F	L	203
Yucca filamentosa	5–10	E	P	white		DR	82
— flaccida	5–10	E	P	white		DR	82
— — 'Ivory'	5–10	E	S	white		DR	265, 267, 269
— gloriosa	7–10	E	S	white		DR	82
— recurvifolia	5–10	E	S	white		DR	82, 242

INDEX

Page numbers in italics refer to illustrations.

Fish, Margery, 259
Fleischmann, Ruby, 198
foliage
    black, 178
    and effect, 39, 43, 57, 85–86, 93–96,
        133–34
    filigree, 40, 71, 162, 266
    function and shape, 91
    glaucous, 125–26, 131, 228;
    described, 162
    as guides in cultivation, 91–92, 125, 128
    and perspective, 90
    variegated, 9, 82, 90, 91, 94–96, 133,
        203, 226, 227, 248, 262
    See also colour
forest fire, 59
fork, "lady's fork", 302–3
Fortune, Robert, and jasmine, 136
fragrance
    of arborvitae, 277
    of azaleas, 41
    of chrysanthemums, 179
    of crocus, 58
    of *Daphne*, 49
    of *Elsholtzia*, 28
    of Flowering Current, 133
    of honeysuckles, 204
    of hostas, 180
    indoors, 3
    of ivy, 261
    of *Iris*, 18, 162
    of jasmine, 135–37
    of lily-of-the-valley, 57
    of *Mahonia*, 4
    of *Narcissus*, 30
    of *Perovskia*, 27–28
    of phlox, 174
    of privet, 248
    of rhododendrons, 41, 44–45, 73, 75–77,
        125, 133
    of *Scilla*, 23
    succession of, planting for, 116–21
    of Sweet Peas, 138, 140

of *Viburnum*, 9
of *Wisteria*, 130
    See also roses: fragrance of
Freeman, Miss, at Cooldrinagh, Leixlip
    (Laois), 197–98

Gallicas, 169
garden, the
    as art/craft, xxii–xxiii, 21, 100, 115, 241
    in evening, 45
garden design
    and climate, xxiv
    compared with interior design, xxvi
    to contrast with green, 185–87
    with dark colours, 307–9
    factors in planting schemes, xxvii–xxviii,
        164, 187
    and foliage, 90–92
    formal vs. informal, xxv
    and fragrance, xxv–xxvi
    with herbs, 225–29
    history of, xxiii
    Japanese, 189–92, *190*
    and local conditions, xxiv, xxvii, 161
    mixed planting, 114–15
    nineteenth-century rose, 102
    and parterres, 212–15, 225
    and paths, 157–58, *157*, 215
    vs. plant collecting, xxvii, 100
    and pools, 207–10, *209*
    principles of good, xxvi, 33, 81–82
    with single color, 185–88
    small, 112, 128–37, 187, 188, 237, 239
    use of white, 186, 308
    use of yellow, 94
    See also heather; seaside gravel garden;
        trees
gardening, and the elderly/handicapped, 51
Glasnevin, Dublin, 85, 143, 198
Graham Stewart Thomas Rose Book, The (Thomas),
    151
Graigue Conna, near Bray, Co. Wicklow, Ire-
    land, 227

Newby Hall, 148
New Mexico, 196
New Zealand, 82
Nicholson, William, 243
noise, 80
Norfolk, 296
nutrition
    bonemeal 24
    humus, 24, 79–80
    leaf-mould, 69, 79, 80, 108, 311
    peat, xii, 69, 311

odour, plants with unpleasant, 7, 124, 221,
    248, 277
Oregon/British Columbia, plants from, 54
origins of ancient plants, 167
Oxford, Botanic Garden at, 146

Parkinson, John, *Paradisi in Sole Paradisus Ter-
    restris*, 225
parterres. *See* garden design: and parterres
Patagonia, 141
paths. *See* garden design: and paths
Paul, William, at Cheshunt, 102, 124
pea-shingle, 81
pergola, *200*
    construction, 201–2
    defined, 199
    design, 200
    function, 200, 202
    plants for, 202
perspective, viewing, 112–13, *113, 114*
Peru, 271
pests, 26, 46–47, 48, 50
"pippin", origin of word, 297–98
plant associations, xxviii
plant kingdom, divisions of, 272
pools, artificial. *See* garden design: and pools
privet
    as opprobrious term, 246, 247, 249
    as topiary, 248
    trimming of, 247
prostrate plants, minitature, 49, 81

pruning, 25, 85, 204
    reasons for, 317
    rule for, 316
    rules against, 318
    shrubs with berries, 317
    spur-, 202–3
Purdy, Carl, 54, 55

rake, 303–4, *303*
restoration of gardens
    considerations of site, 321
    initial archival work, 319–20
    and layers of history, 320
    and maintenance, 320
    process of, 322–25
rhododendrons, "king" of, 44
Roads Beautifying Association, 235
Robinson, G. W., at Oxford Botanic, 146
Robinson, William, 64, 243, 260
rock gardens, 190, 239
rocks, use of, 190
Roseraie de l'Haÿ, near Paris, 102, 169
roses
    fragrance of, 20, 99, 119–20, 151,
        152, 154, 165, 167
    in garden design, 102
    and garden ornaments, 102
    historic collections of, 169
    hybridising of, 20, 99, 101–3, 151–56,
        165, 169–70, 192
    long period of colour, 102, 156
    medicinal properties of, 165
    new colours of, 152
    origins of Damask, 167
    second season of beauty, 132
    upsurge in growing, 101
    standards, 102
    tea-scented species, 151
rose-water, 99, 165
Rowallane, Co. Down, Northern Ireland,
    109, 196
Royal Horticultural Society, Dublin, 197
Russell, James, 145

Ruys, B. 66

St Anne's, near Dublin, 196
St Nicholas, at Richmond, Yorkshire, 306
Sangerhausen collection, Germany, 169
Saunders, Sylvia, and hybrid peonies, 108
Savill Gardens, Windsor Great Park, Berkshire, 15, 54, 69, 81
Scotland, xxix–xxx, 70–71, 185, 296. *See also specific sites*
scythe, 300–301, *300*
seaside gravel garden, 81–83
secateurs, clippers, 305
shade, xxiv, 39, 199, 203, 204
     plants for, 5, 6, 32, 59, 78, 92, 159–60, 161, 163, 179, 182, 196, 206, 264, 288
     at roots, 250–51
Shakespeare
     The Merchant of Venice, 184
     Sonnet LIV, 151
Sherriff, George, and poppies, 70
shovel, 302
shredders, 80
shrubs
     with double seasons, 129–32
     and invention of greenhouse, 122
     and planting compartments, 112, 113–14, *114*
     placing variegated, 94–95
Shugborough Hall, Staffordshire, 141
Sicily, 138
Sissinghurst Castle, Kent, 140, 155, 186–87, 302, 308
Slinger, Leslie, at Slieve Donard, 70
Smith, G. N., and Daisy Hill Nursery, 193
Smith, Tom, and Daisy Hill Nursery, 85
soil
     acid, xxi–xxii, xxvii, 23
     lime-free, 3, 130–32, 214
     limy, xxi–xxii, xxvii, 39, 55, 59, 73, 80, 126, 221, 257, 311
     clay, xxvi; and "wet necks", 81

as factor in design, xxiv, xxvi, 33
Somerset, 259
sound of water, 209
South Africa, 167, 178
spade, 301–2, *301*
Stephens, Theo. A., and *My Garden* magazine, 63
Stern, F. C., 55
Stevenson, J. B., at Ascot, 45
Stormonth, J., nursery at Carlisle, 65
Stourhead, Wiltshire, 231
succession of bloom, 20, 28, 59, 114–15, 128–29
     of azaleas/rhododendrons, 73, 74
sun, plants for, 18, 33, 94–95, 114, 138, 142, 155, 158–59, 163, 178, 180, 183, 196, 206, 227, 248, 284
sunken gardens, 102
Surrey, 8, 15, 16, 141, 154, 184. *See also* Jekyll, Gertrude
Sussex, 15. *See also specific sites*

texture, xxviii
Thomson, J., *Spring*, 51
Thornton, R. J., *Temple of Flora*, 123
trees, xxv, *218*
     bark of, 219
     columnar, 235, *235, 236, 237*
     diseases of, 231, 236
     factors to consider in planting, 216, 217–18
     fastigiate, 222, 236
     little, 220–24
     pruning of, 222–24
     shaping of, 218–19, *219*, 238
     specimen, 219
     topiary, 221–23
     training shrubs as, 220–21
     weeping, 230, *230*, 232–34; propagation of, 231; shaping "umbrella", 232
     See also climbing plants
Trees in the Landscape (Thomas), 216
treillage, 102

NOTES

GLENDALOUGH
JUNE 1949